D0919282

Staying
on
Alone

Staying on Alone

LETTERS OF ALICE B. TOKLAS

Edited by Edward Burns

WITH AN INTRODUCTION BY GILBERT A. HARRISON

ANGUS & ROBERTSON

ANGUS & ROBERTSON
LONDON SYDNEY SINGAPORE
MANILA

FIRST PUBLISHED BY ANGUS & ROBERTSON (U.K.) LTD. IN 1974

ISBN: 0-207-95569-7

The publishers wish to thank the Estate of Alice B. Toklas for permission to publish the letters contained in this book.

1.987654321

Designed by Betty Binns
MANUFACTURED IN THE UNITED STATES OF AMERICA

Contents

List of Illustrations

List of Illustrations

List of Illustrations

Manuscript Locations

I. Institutions

ATLANTIC	*The Atlantic Monthly*
BANCROFT	Bancroft Library, University of California at Berkeley
BOSTON	Mugar Memorial Library, Boston University
CALIFORNIA	Research Library, University of California at Los Angeles
COLUMBIA	Columbia University Library
HARVARD	Houghton Library, Harvard University
INDIANA	Lilly Library, Indiana University, Bloomington
LIBRARY OF CONGRESS	Library of Congress, Washington, D.C.
METROPOLITAN	The Metropolitan Museum of Art
PRINCETON	Princeton University Library
ROSENBACH	The Philip H. & A. S. W. Rosenbach Foundation, Philadelphia
TEXAS	Humanities Research Library, University of Texas at Austin
VIRGINIA	University of Virginia Library
VIRGINIA-BARRETT	Gertrude Stein Collection, Clifton Waller Barrett Library of the University of Virginia Library, University of Virginia
YALE	Yale Collection of American Literature, The Beinecke Rare Book and Manuscript Library, Yale University

II. Private Owners

BALMAIN	Pierre Balmain
BEATON	Sir Cecil Beaton
BENNO	Benjamin G. Benno
BROWN	John Brown
CAMPBELL	Sandy Campbell
CHAPMAN	Mrs. Gilbert W. Chapman
CLAFLIN	Philip W. Claflin
EAKIN	Jane Eakin
EDER-DYDO	Ulla Eder-Dydo
FAŸ	Bernard Faÿ
FREDERICKS	Claude Fredericks
GALLUP	Donald Gallup
GYSIN	Brion Gysin
HAAS	Robert B. Haas
HARRISON	Gilbert and Nancy Harrison
KNAPIK	Harold and Virginia Knapik
LOOS	Anita Loos
LOW-BEER	Anne de Gruchy Low-Beer
LUCAS	John Lucas
MERRILL	James Merrill
PIVANO	Fernanda Pivano
PORTER	Russell Porter
ROGERS	W. G. and Mildred Weston Rogers
ROREM	Ned Rorem
SELDES	Marian Seldes
SUTHERLAND	Donald Sutherland
TAYLOR	Louise and Redvers Taylor
WEISSBERGER	L. Arnold Weissberger
WILCOX	Wendell Wilcox
WILDER	Isabel Wilder and Thornton Wilder
WILSON	Robert A. Wilson

Introduction

Mabel Dodge looked puzzled: "I can't understand you. What makes you contented? What keeps you going?" "Why," Alice Toklas replied, "I suppose it's my feeling for Gertrude." From the day they met in 1907 at the Paris apartment of Miss Stein's eldest brother, Michael, Gertrude Stein held Alice's "complete attention" and held it "for all the many years I knew her." Long after, she remembered Gertrude as "a golden brown presence, burned by the Tuscan sun and with a golden glint in her warm brown hair." She remembered "a warm brown corduroy suit and a large round coral brooch," and when Miss Stein "talked, very little, or laughed, a good deal," Alice thought her voice came from the brooch: "It was unlike anyone else's voice—deep, full, velvety like a great contralto's, like two voices. She was large and heavy with delicate small hands and a beautifully modelled and unique head."

At that first meeting, it was arranged that Miss Toklas would call at the rue de Fleurus the following day, and the two of them would stroll through the Luxembourg Gardens nearby. "Alice," Miss Stein said as they walked, "look at the autumn herbaceous border." But Miss Toklas was not yet ready for that; she "did not propose to reciprocate the familiarity." To Gertrude Stein a name was a name, to Alice it was a relationship, and through the thirty-eight years they lived together it was Alice who let friends know when the time for first names had come.

To the question "What keeps you going?" a more prosaic answer could have been given. Alice marketed, cooked, gardened, walked the dogs, knitted gloves and blankets, embroidered rose is a rose is a rose, small as a dime, on handkerchiefs, transcribed Miss Stein's sloping penmanship into neatly typed pages, negotiated with printers, replied (signing herself A. B. Toklas) to inquiries about why Miss Stein wrote as she did, poured tea, sat with the wives of geniuses, and turned away the curious who came *de la part de* nobody. The well-ordered household permitted Gertrude Stein to concentrate on her writing, usually at night and continuing until just before dawn. Authors were brought to the rue de Fleurus by other authors, and were instructed by Miss Stein on the difference between remarks and literature.

Errant poets, composers, painters were welcome, if they were interesting. "What's your news" was Alice's opener. She meant gossip, not newspaper news. But there were limits to her tolerance of impropriety. People get into scrapes, scandals could be relished, but Alice had a genteel streak. She would have liked to have been descended from Polish nobility and sometimes was sure she was. As a girl, so she told Joe Barry, she was taught "to open a bottle of champagne by breaking it cleanly at the neck, and, sweeping up the day after a champagne party, to be careful about the diamonds in the dust." That is what it meant to be raised in "necessary luxury." She learned to type rapidly and accurately, but a typewriter was for business letters or manuscripts, not personal correspondence. As for her spidery script, it could be said as Gertrude Stein said of the handwriting of the Baronne Pierlot, that its beauty and illegibility were quite independent.

Whatever her distant origins, there is no doubt that Alice's mother's grandfather settled in California before it became a state, owned land in the San Joaquin Valley, and that Alice was born in San Francisco. Her sedate childhood was enlivened by one trip to England where she was parked briefly with two cousins, "sweet companions" but unpredictable. She was awakened one night by one of them: "Come quickly, Adela is walking in her sleep on a balcony without a railing." Alice found that "frightening but romantic." Quite as romantic was the elephant tusk jelly served by an Indian colonel for tea.

She was proud of being a Westerner and as a child travelled to Southern California by "carriage, by buckboard, by horseback and by muleback," which was "amusing but fatiguing." She attended private schools in California, studied piano with a pupil of Liszt, played in concerts, graduated from the University of Washington with a degree in music, then gave up music completely.

Her mother was "an ardent gardener" and had a taste for fine distinctions. They were alike in both. "You have such lovely watery periwinkle blue eyes," Alice once told her mother, and was corrected: "You mean, dearest, liquid eyes." Her father appears to have been a man of monumental aplomb. According to Alice, when their house was violently shaken by the San Francisco earthquake, she hurried to his room, pulled up the shades, pulled back the curtains, opened the windows and urged him to "get up, the city is on fire." To which he replied: "That will give us a black eye in the East."

Alice was thirty when she and her friend Harriet Levy set out to "do" Europe, her father having consented by way of a "noncommittal sigh." It was a hot summer and on the train to Italy Alice threw her cerise ribbon girdle out of the dressing room. "What a strange coincidence," Harriet said when Alice returned to their compartment, "I just saw your cherry-colored corset pass by the window." In Paris, they roomed in a series of hotels, but it was not long before Alice had maneuvered Miss Levy's return to America and was established in the Stein household—"two stories with four small rooms, a kitchen and bath, and a very large atelier adjoining." The studio walls were covered with pictures by Cézanne, Matisse, Picasso. There was an octagonal Tuscan table with heavy-clawed legs and a double-decked Henry IV buffet with three carved eagles on the top. Alice said that only after wiping these and other pieces of furniture did she fully appreciate their "beauty, their details, their proportions."

There were two visits to England, occasional vacations in Italy and Spain and a lecture tour of America in 1934, but Paris was their hometown. For fourteen summers they rented a manor house at the foot of the Alps, east of Lyon, where, in May, Alice gathered salads, radishes and herbs and felt like a mother about her baby—"how could anything so beautiful be mine." The weeds ran a race with the vegetables and lost. Guests were handed a hoe, but also each morning on the terrace a breakfast tray with fresh rolls and wild strawberry jam. They drank only wine, and sparingly. They ate what Alice grew, and with what discrimination they ate! "What is sauce for the goose may be sauce for the gander," Alice wrote in her cookbook, "but is not necessarily sauce for the chicken, the duck, the turkey or the guinea hen." Good food could not be prepared quickly or cheaply. A marinade was "a bath of wine, herbs, oil, vegetables, vinegars and so on, in which fish or meat destined for particular dishes repose for specified periods and acquire virtue." Her omelette required breaking eight eggs into a bowl and mixing well with a fork, adding salt but no pepper. Then, "pour into a saucepan—yes, a saucepan, no not a frying pan. Put the saucepan over a very, very low flame, keep turning them with a fork while very slowly adding in very small quantities of ½ lb. butter—not a speck less, rather more if you can bring yourself to it." She was addicted to cookbooks and could never settle on where her treasure of recipes should go. She kept revising her will, leaving them to one beneficiary, then another. When things got "too black," she would peer into a cookbook and become "immediately lost to everything outside." She spent hours of each day in the kitchen, but if something interesting was being said by a visitor in the sitting room, she would be summoned by Gertrude: "Listen to *this*."

Alice claimed that Picasso saw around corners. So did she. Arriving late at the Del Monte Hotel in California during their American tour, they were telephoned by Mabel Dodge. Alice, who answered, recounts the conversation: "She said, Hello, when am I going to see Gertrude? and I answered, I don't think you are going to. What? said she. No, said I, she's going to rest. Robinson Jeffers wants to meet her, she said. Well, I said, he will have to do without." Later that week in San Francisco, "it had been understood that Gertrude Stein would sign books, but there were a number of people who said to me, when that is over can we meet Gertrude Stein and drive you back to your hotel: One of them said to me, you know, we were tremendously fond of your father, your mother was an angel, and you are very dear to us." "I noted the descending order," was Alice's comment.

No *femme de ménage* satisfied: Leonie was "too hardworking for her years, her boundless energy and recklessness frightened me. With her long arms and frail body she would climb a stepladder with an agility and the unnatural smile of a professional acrobat." Of another she wrote: "If no word has come to you from me before, it is because the very naughty *femme de ménage* has not turned up. . . . She has said it is because a dear cousin died, because her daughter returned from the country and had been unprepared to enter a technical school—she will give me a further choice when she finally comes back in three days." Alice kept a firm hand on what went on in the kitchen, but also on "recalcitrant gas companies or gentle but obstinate carpenters." Observing her give one French plumber to understand that the job he had contracted to do was not done, W. G. Rogers heard

Miss Stein suggest, in English, that Alice not be quite so severe. Not at all: the only way to get anything done was to holler for it, and Alice intended to holler.

She usually made her point more deftly. Of one of Miss Stein's nephews: "Both Matisse and Picasso had painted portraits of him, the greatest distinction he was to know." When Marie Laurencin was born, Alice recalled, "her mother never saw the father again. Nor would she see any man thereafter, so that when she and Marie established themselves in the Paris flat no man was admitted." "That," Alice added, "would not have been Marie's idea." She scorned Ernest Hemingway's braggadocio and said the real people (she could identify them) were far more interesting than what he made of them in *The Sun Also Rises.* Hemingway repaid her by never mentioning her name in his memoir, referring simply to "Miss Stein and a companion."

The "companion" of those days could not be easily forgotten. Mabel Dodge described her "beautiful gray eyes hung with black lashes. . . . She had a drooping Jewish nose, and her eyelids drooped, and the corners of her mouth, and the lobes of her ears drooped under the black, folded Hebraic hair, weighted down as they were with long, heavy oriental earrings. . . . Her hands were small and fine and with the almond-shaped, painted, glistening nails they looked like hands of a courtesan. . . . Pensive, pale . . . 'tender-eyed,' like Leah." In Spain, Alice toured the cathedrals with Gertrude in what she called her Spanish disguise—a black silk coat, black gloves and a black hat. In later years, smaller, more stooped, her only concession to the exotic was a more than faint mustache and hats which she decorated. She wore simple sandals and a thick tweed suit made for her by their protégé, Pierre Balmain.

For twenty years after Gertrude Stein's death in 1946, Alice lived alone, resigned to the Lord's letting her go on long after her work was finished—getting Gertrude's unpublished manuscripts into print. To do that, she quietly and through an intermediary sold Picasso drawings at less than their worth. She never discussed the cash value of art; it didn't interest her. She stayed in touch with old friends—Thornton and Isabel Wilder, Donald Gallup, Joe Barry, Carl Van Vechten, Virgil Thompson, Janet Flanner, Donald Sutherland, Francis Rose. She made some new friends, not many—Virginia and Harold Knapik, Doda Conrad, John Brown. There was one meal a day to be enjoyed, the white poodle to be let in and out and groomed and taken to the vet. And there were letters to be written, hundreds of them, to report that someone turned up without his wife, that it rained for a month, that a gushy visitor had been "underwhelming," that she had been invited to Iceland ("screamingly funny"), that she had read a new book about Gertrude and nobody should. When she could no longer cook, a caller would guide her out of her apartment on the rue Christine, down steep steps, into a taxi and off to an excellent lunch. An eye operation in her eighties restored enough sight for her laboriously to read Ivy Compton-Burnett ("witty and amusing beyond words"), holding a huge magnifying glass over the pages. A chain smoker, she gave up cigarettes at eighty-seven. By then she could no longer walk. The white poodle, Basket II, was dead. The Paris winters had turned colder.

She was fiercely protective of friends from the past. A one-time professor at the Collège de France who accepted the directorship of the Bibliothèque Nationale under the Nazi occupation was subsequently convicted of collaboration and took refuge in Switzerland. But he had been devoted to Gertrude Stein and her writing, and Alice conspired loyally to secure his rehabilitation. Less than a year before she died, a visitor tactlessly suggested she needn't bother seeing Picasso's latest paintings, they weren't that interesting, "*You* may not like them," she shot back, "but you cannot say that I would not like them. I'll see them for myself."

She had by then been expelled from the rue Christine, the owner wanting the apartment for someone else. She was moved across Paris to a newer, lighter apartment where the walls were so thin that "a neighbor sneezed the other day and I heard it distinctly." It had an elevator, it was more modern. But, she cried, "Gertrude is not *here.*" The frayed horsehair couch and chairs were there and the octagonal Tuscan table. The paintings, in which she had a life interest, had been removed by court order initiated by the heirs of Michael Stein, to whom they would go on Alice's death. She scarcely noticed their absence. She remembered them as they were, and had they remained on the walls she could not have seen them. A single landscape by Dora Maar rested on the floor. It was sent to Yale. It must be mine to give, Alice said, since they have not taken it. She had been in France for over half a century and her accent was still flat Californian—"You bet!" Conversation turned more and more to something Gertrude had said, then silence. There had to be a heaven. How else could they be reunited?

She was admitted to the Roman Catholic Church, and on March 7, 1967, just short of her ninetieth birthday, her heart stopped. Flowers were banked against the outside entrance to the apartment on the rue de la Convention. The plain coffin was driven one block to the parish church, then on through the thickest Paris traffic, winding about the Père Lachaise Cemetery until the opened vault of Gertrude Stein was reached. A dozen mourners filed by, each dropping a flower. The grave was closed, blanketed by blossoms, and a tall, white-haired, black-clad master of ceremonies said, "ladies and gentlemen, it is over."

GILBERT A. HARRISON

On Collecting the Letters

After Gertrude Stein's death in 1946, Alice Toklas "took on" letter-writing, referring to it as "my work." She would sit in the low, horsehair armchair in the apartment on rue Christine, her attaché case opened and beside her on a small table a bottle of ink (frequently spilled), a pen with a Spencerian nib, a large box of matches, an ash tray, a package of Pall Mall cigarettes and, if it was morning, a crushed copy of *Le Figaro.*

In preparing this collection, I have gathered and transcribed over three thousand of her letters. Initially, I wanted to include those from all periods of her life but abandoned the idea. Miss Toklas' letters to her father, written with regularity from 1907 to his death in 1922, could not be found. Her letters to her childhood friend Clare Moore de Gruchy were all destroyed by Mrs. de Gruchy shortly before her own death. In the late 1920's Annette Rosenshine, another childhood friend, destroyed all of Alice's early letters to her. Alice's closest friend, Louise Taylor, lost most of the pre-1946 letters when her valise was stolen from a train during World War II. Rather than include only a fragmentary selection of early letters, it seemed wise to concentrate on the last twenty years of Miss Toklas' life. In so doing, I have included letters that are of biographical, literary, and artistic significance to Gertrude Stein and her circle; letters that illustrate the catholicity of Alice Toklas' friendships and associations; letters that reveal the quality of her sensibility; and letters that delight for their description of her "daily living."

It has been necessary to delete opening and closing sentences that follow a set pattern, as well as information of interest only to the recipient or which is duplicated in other letters.

All of the letters (with the exception of the one letter to Julian

Sawyer which came from a printed catalogue) have been transcribed from an original manuscript or photostat. Mercedes de Acosta felt that Miss Toklas wrote with the "eyelash of a fly," and complicating the problem of her minute handwriting, there was the difficulty of reading or copying letters written on almost translucent, tissue-thin paper. Where I have guessed at a word I have followed it by a question mark in square brackets. Completely illegible words are printed as "word" followed by a question mark and set in square brackets. An occasional unimportant word that has been inadvertently omitted, a name that has been added for clarity, a missing address or date that has been supplied by sources other than the letter itself have all been inserted in square brackets. Abbreviations have been opened up where clarity demanded, and the printing of titles has been standardized.

Miss Toklas was generally a good speller. Occasional slips of no special significance have been corrected. Her use of French was not always accurate. Where she freely "adapted" an idiom and her general sense is clear, no correction has been made.

She usually punctuated with short dashes, which she used to represent every stop. End marks proved difficult to decipher—particularly when followed by "I" or a proper noun. In such instances I have punctuated as meaning would suggest.

Miss Toklas used every inch of her paper (a habit she acquired during World War I when paper was scarce); only occasionally would she insert a tiny "x" to indicate the start of a new paragraph. I have paragraphed freely as sense demanded.

Gratitude is expressed to the following persons and institutions for granting access to Toklas letters which they own or which are part of their holdings, and to those listed below who gave information on the whereabouts of letters and identification of correspondents, assisted in the annotation, or gave other less easily defined aid and encouragement: William Alfred; J. Richard Phillips, Special Collections Librarian, Amherst College Library; *The Atlantic Monthly;* Madame Denise Aimé-Azam; Pierre Balmain; Hélène Baltrusaitis, Cultural Consultant, Fine Arts, USIS, American Embassy in Paris; Alfred H. Barr, Jr.; Joseph A. Barry; Sir Cecil Beaton; Virginia Becker; Benjamin G. Benno; Dr. and Mrs. Max Berg; Emma R. Bethill; Elizabeth Bishop; Mrs. Robert K. Black; Howard B. Gotlieb, Curator of Special Collections, Mugar Memorial Library, Boston University; Christiane Botrel, Assistant Regional Programs, USIS,

American Embassy in Paris; Paul Bowles; Mrs. William Aspenwall Bradley; John Breon; John and Simone Brown; James Hart, Director, Bancroft Library, University of California at Berkeley; Sandy Campbell; Kathleen Cannell; Dr. and Mrs. Antoine Chapman; Mrs. Gilbert W. Chapman; Philip W. Claflin; Kenneth A. Lohf, Librarian for Rare Books and Manuscripts, Columbia University; Mrs. Mary A. McKenzie, Librarian, Connecticut College Library; Doda Conrad; Katharine Cornell; Mina Curtiss; Michel Duc; Ulla Dydo; Donald Downes; Tony de Lille; Jane Eakin; Mr. and Mrs. Albert Eichel; Bernard Faÿ; Janet Flanner; Loren and Lloyd Frankenberg; Claude Fredericks; Joseph Fuchs; Brion Gysin; Robert B. Haas; Nancy Harrison; William H. Bond, Librarian, and Rodney G. Dennis, Curator, both of The Houghton Library, Harvard University; Helen Hayes; Joan Hofmann; Eileen Hose; Mrs. Elfrieda Lang, Curator of Manuscripts, The Lilly Library, Indiana University; the late Daniel C. Joseph; Mr. Daniel-Henry Kahnweiler; Sanford and Nancy Kreger; James Laughlin; Michel and Louise Leiris; Calman A. Levin; Roy P. Blaser, Reference Department, Manuscript Division, The Library of Congress; Anita Loos; Anne Low-Beer; Mr. and Mrs. Murray Lubasch; Herbert and Virginia Lust; William Meredith; James Merrill; Thomas P. F. Hoving, Director, and Mrs. Patricia Pellegrini, Associate Archivist, both of The Metropolitan Museum of Art; Jim Morley; William S. Lieberman, Curator of Drawings, The Museum of Modern Art; John Bernard Myers; David Noakes; Lucille Ostrow; Paul Padgette; Norman Holmes Pearson; Sir Roland Penrose; Fernanda Pivano; Russell Porter; Margaret Potter; Mrs. Wanda M. Randall, Assistant to the Curator of Manuscripts, Princeton University Library; Elizabeth Shenton, Assistant to the Director, The Arthur and Elizabeth Schlesinger Library on the History of Women in America, Radcliffe College; Juliet Rago; Man Ray; W. G. Rogers and Mildred Weston Rogers; Ned Rorem; Don Roscher; Sir Francis Rose, Bart.; Lady Frederica Rose; Clive E. Driver, Director, The Philip H. and A. S. W. Rosenbach Foundation; Daniel and Eleanore Saidenberg, Virginia B. Trodden, Executive Secretary, Saint Mary's Cathedral, San Francisco; John Schaffner; Rev. Donald R. Espen, Assistant Chancellor, Archdiocese of Seattle; Marian Seldes; Roger Shattuck; Joseph Solomon, for permission to use photographs from the Estate of Carl Van Vechten; Ettore Sottsass, Jr.; Frances Steloff; Samuel M. Steward; Lawrence D. Stewart; Donald and Gilberte Sutherland; Father Edward Taylor; Louise and Redvers Taylor; Professor Ruth Z. Temple, the City University of New York; David Farmer and June Moll, Librarians, Humanities Research Library, The University of Texas at Austin; David Vaughan; Edmund Berkeley, Jr., Curator of Manuscripts, and Mary Faith Pusey, Assistant in Manuscripts, both of the University of Virginia Library; Eugene Walter; Mrs. Bernadette Gualtieri, Head of the Reference Section, University of Washington Libraries, Seattle; L. Arnold Weissberger; William Whitehead; Wendell Wilcox; Isabel Wilder; Thornton Wilder; and Robert A. Wilson.

In the typing of the manuscript I have had the assistance of Julie Kurnitz, John Herbert McDowell, Josef Bush, and Joan McCullough. Theo Barnes transcribed and helped to check the great majority of the letters, controlled a voluminous flow of correspondence, and conducted much individual research. I am especially grateful to Donald Gallup, Curator of the Yale Collection of American Literature, Beinecke Rare Book and Manuscript Library, Yale University; to Leon Katz; and to Harold and Virginia Knapik.

EDWARD BURNS

Staying
on
Alone

1946

To W. G. Rogers, New York, Telegram/MS Rogers

27 July 1946 Paris

Gertrude died this afternoon. I am writing. Dearest love

Alice

To Carl and Fania Van Vechten, New York/MS Yale

[31 July 1946] Wednesday 5 rue Christine, Paris VI

Dearest Fania and dearest Papa Woojums—

When I came back Saturday evening I sent off the wire and put out the envelope and paper and now I'm trying tell you everything. For us who loved our Baby Woojums so completely it should be easy to say it all—but the emptiness is so very very great—and more intensely when I am with you. But there are many many things you must know and gradually you will know them all. Baby told me all over again about a week ago how you had been her most loyal friend from the beginning and how wonderful it was that you had done the perfect introduction. It was one of the three last pleasures Baby was given—it and the two first copies of *Brewsie and Willie* and the telegram from Montie saying the play was going on. It was a miracle that everything happened in time. I must not wait longer but try to tell you at once everything that happened. After the trip to Belgium just before Christmas Baby complained of being tired and said she wouldnt go about so much and we'd see fewer people—it had been too exhausting—the occupation and seeing nearly the whole American army. But in April the doctor said she needed to be built up and then an operation. And Baby said she wanted to feel strong again but refused the operation—and then she felt better but was growing very thin. And finally she consented to go away from Paris to the Sarthe to a lovely house a friend was lending us. But there suddenly the day after our arrival there was a short but very painful attack and when it was over Baby felt better and we stayed on until Thursday when she finally consented to go back to Paris—and we went to the American Hospital at Neuilly—both of us full of hope—planning to return to the Sarthe in September. All the great specialists were called and said that Baby must be given a treatment for several days to insure success—and then last Friday morning they refused to undertake it. Tired suffering Baby dismissed them all and said she never wanted to see any of them again. She was furious and frightening and impressive—like she was thirty years and more ago when her work was attacked. And then we got Valery-Radot and Leriche and they consented because she implored them to. And Leriche told me that three years ago the risk would have been very great. And he said never had any one been so sick and not suffered a hundred times more—just two weeks of suffering—that her body was as strong and as sane as her mind. And oh Baby was so beautiful—in between the pain—like nothing before. And now she is in the vault at the American Cathedral on the Quai d'Orsay—and I'm here alone. And nothing more—only what was. You will know that nothing is very clear with me—everything is empty and blurred. Papa Woojums—she said it to me twice—you are to edit the unpublished manuscripts and I am to stay on here and the Picasso portrait goes to the Metropolitan Museum—and on Sunday Jo Barry takes me down to the Sarthe to bring back Basket and the trunks. There are many things more to tell you but they fade off and perhaps anyway I've told you. All the manuscripts and letters got off to Yale three weeks ago—but a lot of printed matter is still here. I'll tell you about that next letter. Later too I'll send you the wires and things for Fania and you. And they want photographs for a *Hommage* the good friend of Jean Denoël is doing for [Fontainebleau?] and if it's one of yours he wants and he says it is will you forgive me if I give it to him. J. [Janet] Flanner said she would keep the French papers—and I'll send you them all. Forgive me and give me a little of the great affection you had for our darling Baby Woojums. Ever your loving but so very loving and lonesome

Mama Woojums

Woojums: A term of endearment used by Alice (Mama W.), Gertrude (Baby W.), Carl (Papa W.), and Fania (Empress or Madame W.). Carl Van Vechten, writer, critic, and photographer, first made Stein's acquaintance through her *Portrait of Mabel Dodge at the Villa Curonia* (1911), which Mabel Dodge had brought back with her from Florence and which she kept on a small table in the foyer of her home at 23 Fifth Avenue. In 1913 Van Vechten arrived in Paris with a letter of introduction from Mabel Dodge. His friendship with Stein and Toklas was immediate and lasting. Over the years he helped keep Stein's name before the public, placing many of her works in magazines, and securing book publication. Stein appointed him her literary executor and charged him with the responsibility of publishing all of her unpublished works. Van Vechten, with Alice's assistance, carried out this task through the Yale Edition of the Unpublished Works of Gertrude Stein.

introduction: Selected Writings of Gertrude Stein, with Notes and an Introduction by Carl Van Vechten (New York: Random House, 1946).

Brewsie and Willie: Stein's narrative about the G.I.'s, published by Random House in 1946.

Montie: Lamont (Montie or Monty) Johnson, actor and director, had cabled Stein on July 24, 1946, announcing that arrangements had been completed for a New York production of her play *Yes Is For A Very Young Man.* This plan, however, fell through. Johnson and his colleague Robert Claborne did realize their hopes for a New York production when the play opened at the off-Broadway Cherry Lane Theatre on June 6, 1949.

Sarthe: Bernard Faÿ had loaned Stein and Toklas his house, Le Prieuré St. Martin, Luceaux, in the department of Sarthe.

Valery-Radot and Leriche: The two doctors who operated on Stein for cancer at the American Hospital in Neuilly. Valery-Radot was a member of the Académie de Médecine and head of the French Red Cross.

Janet Flanner: "Gênet," the French correspondent of *The New Yorker* and a friend of Stein and Toklas' since the 1920's.

To Carl Van Vechten, New York/MS Yale

2 August 1946 — 5 rue Christine, Paris VI

Dearest Papa Woojums—

Your wonderful letter has just come and you say everything I wanted to hear and thank you with all my heart. It is most likely that our Baby Woojums will stay in Paris that she loved so much—at Père Lachaise—with friends and amongst the French great. I hope that you think that that is right—she never said anything about any such thing it couldnt and didnt interest her at all —dead is dead—you remember in *The Makings*. From time to time I long to have you here—but now that our Baby never will be again distance is nothing. She is and often you are—and that is every thing. The French law will make things drag on but it all will be beautiful. Virgil has just spent the afternoon with me—he has just returned from Venice—and I told him in case of any doubts of interpretation (apropos of the opera) or anything else he would have to consult you. And he said he did not wish to have the text appear before the opera was played and to that I answered that was for you to decide. We have a long habit of each other.

GERTRUDE STEIN, CARL VAN VECHTEN, AND
ALICE B. TOKLAS, NEW YORK, 1935

Photograph by Carl Van Vechten

You will tell me if I do anything you dont like—please. She always said you knew.

There are two articles in literary reviews to appear and the French radio devotes a half hour Thursday to her memory. I am to have the script to send to you. Has Mr. Morgan the lawyer sent you a copy of the will—he should have yesterday. She gives the Picasso portrait to the Metropolitan—the rest to me—and then to Allan's children—so I definitely stay on—the landlady is agreeable to this. Sunday Joe Barry who is a comfort is going back to Luceaux with me just for the day—in the two hours we will have there I hope to be able to pack—pay—and follow as she used to say—and bring back Basket. I am walking a little more every day so as to take him on the walks they used to love. My dearest love to you both.

Mama Woojums

You will tell me if I do anything you dont like—Please. She always said you knew.

dead is dead: The "Dead is dead" section of Stein's *The Making of Americans* (Paris: Contact Editions, 1925, beginning on page 498). Throughout Toklas uses a short title, *The Makings.*

Virgil: Virgil Thomson, composer and critic, first read Stein's works while a student at Harvard. In the fall of 1926 he came to Paris and met Stein and Toklas. Thomson has set a number of Stein's works to music. In addition to his celebrated collaboration on *Four Saints In Three Acts* (composed in 1928), he composed music for a number of her poems and portraits, including "Susie Asado" (c. 1926), "Preciosilla" (c. 1927), "Capital Capitals" (c. 1927), "Portrait of F.B." (c. 1929), and "Film: Deux Soeurs Qui Sont Pas Soeurs" (c. 1930). Thomson has also written musical portraits of both Stein and Toklas: a 1928 violin portrait, "Miss Gertrude Stein as a Young Girl," and the 1930 portrait "Alice Toklas," for violin and piano. Stein's last work was a libretto based on the life of Susan B. Anthony, *The Mother of Us All,* which Thomson set to music in 1947 and which had its premiere at Columbia University on May 7, 1947.

Allan: Allan Daniel Stein, only child of Gertrude's oldest brother Michael. He, and after him his children—Daniel by a first marriage, and Michael and Gabrielle by a second marriage—were the beneficiaries of Stein's will after Toklas' death.

Joe Barry: Joseph (Joe or Jo) A. Barry, writer and journalist, knew Stein and Toklas when he was attached to the American Army just after World

War II. Stein based her character Jo the Loiterer in *The Mother of Us All* on Barry.

To W. G. and Mildred Rogers, New York/MS Rogers

5 August 1946 5 rue Christine, Paris VI

Dearest Kiddies–

Thank you for every thing–the wire and the letter but most of all for being the loyal faithful Kiddies who gave Gertrude so much pleasure and whom she loved so dearly and every thing was always perfect until now. She was always the happiest and the strongest and the most vibrant and so full of energy–until this year when you know she wasnt quite so fit and then in late spring she was better and we both thought the rest in the country would do everything–but it was years too late but we didnt know because she had no pain and then even there were no signs until nearly the end and she was all happy again with *Brewsie and Willie* and the wire about *Yes*. And now Gertrude is gone and it's not possible to say more about it now. I went to the country and got Basket Sunday and he and I will stay on here and you will write to me wont you. There is a lovely happy snap of Mr. Kiddie and Gertrude singing on the wall of the terrace at Bilignin the song you brought her the song of the lonesome trail. God bless you dear Kiddies.

Love from
Alice

Rogers: William Garland Rogers had been a "doughboy" attached to the Amherst College ambulance unit in 1917 when he first met Stein and Toklas and they christened him "the Kiddie." They corresponded briefly after the war and then lost contact. He wrote to them again in 1934 just before the first performance of *Four Saints In Three Acts,* and then visited them in Bilignin. He and his wife, the poet Mildred Weston, were responsible for

W. G. ROGERS AND GERTRUDE STEIN, BILIGNIN, 1934

There is a lovely happy snap of Mr. Kiddie and Gertrude singing on the wall of the terrace at Bilignin the song you brought her the song of the lonesome trail.

encouraging Stein to undertake the American lecture tour in 1934–35. For a detailed account of his friendship with Stein and Toklas see his memoir *When This You See Remember Me* (1948). All future references to "the Kiddie" or "the Kiddies" are to Rogers and his wife.

song: Toklas means "Trail of the Lonesome Pine," which became one of Stein's favorite songs.

To Bennett Cerf, New York/MS Columbia

18 August 1946 5 rue Christine, Paris VI

Dear Bennett—

If Gertrude hadnt got *Brewsie and Willie* in time and the news that her play was going on in New York it would have been unbearable but she did and they were the last happy moments we had for very shortly afterwards we knew how great the risks were —at best. And now Basket and I are in the flat alone where we definitely stay on. There is nothing you can do for the moment —but later very likely there may be and then you will. I count on you just the way we used to.

Love to you always.

Alice

Bennett Cerf: Publisher and writer, founder of Random House in 1927. Cerf became a friend during Stein's American lecture tour and later visited in Bilignin. Under his aegis Random House published a number of Stein's works including *Four Saints In Three Acts* (1934), *Portraits and Prayers* (1934), *Lectures in America* (1935), *The Geographical History of America or The Relation of Human Nature to the Human Mind* (1936), with an Introduction by Thornton Wilder, *Everybody's Autobiography* (1937), *Ida A Novel* (1941), *Wars I Have Seen* (1945), *Brewsie and Willie* (1946), *and Selected Writings of Gertrude Stein* (1946).

To Samuel Steward, Chicago/MS Bancroft

26 August 1946 — 5 rue Christine, Paris VI

Sam dear—

Basket and I stay on here alone—so if you come over we'll try to welcome you prettily in Gertrude's home.

Always affectionately
Alice

Steward: One of the young writers Stein and Toklas had met in 1934–35. His novel *Angels on the Bough* (1936) had impressed Stein.

To Saxe Commins, New York/MS Columbia

22 August 1946 — 5 rue Christine, Paris VI

Dear Mr. Commins—

Carl Van Vechten has written me of your kind message. I appreciate it very much. Random House did give us such a good time in '34 and '35. Gertrude was never happier. And now she is gone and there can never be any happiness again. There are a few things for me to still do for Gertrude and I will at once ask your help. First will you please have ten additional copies of *Brewsie and Willie* sent to me at once. There are friends over here to whom it must be given. Second can you tell me about when Random House received from Maurice Fridberg the advance copy of *The First Reader*. Gertrude was more than surprised not to have received one at the same time—indeed no copy came to her in all the time since and when I know how long Random

House has had a copy I will write to Fridberg. I should not be asking you to do these things for me—please pardon—and will you have the right persons attend to them at once.

I am always cordially
A. B. Toklas

Saxe Commins: An editor at Random House.

The First Reader: The Gertrude Stein First Reader & Three Plays (Dublin and London: Maurice Fridberg, 1946), illustrated by Sir Francis Rose.

To Carl Van Vechten, New York/MS Yale

3 September 1946 5 rue Christine, Paris VI

Dearest Papa Woojums—

Your long letter came three days ago but it is only now that I've found a long moment to answer it. (The char didnt come and Basket pulled and my finger was caught in the door and there's not much courage left to go on with and now that this has been [said] we'll forget it and commence over again.)

No Gertrude certainly wanted *everything* to be published—neither Baby nor I seemed to think that there was much of the early work unpublished—Baby always concentrated on the present—the continuous present—but she certainly meant everything. Baby mentioned it at the hospital—she told me [she] had asked you to do it because she had *all* confidence in you and in no one else—but she thought without doubt to the end that the continuous present was for her as well as for the manner of her creation.

Wouldnt the three plays make a slim book—on rereading your letter I see that this was not your intention excuse me. The play at Yale is only a very few pages and was called "A Play on Names."

Four in America may perhaps have been given to Thornton Wilder. About eight months ago he wrote Baby he wanted to edit it—(*de luxe* not mentioned but suggested)—which she said yes to—since then (up to date) silence from Thorny— (he was always a mad correspondent or none at all) . The lawyer here says he sent you a copy of the will—have you received this? The Baltimore lawyer is getting himself named administrator—as foreign residents Allan and I cannot act (state of Maryland). Has the administrator notified you?

Oh dear no Houghton Mifflin never—I'm furious with their business before anything. Bennett [Cerf] whom you found for Baby has been wonderful—it would be the blackest villainy to think of any one else. (The *Picasso* was given to Scribner's after Random House—during Bennett's absence I think—refused it.)

I am trying through Jo Barry to hear the Columbia broadcast of *Yes.* Monty is very impressive—very clear-headed we thought. And Toni's inarticulate growing pains are tender and early spring morningish—we got very fond of them indeed—Baby was confident they would pull it off.

Janet Flanner's promise to keep clippings consisted mostly in *N.Y. Herald Tribunes*—the more interesting French ones werent included so I immediately got in touch with the French clipping service but they dont work retroactively so I've only the two best —Julian Green's and Marcel Schwob's—which I will send with some other things. I thought to send you all the letters and wires —to be turned over to Yale if you thought fit. Would you send to Yale the many magazines in which Baby's pieces have appeared—would you send dedicated (mostly) first edition presentation copies to Baby—yours—Jean Cocteau—Fitzgerald—to Yale. Because Allan will not know what to do with them—he is going to give me legally carte blanche for such things—now he says whatever you want please dont ask me. (He has lately become interested in pictures but books are closed to him.)

Richard Wright came in one evening having previously sent word that he wanted the picture of Francis Rose that he had bought through Baby. I answered that when I came across it I would have it delivered to him. Then Jo Barry said he had taken it just before we left for the Sarthe—so I told all this to R. Wright. Pierre Roy came in (he'd phoned beforehand) while Wright was describing the two kinds of lives his Julia might have. Pierre Roy couldnt understand him either in American or French so R.W. left and I dont hope to see him again.

Yes there were some letters from Sherwood [Anderson] a dozen or more—very sweet not long and not literary—indeed none were that except Thornton Wilder's and students'—none of her friends.

There surely are no letters of Baby's to Picasso or any one else giving advice—because Baby *never* wrote anything like that—she never gave much advice *viva voce* either. Baby said the eternal truths that nearly every old woman in a village knew could be counted on your ten fingers. Her last one was "go home and be a martyr—that's what you both need—your country and you." And one G.I. said What about you Miss Stein—I will if you do. Go on—I gave my proof long before you were born—was her answer. So there is absolutely *nothing* to offer *Harper's Junior Bazaar*. Baby's own adolescence was a painful memory—she always had sympathy for the young who were suffering from those pains but she didnt think there was any advice to give—you just got through them as best you could. She quoted a friend who used to say any advice is good as long as it is strong enough.

Virgil is leaving in about ten [days] as I understand (he is still in Germany) and he will take something of Baby to you—how much will depend upon the room he will have—but surely the coral seal of *A rose is a rose* because that takes no room—there are other things which you must have—and there is a Chinese coat and skirt (which they [the Germans] didnt take because it was put away years ago high up) for Fania to be taken to her. Oh Carlo could such perfection such happiness and such beauty have been and here and now be gone away. Perhaps I'd better take Basket out for a walk and mail this before it pours—the weather is horrible—the sun never shines. This is not all the answers to your letter for there is still Olga Picasso to tell you about—next time I will find time. Did I tell you Fernande [Olivier] wrote to me?

All my dearest love to you both.

Alice

three plays: It is not clear to which plays Toklas is referring. In the Yale catalogue there is no listing for "A Play on Names."

Thornton Wilder: Stein and Toklas first met Wilder in November 1934 when Stein lectured at the University of Chicago. When they returned to Chicago in March 1935 they stayed in Wilder's apartment (it was there that Stein wrote the lectures *Narration*). Wilder had many conversations with Stein and became interested in the book she had just finished, *Four in America.* Toklas secured a copy of the typescript from Van Vechten and made a copy for Wilder, thus his familiarity with the book stems from 1935. When the book was published in 1947 by the Yale University Press it contained an introduction by him.

the *Picasso:* Stein's long essay on Picasso was originally written in French and then translated by Toklas into English. It was published in 1939 by B. T. Batsford in England and Scribner's in America. A corrected edition, with an essay on the publishing and translation history, was published by Liveright in 1970 in *Gertrude Stein on Picasso.*

Toni: Toni Merrill, an actress who had been reading the part of Constance in *Yes.*

Richard Wright: Wright had written a review of Stein's *Wars I Have Seen* that was published in *PM* on March 11, 1945. Stein wrote to him about his autobiographical book *Black Boy.* When Wright left America in 1946 to settle in France, Stein and Toklas were members of the reception committee that welcomed him.

Francis Rose: English painter and writer. Stein first began collecting his work in 1929–30. Both she and Toklas did much to promote his career.

Pierre Roy: A French painter.

Fernande: Fernande Olivier was among those who occupied 13 rue Ravignan, nicknamed the "bateau lavoir" after the laundry barges on the nearby Seine. She first met Picasso, whose mistress she became, in 1904, one year after he had arrived in Paris.

To Julian Beck, [on tour in California]/MS Wilson

8 September 1946 5 rue Christine, Paris VI

Dear Mr. Beck—

Thank you for writing to me and from my own California which Miss Stein and I visited in the spring of 1935 and which I will never see again. I am staying on here alone now.

Sincerely yours
A. B. Toklas

Julian Beck: Together with his wife, Judith Malina, Beck founded the Living Theatre. They first performed Stein's plays in the New York apartment of Beck's parents in the 1940's. Later, at the Cherry Lane Theatre, they produced *Dr. Faustus Lights The Lights* and *Ladies Voices a Curtain Raiser.*

To Louise Taylor, England/MS Taylor

29 September 1946 or perhaps 30—or 1 October 5 rue Christine, Paris VI

Dearest Louise—

This afternoon Mrs. Murphy (Noël) told me that she was going to London and I jumped at the chance to have her take you a brooch of Gertrude's that I had hesitated to give to Frederica [Rose] to take to you. About the lovely lace you sent Gertrude you will let me explain and you will understand and then we wont speak of it again. Gertrude was very happy and proud in its possession and it was understood that Pierre Balmain (who was unusually moved by its beauty and quite inspired to do something wonderful with it) would create something marvellous for Ger-

ALICE B. TOKLAS AND BASKET II IN THE LUXEMBOURG GARDENS, 1949

Photograph by Carl Van Vechten

I am staying on here alone now.

trude for this winter. But now there is no winter and decidedly it should not be used for any one else. I know you agree with me that something so personal to you and to Gertrude—so rarely lovely should not be worn—even after my time—by any one else. And so my dear it must be yours again. Gertrude had all the pleasure she was to have in it—and it was enormous. And it was sweet that it should have been you to have given her it. Bless you always.

I am at work getting Gertrude's manuscripts and letters and books ready to send to Yale. And then I will write to you again. Love to you both.

Alice

Louise Taylor: Louise Hayden Taylor had met Toklas as a young girl when both were studying music. Brought by her mother to Europe in 1900, Louise first studied piano in Munich and then in Paris. In 1922 she married Colonel Emmet Addis and returned to the U.S. In 1939 she married an English Lieutenant Colonel, Redvers (Red) Taylor, and settled in England. With few exceptions, she visited Alice every year.

Mrs. Murphy (Noël): An American singer who had lived in France during the occupation.

Rose [Frederica]: Lady Frederica Rose (Dorothy Carrington), then wife of Sir Francis Rose.

To Carl Van Vechten, New York/MS Yale

6 October 1946 5 rue Christine, Paris VI

Dearest Papa Woojums—

Now I am waiting so impatiently for *Selected Writings*—I do hope Bennett [Cerf] had it sent by air mail. Even if it does come off the royalties—but they are really for you to use. About instructions from the lawyer to you—there shouldnt be any—you are free to do as you think best—the funds in the bank in Baltimore are for you to draw on. Baby left you carte blanche—surely that is the only reading of her will.

Finally I've commenced to type—Darantière wants *To Do* this week—there are nearly 100 pages—but I commenced—with the two blank books in Baby's attaché case—the fragment on the atomic bomb and the thirty meditations. The three last meditations seem to me as beautiful as anything Baby ever wrote—and appallingly prophetic—they stir me profoundly—are they not the pure essence of Baby—of her writing—they come so directly from her—her most precious gift to us. When everything is in order here—there will be nothing left—*all* the letters and photographs and manuscripts—nothing will remain except the furniture and objects—everything that was personal—and there was so little—because they [the Germans] took so much in '44 and I only feel I have the right to dispose of what I gave Baby—the rest will be Allan's—but gradually I will find things and then I will send you something more. But these last three meditations come so directly from Baby everyday as a new gift—precious precious Baby.

Jean Denoël brought Marcel Brion the other day. In '25 he wrote enthusiastic pages when *The Makings* was published—not only enthusiastic but very intelligent and thereafter serious—equally enthusiastic of each book as it appeared in English and then in translation. They only met once for an instant and now he wanted to come and sit in her room—he was so sympathetic and so intelligent and then I told him how Baby had kept her old energy to the end—how she had dismissed all the specialists when they refused to operate. Ah—said he *elle a choisie sa propre mort comme elle a toujours choisie sa vie.* He is going to come to see me again this week before he leaves for his home in the south. Baby never made any effort to know him. I used to ask her to write him a line—she was never inclined to—nor was he—she sent him dedicated books and he wrote formal thanks. And now he tells every one about his feelings for her—and wants to talk about her all the time Jean tells me. He looks like a French primitive.

Tomorrow an ex-G.I. is calling for me in an ex-Jeep to take Basket to the vet's—he has to have something done to what if he were a chicken would go over the fence last. He's such an original dog—who but he would have thought of contracting such an inconvenient *maladie*—happily it is nothing—he will spend the day there and in the evening the jeep willing we'll call for him. I've wanted to tell you and always forgot such a strange thing that happened—the other morning. Marketing is such a hectic experience—lines for everything from geese to parsley—the street is [so] filled with us that we really only tolerate truck traffic—we hold up private cars by numerical strength. One of the streets we invade leads directly from the Seine to the Senate—where the peace conference is going on—so that frequently smart limousines try to push their way through. On my left arm I have my market basket —an umbrella and my bag—in my right the leash with Basket. All the market streets and there are four of them know him—that is the shop keepers and stall keepers. New customers discover him joyously—a sheep—a cub! Well one day I was struggling along—my basket on the left side was heavy and Basket on the right was pulling when I suddenly realised someone was speaking English. That's Basket—surely that's Basket—it came from inside a car that was leaning towards us as it forced its way through—and then very loud—Is it Basket? I nodded my head but I think they had already gone. You know in an American hospital once I followed Gertrude and the doctors with Basket and a soldier from his bed said to one next to him—I wish I was as famous as that dog. Basket isnt very much occupied with such things but he obviously understood he was being well spoken of. He is very sweet and patient. Now I must hastily get to bed so that I get some more typing done tomorrow morning. Good night—dearest Papa Woojums.

Alice—Mama Woojums

Darantière: Maurice Darantière, a French printer, had previously set the type for three of the volumes in Toklas' Plain Edition series: *How to Write* (1931), *Operas and Plays* (1932), and *Matisse Picasso and Gertrude Stein* (1933). His plan to print *To Do: A Book of Alphabets and Birthdays* never materialized because of difficulties with the Bibliothèque Nationale, whose ancient typefaces he hoped to use. *To Do* eventually appeared in *Alphabets and Birthdays* (New Haven: Yale University Press, 1957) with an introduction by Donald Gallup.

atomic bomb: One of Stein's last works, "Reflection on the Atomic Bomb," was published in the *Yale Poetry Review* in 1947.

To Mrs. Charles B. Goodspeed, Chicago/MS Chapman

11 October 1946 — 5 rue Christine, Paris VI

My dear Bobsie—

You know Gertrude left her manuscripts and correspondence (40 years) and her photographs to Yale and I've been going over them to label them—and there were so many you took and such excellent ones—and it brought back to me all those happy happy days so vividly—now they are off to Yale—and I'm busy typing. Darantière is going to bring out two books very limited *de luxe* editions and I get up so early but dont get things done—there is still so much to do—everything must be put in order as soon as possible.

I have just heard from Thornton—it was strange he should not have written to Gertrude but a brief note immediately after the liberation and one letter since. Going to the war I imagine was too upsetting—and then his mother died which I had not known. He suffers so much—he seems to have so little protective covering. It was through him that the manuscripts etcetera went to Yale. Dear Bobsie—it is very sweet of you to order food for me from Denmark—but you really musnt as we dont do so badly now—everything is infinitely more abundant than it was—we have more meat than you have—fats butter etcetera are nonexistent through the regular legal channels but we who weathered the occupation know how to make a little go very far and can therefore with care afford the necessary amount for health through the black market. So thank you many many times but you really musnt feel that we are undernourished. Indeed Natalie Barney who passed the occupation near Florence when she came back to her home here said she thought it was time for us to send packages to U.S. even if it were only what we had received from there. It is hard from the newspapers to make out just what the conditions are—except that prices seem prohibitive but they are that the world over now.

Fondest love to both of you.

Alice

Mrs. Charles B. Goodspeed: Bobsie Goodspeed, now Mrs. Gilbert W. Chapman, had been introduced to Stein and Toklas in 1934 by Fanny Butcher of the *Chicago Tribune.* It was at the home of Mrs. Goodspeed and her husband Barney that Stein and Toklas stayed during their first visit to Chicago.

Natalie Barney: An American writer who maintained a famous literary salon at her home on the rue Jacob.

To Carl Van Vechten, New York/MS Yale

17 October 1946 — 5 rue Christine, Paris VI

Dearest Papa Woojums—

It has been decided that prayers will be said for Baby in the crypt of the church with only a few friends present next Tuesday morning at 10 o'clock—then they will take Baby to Père Lachaise with just Allan and me going along. It is a new separation—it seemed that perhaps in time it would be alright for Baby to be there near the Seine she loved so much—she had left the hospital but she was there. But now this new separation—this going away again is very hard—it makes a new pain and the old one still is like it was and always will be.

Mama Woojums

Père Lachaise: The Paris cemetery famous as the burial place of many literary figures. In 1967 Toklas was buried beside Stein. Neither Stein nor Toklas had made any arrangements in case of death, hence the two month delay between Stein's death and her burial while Toklas arranged for a cemetery plot.

To Carl Van Vechten, New York/MS Yale

22 October 1946 5 rue Christine, Paris VI

Dearest Papa Woojums—

I dont want to go to bed without writing to you. We took Baby from the crypt of the American Cathedral out to Père Lachaise this morning. Dean Beekman whom Baby knew and liked for years read prayers—three psalms and such parts of the service from the Book of Common Prayer as Baby would have subscribed to—with just Allan and his wife and ten of Baby's intimates there—and then just Allan and his wife and me following to Père Lachaise—there were lots of lovely flowers that she would have loved—a mild morning but the sky overcast and now Basket and I are more alone than ever—as he was alone all morning for the first time he's upset and restless now and constantly wakes up from bad dreams and comes to me to be consoled. Dearest Papa Woojums I send you all my love and to Fania Woojums too of course.

Alice

To Mrs. Charles B. Goodspeed, Chicago/MS Chapman

25 October 1946 5 rue Christine, Paris VI

Dear Bobsie—

I know how I am adding to the many worries—and duties you already have now but because of Gertrude's insistence I feel you will understand and forgive me. It is about Bernard Faÿ and his still being in prison. You know that Gertrude had a long and intimate friendship—it had its moments of more or less intensity but since we came back from U.S. in '35 it never varied. Gertrude completely disagreed with his political ideas—fairly left for U.S. and royalist for France—she didnt agree with a number of other ideas of his. I tell you this to show you she knew—understood—appreciated and finally became very very fond of him—and she never had any doubt as to his complete loyalty to his friends and to his two countries. He made many personal enemies—he once said he collected them. He has been in prison since the liberation—he is anti-mason—anti-communist—those are no crimes—but dangerous opinions just now and he courageously expressed his opinions and he was always since the other war a friend of Marshal Pétain—*not* of Vichy or heaven forbid the Germans. If he accepted the directorship of the National Library it was to save its treasures from German spoliation—which he did—there wasnt one item missing the day he left it for the last time and Göring had asked to have various items sent to him to look at at his leisure but B.F. failed the awful creature (he also saved the Byzantine Library owned by Americans from the Germans). His trial has been postponed but according to the French law the judge can call witnesses to testify so that he may prepare his charges. Gertrude wanted to but as a foreigner she wasnt allowed to appear but her written statement was accepted. In the meantime the confinement has seriously affected his already delicate health. It seemed as if nothing could be done from the outside that is by Americans except a very carefully prepared press campaign. All this weighed very heavily upon Gertrude's mind—prison was always a horror to her—not to be free—not to move about—the whole thing got so on her mind particularly as she saw the G.I.'s who kept saying we dont want to be pushed about. Well in spring Francis Rose came over and he met Mrs. Dewey at some dinner party and they mentioned Bernard and Mrs. Dewey wanted to do something for him and said she could—but Francis was leaving the next morning early and said Gertrude had all the information and would do anything if her name would help—so Mrs. Dewey came over and they had an hour's conversation—all Gertrude wanted was to get him in a nursing home under his doctor's care with police surveillance. Mrs. Dewey whom I met for a moment said she thought something could be done about securing that from U.S. About two weeks after that we went down to Bernard's country home in the Sarthe—an old priory he had lately made into a charming house where I hoped and Gertrude was sure she would have the quiet rest she was looking forward to. We were only there five days when I brought her to the hospital. All this time she was constantly saying Mrs. Dewey says it can be done and that she will do it. Then just a few days before the end but when we were completely hopeful of the outcome Gertrude said to me if we dont hear from Mrs. Dewey within a week we will write to her. And then when I came back here alone I started at once to find Mrs. Dewey's address but when I was in despair from not finding it a very kind letter indeed from Mrs. Dewey came to me and when I thanked her for writing to me I mentioned Gertrude's eagerness—her being possessed by the idea of freeing Bernard—but no one has heard a word and she left here nearly four months ago. Is there any other way of working the miracle—can nothing be done. To me it has become a sacred trust—it was so near to Gertrude and the only real sadness she had known—indeed since Juan Gris died nearly twenty years ago—nothing made Gertrude sad like this—it profoundly upset her—and then there was this hope. I have told you the whole story so that you may understand the situation—I leave it in your hands to decide if you wish to do anything and the means of approach to any effort. I trust your feelings for Gertrude absolutely and you must trust the feeling she had for Bernard—neither of you were mistaken in their friend. Dear Bobsie forgive me for taking so much of your time—there are many small things I can do for Bernard but not one thing that changes a minute of his long imprisonment.

Best wishes and much love to you both.

Ever yours
Alice

Bernard Faÿ: Stein and Toklas had met Faÿ in 1924 through the French writer René Crevel. Faÿ was then a professor at the University of Clermont-Ferrand; later he held the chair in American Civilization at the Collège de France. In 1941 he became head of the Bibliothèque Nationale under the Pétain government, and in that position he was able to help Stein and Toklas secure extra bread and gasoline rations. Faÿ was accused of collaboration and arrested in his office on September 19, 1944. He wrote an excellent preface to the abridged version of *The Making of Americans* (New York: Harcourt, Brace and Company, 1934).

To Carl Van Vechten, New York/MS Yale

25 October 1946 [5 rue Christine, Paris VI]

Dearest Papa Woojums—

Edgar Allan Poe (is it possible?) has been named administrator instead of his partner Kemp Bartlett—(or Bartlett Kemp—I have no memory of seeing his name written and my poor old head seems to consider either equally acceptable) who is absent from Baltimore and he was writing to you when he wrote to Mr. Morgan. Edgar Allan Poe was concerned about Baby's having given her manuscripts so unconditionally to the Yale Library—did they understand that they had no right to publish—did they expect to have any royalties from such publication!!! He seems to be a rather fussy but nice grandpapa. I hope he has made everything clear and easy for you.

Pierre Balmain talks of a three week American trip to U.S. next month. I am giving him a letter to you because Baby told him she would. I am only doing what Baby would have done. I try to—I mean—and so the days pass twenty-four long hours and no time to do anything because the door bell seems to ring almost half as often as it used to—which is easily explained because the old friends want to come and talk about Baby or they ask what Baby would have said about something or what she felt—and sometimes like Henri Kahnweiler who is sad and just sits a while and goes away. Today Pierre Reuloz brought a Mrs. Sandburg whose American husband (she is French) is in business in New York. She is about to do something in Franco-American relations she wants a better understanding between the two countries—it's a deadly commonplace—and nothing seems to come of such efforts—but Baby would have been interested because she would have made something happen. When I told Pierre this he said when they ask you tell them how she looked when she did it—that wil give them some idea of the force it needs.

So much love to you both always.

Alice

Pierre Balmain: Stein and Toklas first knew Pierre Balmain during the occupation when he delivered clothing they had bought at his mother's specialty shop in Aix-les-Bains. After the war they helped to launch his first collection in Paris.

Henri Kahnweiler: Daniel-Henry Kahnweiler, the noted picture dealer, writer, and publisher had been a friend of Stein and Toklas' since 1907 when he opened his first gallery, the Galerie Kahnweiler, on the rue Vignon. He has been the dealer of Picasso, Braque, Gris, Léger, Masson, Lascaux, and others. Under the imprint of Galerie Simon he published Stein's *A Book Concluding With As A Wife Has A Cow* (1926), with lithographs by Juan Gris. In 1928 he published *A Village. Are You Ready Yet Not Yet. A Play in Four Acts,* with lithographs by Élie Lascaux.

Pierre Reuloz: A young French scientist whom Stein and Toklas had first known as a neighbor in Bilignin. He was also working to free Bernard Faÿ.

To Donald Gallup, New Haven/MS Gallup

28 October 1946 5 rue Christine, Paris VI

My dear Donald—

I must thank you for sending me a copy of your excellent review of *Brewsie and Willie* and tell you how much I liked it—how very much—Gertrude would have liked it because it clarified instead of making mysterious the uncomplicated but essentially simple truths that were the foundation of all Gertrude's writing—certainly her later writing—but which were usually set down in such a long breath. Only active minded readers followed and I do think it was because her thought and expression held out at least twice as long as any other writer's of her time except Proust and Henry James. I wonder if you think this is true.

Now I would like your advice and perhaps your help. When I got the manuscripts and letters together to be sent to the Yale Library—Gertrude said that eventually they should have the dedicated books she had received—so I am sending them without asking the library—but the catalogue that you prepared I can find nowhere though I've gone through every thing—by mistake was it amongst the manuscripts which left the house in July. There are two reasons I wanted it just now—one was to know what had been published. The other—what books of hers—not manuscripts—were missing from the Yale Library—I could help fill out with some. And would it be more correct for me to ask the Yale Library formally and in which case to whom would I write or could and would you do it for me. Whatever you answer I am very grateful to you for helping me—with a very fond remembrance.

I am always affectionately yours.

Alice

Donald Gallup: While a soldier in World War II Gallup met Stein and Toklas. His familiarity with Stein's work, however, predated his meeting her. In 1940–41 he and Robert B. Haas prepared for the Yale University Library *A Catalogue of the Published and Unpublished Writings of Gertrude Stein.* In July 1947 he became curator of the Yale Collection of American Literature (hereafter abbreviated as YCAL), and in 1958 he succeeded Carl Van Vechten as the literary executor of the Stein estate.

To Carl Van Vechten, New York/MS Yale

1 November 1946 5 rue Christine, Paris VI

Dearest Papa Woojums—

I have asked Gallup to ask the Yale Library if they want to fill out their books of Baby. Surely you have *all* of them—if you havent let me know at once and I'll send you what is missing if it is here. They're not all here by about a third. Baby used to lend the last one to some one and then not ever see it again. You know what Jane Heap said long ago—Gertrude Stein may not be the most read author—but she certainly is the most stolen author.

No—I dont make any notes—I wouldnt know how. I once told Thornton Wilder I was going to write a cook book (I have priceless recipes from three chateaux manuscript cook books—18th & early 19th century besides hundreds of later ones). He looked at me surprised and said reprovingly—But Alice have you ever tried to write.

Tomorrow is All Saint's Day—if I can find some way of getting there I will go to the American Cathedral—getting about is so difficult. Dean Beekman wrote me that he was saying prayers for Gertrude—he feels that she was a parishioner of his which she wasnt at all—but as I dont probably know any one in his parish it would be a comfort to go and sit there quietly while he prays.

I found a book of Max Jacob's poetry with a dedication to Baby ending: *beaucoup de monde est gentils mais vous—ma chère Gertrude est devinement bonne*. Precious Baby.

Love from
Mama Woojums

Jane Heap: Editor, with Margaret Anderson, of *The Little Review,* to which Stein contributed a number of pieces. In May 1929 *The Little Review* printed "J. H. Jane Heap, Fairly Well: An appreciation of Jane."

Max Jacob: French writer and painter. When Stein met Jacob in 1905 he was already a close friend of Picasso (Jacob and Picasso had shared a room together in the Hôtel du Maroc where, being so fiercely poor, they were obliged to share a bed in turns). In 1932 Stein wrote "A Play a Lion for Max Jacob" (*Portraits and Prayers,* New York: Random House, 1934).

To Carl Van Vechten, New York/MS Yale

19 November 1946 — 5 rue Christine, Paris VI

Dearest Papa Woojums—

At last *Selected Writings* has come. It is so beautiful—so perfect—it has completely upset me. Everything is in it—all Baby's life from *Three Lives* to the message—your friendship and love for each other—your devotion to her and over all those years your faith in her work. Baby would have been so happy. I carry it around with me and hold it tight. There'll be no *hommage* to Baby—our own precious Baby—to approach it ever. Your notes are admirable and help just enough—it would have been so easy to condescend to your reader—oh no I know you wouldnt have done that but it's such a tight-rope performance not to. I am reading it like Baby used to read her books when we got the first copy—as if I'd never known them and as if they were by a stranger. I've found two typographical errors but they may have been in the books—*The Autobiography* and *The Makings*—you chose the extracts from *The Makings* with such comprehension that they give the effect of colossal size and weight—it's one of your greatest achievements in the making of the book.

Natalie Barney has returned from the Riviera and a short and unexpected visit to Romaine Brooks at Florence. She came to see me when I was struggling with Mr. Morgan so I told her what a nuisance a lawyer could become when he was paid to help. She said she and her sister once had to go to see Mr. Coudert to have him do something for them. He said it wasnt possible and spent an uninterrupted hour telling them *all* the other things they couldnt do. When he finally finished they said to him—What is the alternative to our idea—is there nothing you can suggest—for we insist upon getting out of an impasse which we didnt create—why we didnt even make the laws that you say prevent us from acting in the way we suggest. To which he didnt answer but said he would see what could be done. And finally he found a solution and Natalie says lawyers *are* obstructionists.

No word yet from R. Lewis—I hope he hasnt lost his enthusiasm—but I couldnt do otherwise—Baby wouldnt have accepted what she called at the time of the Biarritz episode "a hand picked audience" and a "workshop" performance. She reminded me of [a] question a friend of mine put to the conductor of an electric car we were in. There was a large notice pasted on two windows—This car gives transfers to the Ingleside race track on pleasant Sundays. Doris looked up to the conductor and said to his bewilderment but to the delight of all the passengers—And who is the judge of the weather! How would one know who would be a sympathetic audience? She thought they would probably be more anti than pro.

Bernard Faÿ's brother has just telephoned me to say Bernard's trial is next Monday which is great shock to me—it has been postponed many times—everyone including his lawyers felt the longer it was postponed the better and now is not a good moment—after a 25% gain by the communists at last Sunday's elections. He has been at Fresnes prison since the liberation accused of hating the

BERNARD FAŸ AND GERTRUDE STEIN, BILIGNIN, 1932

. . . they didnt agree in politics for twenty years and he was wonderful to her.

communists (who doesnt) acting against the masons (who wouldnt in France) hating the English (the large majority of Frenchmen do) hating the Jews (is he alone?). Well he and Baby were dear friends though they didnt agree in politics for twenty years and he was wonderful to her. It was a great grief that he should be suffering in prison (his health is none too good—he saw his doctor weekly and had a diet and did special exercises and now of course physically he's in a bad way). He was very witty and he liked to turn his phrase not caring to whom or where it was repeated. He stayed two nights with us in the early autumn of '43 and Baby begged him to be more prudent—that it was no time to swim in troubled waters. He told me before he left to reassure her that anyone who had saved the Bibliothèque Nationale could be in no danger from any Frenchman and that anyone who had escaped the Gestapo as often as he had could no longer fear the Germans. It was he who saved [Gertrude Stein's] pictures. Gertrude he said would always understand one's motives but she would worry in war time for her friends which was true. It is fortunate that a foreigner is not allowed to be an oral witness so Gertrude had to write her testimony—which she did—there were some things she knew and said which were not unimportant but it is *au fond* a political trial and facts wont count I'm afraid—and it is no comfort to know that he should not be convicted. I am very upset.

Pierre Balmain is the dressmaker and how—I hope he has described one of his dresses to you—his hands outline his bust—caress his hips—indicate the tight small waist line (he is huge) and then he walks across the room carrying the train over his arm. It is beyond caricature—you and Fania will like this—and him too I hope. All my love to Fania—and to you.

Mama Woojums

Romaine Brooks: An American painter and life-long friend of Natalie Barney.

R. Lewis: Lewis had written to Van Vechten and Toklas about a plan to present *Yes Is For A Very Young Man.* While Toklas accepted his enthusiasm as genuine, she objected to two points in his letter to her: his plan to have a workshop production (a production without scenery) and a specially invited audience. It was for these reasons that Stein withdrew the play from the Theatre at the Biarritz American University in October 1945.

saved pictures: Silver and valuable bric-a-brac had been stolen from the apartment by the Germans, but they were prevented from further theft by the intervention of the concierge who called the French police, by then emboldened to tell the Germans to leave. In an interview in Paris, April 1973, Bernard Faÿ stated that: "Three days before the Germans left Paris Picasso called me and told me—The Germans are preparing to move the collection of my pictures owned by Gertrude Stein, do something. I got in touch with Count Metternich (in charge of protecting works of art in occupied areas) and asked him to act quickly, which he did. The collection of Gertrude Stein was in the custody of the German Administration of Jewish Properties. Metternich told the Administration of Enemy Property to put its seals on Stein's door. The two administrations had a bureaucratic battle and it was impossible for them to move the property. The collection was saved."

To Donald Gallup, New Haven / MS Gallup

29 November 1946 — 5 rue Christine, Paris VI

Dear Donald—

Did I tell you that Darantière is going to do a *de luxe* very limited edition of a text of Gertrude's on Raoul Dufy (oh so delightful but not so entirely on Dufy) with illustrations by Dufy —and in spring he will commence *To Do* by Gertrude—illustrator not yet selected.

Now I have a great service to ask you and if it doesnt suit you to undertake it you will please quite frankly say you would rather not and I will perfectly understand and it wont be the least bit of a grievance to me indeed you may suggest some one else for the unpleasant task. If you do do it—you will do it perfectly because you have the proper feeling for both sides. Well it is this: About five or six weeks ago I had a letter from Thornton Wilder in which he said that the Yale University Press (hereinafter designated as Yup) were probably ready to publish Gertrude's *Four in America* (which T. Wilder likes very much)—it is shortish and to whom should he talk about it. I answered at once Carl Van V. Here I must confide some history of them—T.W. is sensitive changeable—well almost fluctuating with a personal sense of what is worthy. To begin at the end I am fairly sure that he finds C.V.V. unworthy and perhaps common but that may not be the reason why during a long month he hasnt communicated with him. He may easily have changed his mind—about wanting the book published by Yup—he may feel that the book is not what he remembered it to be. Now Carl keeps bothering me about no one's approaching him about *Four in America.* (He can't commence his own work for Gertrude for some weeks yet on account of legal reasons and wants to see something on the way—naturally.) Now—could you diplomatically or rather in just your own way—find out which way the wind blows with Yup. Do they want to—would they be ready to have Carl represent Gertrude as he legally does concerning all unpublished manuscripts—would *they tell you if not* what they feel or want or both. If this isnt easy for you to do please please please dont give it another thought.

About the letters of Gertrude to Picasso they're not many—he probably has them but he wouldnt possibly know where and well you must have more history. Picasso cant write a letter—no he's not illiterate but he cant write—he just writes postals on which he says he is well and working and when he is returning or asks when you are returning. Dont ask me how he writes his poetry—it's beyond me but not beyond a guess or two. Gertrude's letters were never literary as you may easily realise. She didnt write about the method or meaning of her work—rather the contrary—letters were a happy diversion—often intimate and playful. Carl probably received more letters from her than any one person. The correspondence Y.U.L. will soon have is mostly from friends who were often more distinguished in character than by achievement. If you remember her real interest in the G.I.'s (not their cause, but themselves) you will know what I mean. She thought of it as important for the future—say 100 years hence—as expressing our time through various kinds of people from widely different milieux. How my pen runs away with me.

Affectionately
Alice

Raoul Dufy: Dufy had visited Stein and Toklas in their house at Culoz, and Stein had done a portrait of Dufy and his work. Darantière's plan to publish the portrait with illustrations by Dufy was not carried out and only a few page proofs exist in the YCAL. The portrait was published in *Harper's Bazaar* in 1949.

To Carl Van Vechten, New York/MS Yale

19 December 1946 — 5 rue Christine, Paris VI

Dearest Papa Woojums—

I've been cleaning the flat—all the woodwork—the salon and the little library are completely panelled in wood—has been washed and rinsed and wiped dry and everything else has been washed—all the pictures have been taken down and cleaned and put back—all the washable objects washed. Baby and I always did the pictures and objects together—it has depressed and exhausted me—but it had to be done. It is unforgivable for one to live alone in filth. Tuesday evening it will be all done and Basket and I will light some candles for Baby.

Now I must answer your letter. First of all to thank you with all my heart for your article—it is perfect and very moving and just. You moved between Baby's personality and her work—allowing each one to explain the other so subtly that after reading it over and over it's not possible to find just how or indeed even where—you did it. You know you didnt say definitely yes—it was

I think perhaps—you would write again—write a book again when I asked you to—now dont you think you might or rather should. I long to hear that you are—if I am indiscreet forgive me—but I think this generation is finished—it really ended with Fitzgerald—dont you think what's left of it and the new I dont know should have the proof of the virility of yours. However good Faulkner may be he isnt virile—and as for poor Hem and Steinbeck and the rest of them—the least said the better for one's digestion.

Now—a long breath. Gallup has seen the Yale University Press—they "are *very much* interested to do *Four in America*—if Thornton W. will be able to get his part of the work done in the near future! (I was breathless) and if not—that later and something else now. They wonder (a) about the legal rights and I have said C.V.V. is fully empowered to act and (b) what will Cerf have to say. I said I was pretty sure Random House did not have exclusive rights to everything and would almost certainly have no objection to Yup's publishing *Four in America* or any other of the difficult mss. So the next step seems to be to find out what Thornton really intends to do. There is a possibility that he may be being bitter over not having been made literary executor (Gertrude said she had appointed him—you know—in Everybody's A. [Autobiography]. But his friends here feel he is merely *very* busy with his own work (a novel & a play) and is actually relieved at not having the additional labor. At the risk of doing something I shouldnt I think I shall call him soon and see if I cant find out (always I hope diplomatically) what his intentions are. And if his own part of *Four in America* will not be ready for sometime—perhaps we can find something else for Yup to be working on in the interim.)

Well I cant say Gallup didnt find out all I asked him to—since he found out T. Wilder intended or intends perhaps to introduce the *Four in America!* I am writing to Gallup that for the future he should communicate directly with you—that it is *your* not my affair—beside the waste of time—Gallup is a dear—a New England dear like the Kiddie is—the New Englanders are little girls with a curl. I'm telling him to go to see you if he gets to N.Y. I hope this is alright.

Mama Woojums

literary executor: Wilder had visited Stein at Bilignin in the summer of 1936. There they had long talks about her work and about the problems of narration. So impressed was Stein with Wilder and his grasp of her work that she told him she intended to make him her literary executor, a fact she announced in *Everybody's Autobiography* (hereafter abbreviated as *EA*) which Random House published in 1937 (see pp. 300–302). On July 23, 1946, when Stein made her will, she appointed Van Vechten as her literary executor. The reason for the change is not clear, but perhaps Stein felt that the pressure of his own work and his mobility might impede Wilder's attending to the day-to-day tasks that might be required.

To Donald Gallup, New Haven/MS Gallup

21 December 1946 — 5 rue Christine, Paris VI

My dear Donald—

Thanks so very much for being so perfect a diplomat. Now we have all the information thanks to your effort and method and Carl can go ahead. I have just this minute finished my letter to him telling him that for the future you or the Yup will communicate directly with him—which I am now asking you and you will ask Yup to write to him about publications because he and not I will be commencing the work of editing the unpublished manuscripts very soon now. It was a miracle that you were at Yale to unravel the knot made by Carl and Thornton neither of them pliant or willing to stoop to the other even for Gertrude—it's something not quite clear that must have happened to them or rather between them a long time ago. It isnt as easily explained as I've tried to make it out—a natural antipathy—a natural *mépris*—a jealousy concerning Gertrude and it really isnt of the slightest importance—as they move and live in quite different worlds. So all my thanks again.

Henri Kahnweiler brought me his book on Juan Gris—he said he had sent you a copy. It is really admirable—the approach—the material—the clearness. But what Gertrude would have liked best are his portraits of the four painters—Juan—Picasso—Braque and Matisse—she shared his judgements and would so have enjoyed his way of expressing them. He and Juan had a rare friendship—which Lascaux shared to a considerable degree.

It has been terribly cold 9° fahrenheit and no one sufficiently heated. I try to get one room comparatively comfortable and Basket and I stay near the heater all we can. They threaten to turn off all heat in homes—but that's just a menace not a promise—and three months from tomorrow is spring officially—and one knows what spring in Paris is—do you remember how you suddenly can see everything way down the street—that's the first week in May—and the buds on the chestnuts are out. Thirty-eight times we saw it together.

Always affectionately
Alice

book on Juan Gris: Daniel-Henry Kahnweiler, *Juan Gris, Sa Vie, Son Oeuvre, Ses Ecrits* (1946).

To Carl and Fania Van Vechten, New York/MS Yale

[25 December 1946] Chrismas Day 5 rue Christine, Paris VI

Dearest Empress Fania Woojums and Papa Woojums—

The concierge turns the water off at 8:15 every evening to prevent the pipes from freezing and doesnt turn it on again until

8 the next morning. But they have frozen somewhere in the house in spite of all this and since last evening we've been without water—that is except what Augustins goes into the cellar to carry up. There's nothing but loss of time—discussion—exchange of ideas and a return to less than what was normalcy to put the French into good humor. All the tenants in the house cheerfully accept that the plumbers cant come before tomorrow if then—I'm the only grumbler but the concierge who is fed up with pipes.

This afternoon Olga Picasso is coming to see me—she comes at six and stays until 12 and she tells me volumes of the movements and reasons why of every one we ever knew and always ends each story with—What would Gertrude have said—what did she feel about him or her or it. Did she think it was Éluard's fault or did she think André Breton was the influence. She asks me so many questions and to most of them there are answers and she has mellowed so sweetly—it is all very pleasant and Baby had the *rapprochement* with her so even if it takes time I'm continuing to cultivate Olga.

I'm getting to work at the catalogue but so far find nothing that has been published that has not been included in the catalogue. I've been so busy washing the flat and its contents and putting down D.D.T. powder so as not to be eaten up by the moths. Poor Basket has not too much exercise while all this is going on—beside it is too cold—not for him but for me. It's not possible to keep more than one room comfortable—electricity is prohibitive. We ate Madame Cézanne but I dont want—figuratively—to burn a Picasso. And all this time I've been tormented about the horrible fate of Bernard. René Reuloz gave me some information which started me off in several directions. The family and his lawyers wont appeal the case for fear of worse. It's too absurd that an insignificant foreigner and a rising young physicist—neither of them having any pull—still should hope that they can pull something off but we do. It will be a miracle if we do—but I'm convinced what we have to do is the only way to succeed. Picasso told Kahnweiler that if he wanted proof that miracles do happen he had only to notice that his hair grew—wasnt that one? Well it has to happen soon or it will be too late to save the archives and library which are essential for his [Bernard's] future—if he has one. Yesterday I asked one of Baby's friends to come and talk it over with me and I saw clearly that for Baby it would have been done—because they need our good will and she would have found means to impress them. So we must keep at it. Last night Basket and I burned the Christmas candles I found—pretty rose ones left over from the rue de Fleurus days—for Baby—he sweetly remembered it all but was troubled for the first time—poor Basket.

Mr. Morgan rang me up to say he had had a statement from the bank here and it was a larger sum than he had expected—it's a mystery to me to hear those utterly foolish men of the law talk as they do. When I was a child I never felt the surprise expressed by the object that popped out of a jack-in-the-box was contagious—well the lawyers are just jack-in-the-boxes so pleased with their surprise—unconscious that no one is sharing it.

A happy happy New Year to you both and many more of them and may I see you both again. Bless you and all good things to you. My endless grateful love.

Mamma Woojums (a double m for Xmas)

the influence: Olga Picasso, Picasso's first wife with whom he was no longer living, had questioned Alice about the reasons for Picasso's embracing communism.

the catalogue: A Catalogue of the Published and Unpublished Writings of Gertrude Stein (1941).

We ate Madame Cézanne: When World War II broke out Stein and Toklas were at their country house in Bilignin. Early in the autumn they received a twenty-four-hour pass to go to Paris. Once there they collected a few essential household items and brought back to Bilignin with them two pictures, the portrait of Gertrude by Picasso and Cézanne's *Portrait of Madame Cézanne.* During the war, unable to receive funds from America, Stein and Toklas leaned on the generosity of their neighbors Paul and Elena Genin. Without any documents being signed, the Genins agreed to serve as the Stein-Toklas banker. Late in 1943, feeling that they could no longer impose on the Genins, Stein and Toklas made a dangerous journey to the Swiss frontier where they met a Swiss art dealer and sold him the Cézanne portrait. Thus were they able to survive the last years of the occupation and the first year of the liberation. The *Portrait of Madame Cézanne* shortly thereafter entered the collection of Emile Bürhle in Zurich.

René Reuloz: A neighbor from near Bilignin who, with his brother Pierre, was working to free Bernard Faÿ.

To Samuel Steward, Chicago/MS Bancroft

31 December 1946 — 5 rue Christine, Paris VI

Dear Sam—

When I've finished sending things to Yale and done some typing and cleaned the flat and caught up with darning and patching—well then it will be spring and Basket and I will take walks and be in excellent form for when you do come. It's a nice quarter right across from the Pont Neuf and four American blocks from N. Dame and just full of Gertrude. She used to wander all about it and at all hours—except the mornings before noon she never got out and so she always knew the leisurely afternoon life of the population when they could talk endlessly—which they and she did. When you come you'll like them better than ever you did because I think the liberation loosened them up beyond what they were when the Germans first came. There are lots of picture shows too more than there were. And the Petit Palais has all the treasures from all over France gathered together like the exposition of '36 and they say it may last for years. This is the highlight because the Louvre wont be ready for years. It just has a few rooms opened.

Do you remember Francis Rose? He remembers you and sent you his greetings. He has completely reformed—strange to say it is quite becoming though he has lost his looks—married a quite poisonous Frederica who has done him a world of good—and paints beautifully—surer and firmer than when you knew his pictures in '39. He spent the summer in France near Lourdes where he went for a pilgrimage and he painted three or four pictures of it—quite masterly. And now he is doing a big picture a *Hommage à Gertrude*. He lives in London where he can sell his pictures. Frederica writes. It is all so different than it was. Francis has kept his sweetness and pretty ways—but has lost the eccentricity and exotic color of his youth.

Madame Pierlot died during the occupation when she was 92 years old from a cold she caught in the attic going over old papers and letters.

It will in an hour be the New Year so I'm going to bed so as not to know anything about it but once more all my best wishes to you always.

Affectionately yours
Alice

Hommage à Gertrude: This picture is now part of the Gertrude Stein Collection of the YCAL.

Madame Pierlot: When in 1924 Stein and Toklas encountered difficulties in arranging for a hotel in Nice, they decided to spend the summer at the Hôtel Pernollet in Belley. Their only disappointment was that the hotel lacked a garden. Through Étienne Pernollet, wife of the owner of the hotel, they met the Baronne Pierlot who lived in nearby Béon. Their friendship with Madame Pierlot was immediate and lasting. Her reflections, observations, and wit, and examples of her charm often found their way into Stein's writings as they did into Toklas'.

1947

To Louise Taylor, England/MS Taylor

7 January 1947 5 rue Christine, Paris VI

Dear Louise—

Mr. Bristow—whom I liked very much and of whom we will speak later—turned [up] and brought me the exquisite nosegay holder—never have I seen anything so lovely and it gives me so much pleasure. You see when the Germans came and then the [word?] and then—well we wont go into that—they took a great many things but not a picture—not a drawing—not a piece of furniture—so that Gertrude wouldnt ever let me mention anything about it ever because she said we had got off mighty easily—and of course she was right. She absolutely used the pictures every minute of the day and so that was alright—but the rooms lacked the prettiness and elegance they had and sometimes I minded it secretly—but a little more even now because some of the things had been Gertrude's for a long time. And now my dear—all the missing elegance has returned and I thank you very deeply—but you shouldnt have because you two have holes you must fill. If the blitz spared (I've never dared to ask to what degree it spared you)—certainly your far too generous nature has left great gaps in every direction. The first thing I like Mr. Bristow for was his immediate and spontaneous "was there ever in this world such

LOUISE TAYLOR, BELCHAMP ST. PAUL, ENGLAND, 1971

How beautiful—why it's Louise.

generosity." And then Basket lately bathed and always well groomed—came into the room and Mr. Bristow exclaimed—How beautiful—why it's Louise. And then there were other things too. I liked him a lot beside his talking about you and Red. Then he said Red was painting differently but developing all the time—not perhaps towards cubism—but certainly towards abstraction. Well since I heard this I've shaken my head to myself (sounds Irish?) but now we will talk about it just we two. Please dont encourage Red in any change that is a violent one in the direction of abstract painting. On the road there are pitfalls but he would get out of them. It is that there really is no such thing as abstract painting as Red would find out probably quicker than most who have believed and been disillusioned. Gertrude was convinced that it couldnt be done. She had reasons too long for a letter. It had bored me considerably for some months—eventually they are neither paintings nor decorations—not even illustrations. Do I sound interferesome—really I'm thinking of Red's painting that should now have its development that all those miserable war years (not that I dont realise and appreciate what the English effort and his part in it did to save Europe and incidentally Gertrude and me) swallowed up.

Once more all my thanks—and how and with what do I keep it all bright as it is? And much love to you both.

Alice

To W. G. and Mildred Rogers, New York/MS Rogers

2 February 1947 — 5 rue Christine, Paris VI

Dearest Kiddies—

Finally I've snatched a moment to have a nice long talk with you. It is Sunday evening—the heaters are on their *on* hours and the salon is warm. Basket is asleep right up against one. I wont hear the door bell—he will bark to warn me but I will pretend I am out—the telephone is off the hook. Do I sound as if the flat was usually beseiged—not so—but there is the unexpected annoying interruption which I am guarding against. To commence at the beginning—the middle and the end—the cold is not so cold thank goodness—but quite sufficiently so still. It has been frightful—two consecutive electricaless days have just gone into effect for the rue Christine. We were on the current that supplies the law courts but they've discovered how or where to disconnect us. But I turn them on full force the night before and so it isn't so bad. Why I should be spending a page of paper telling you this I'm sure I dont know—particularly on top of Mildred Kiddie's saying you worry. But if you mention this in your answer I will tear up your letter unread and not piece it together afterwards. If I like to complain to relieve my *past* discomforts you must *not* remark my bad manners. It is to [be] hoped that you keep yours by doing what you are asked to do. So there.

How is the book getting on? Have you actually commenced it. What will be its name. Is it in chapters. Is it chronological? I long to see it. What does Mrs. Kiddie say when you read it aloud to her.

Now about all your questions for your book—I put it all off to the last because I'm so afraid of throwing the hammer into the works (that is it isnt it?). Well we met in the hall of the Luxembourg Hotel—and the same day you went up to the garage on foot with Gertrude and then we went somewhere in the car possibly only in Nîmes. And we must have had several picnic lunches—if it wasnt too cold Gertrude preferred it. And we went to Aigues-Mortes by way of Saint-Gilles with its unique church and coming back you climbed the sign posts to read them by the light of your flash (there were no milestones on the small roads of the Camargue) and we went over a bridge of boats and to the Chapelle Sainte Gabrielle where we ate a picnic lunch—on the terrace in front of it. And all the time you gave us cigarettes called Darlings—because France was indulging in its first shortage—at least within my memory. And this is all I remember except how very sweet and winning you were and that we scolded you because you were staying in the ambulance service—when you should with your intelligence and all have been in something more important—I think it was aviation because you said you had flown (we know better now—aviation doesnt require brains and the Kiddie shouldnt have been in aviation—far too dangerous for our Kiddie). What we were out to show you on the way to hospitals—at your request—were Roman remains and beauty spots. You didnt think some of the latter overpowering.

I'm always forgetting to tell you that I dont in the least mind typewritten letters—all my regular American friends write on a machine. Carl does always—so dont feel it's not mannerly. It doesnt happen to be one of my tests of good manners. I dont use the machine because it's not comfortable on my knees and its table is too cumbersome to move about. And beside I never did have the habit. You will do as it suits you best—but it's alright with me. I do so love that phrase—perhaps it's *démodé* now. Well lots of love to you both.

Alice

the book: Rogers' memoir, *When This You See Remember Me* (1948).

To Mrs. Charles B. Goodspeed, Chicago/MS Chapman

10 February 1947 — 5 rue Christine, Paris VI

My dear Bobsie—

The portrait of Gertrude is still here. The Metropolitan has made no sign. The lawyer in Baltimore is to ask them to act—for it's [a] considerable responsibility for me—though you will understand how I cant bear to think of its not being here. Gertrude always sat on the sofa and the picture hung over the fireplace opposite and I used to say in the old happy days that they looked at each other and that possibly when they were alone they talked to each other.

Now I must let Basket out on the terrace—it is all the exercise he has these bitterly cold days—but he plays with his bone and it is exercise however attenuated.

I send my dearest love to Barney and to you. I think of you constantly.

Alice

To William Whitehead, Tasco, Mexico/MS Yale

12 February 1947 5 rue Christine, Paris VI

Dear Whitehead—

As the winter drags on and the days grow colder and darker and wetter it is pleasant to think of you basking in the Mexican sun —of course the snaps—for which I thank you—help me to realise not only what the sun has done for you—but being a free civilian again helps one to achieve that *bien être* which one cant very well do without. It would seem that you chose very wisely in escaping U.S. this winter—all the returned soldiers are complaining of the restlesness—confusion and misunderstanding about them and wishing they saw an end to it all. It's very distressing to think that can be the state of things at home. We used to see too simply and too clearly and now here we are making everything as complicated as poor war worn Europe feels it to be.

But to turn to brighter subjects—how about your youthful heroine —am I never to see her in print. I long to—for she interested Gertrude Stein a lot and dont you write any more verse. And did you see Gertrude Stein's last book *Brewsie and Willie* of which she said she had always wanted to do narration and now she had. It was all there. It has been astonishingly well translated into French. There is a question of doing all her books into French—some eight or nine that have not yet been translated. She would have liked that so very much. It was Elliot Paul who years ago said to her—just wait—you'll be discovered by your home town—meaning of course Paris.

What is going on in Paris is hard to say. Sartre is considered *démodé*—Jean Cocteau's new piece—*L'Aigle a Deux Tête*—is praised but not enthusiastically—there is a great deal of mediocre music played at far too many concerts. [Serge] Lifar is dancing again in London and Monaco—not in Paris yet—he has his lovely green color still but looks too heavy for good dancing.

If everything goes well with you which I very much hope it will and you come over during the summer of next year you will find plenty to interest and distract you—for in spite of the fact that life does not return to what it was in '39 it does become a little more possible all the time—so that one is surprised to remember how much more difficult it was only a few months back. In the meantime make the most of your physical comforts and certain civilities we do specialise in—for after forty years in France I still regret and miss them.

Ever cordially
Alice Toklas

William Whitehead: Whitehead was an actor and a writer and with the American Field Service in France when he met Stein and Toklas.

Elliot Paul: Paul, an American writer, had been editor of the Paris editions of *The Chicago Tribune* (1925–26) and *The New York Herald* (1930). He was co-editor, with Eugene Jolas, of *transition* (1927–28), which printed a number of Stein's pieces.

To W. G. Rogers, New York/MS Rogers

17 February 1947 — 5 rue Christine, Paris VI

Dearest Kiddie—

You're too generous and *la veille grandmaman* (that's what they called me at the *Mairie* the other day—little do they know what I've accomplished before they wake up) isnt going to allow you to spoil her. (I've been given a fountain pen by the last of the G.I.'s and it's not a bad one but it skips a letter like a typewritter when it's run down—except the pen seems to have been born run-down.)

The president of the Guaranty Trust and the lawyer came over to arrange to take the portrait early next week. So much chichi—all these years it travelled about with us—we had it in Bilignin during the war and now they want Pablo to sign a paper guaranteeing it to have been painted by him and I just said I wouldnt insult him by asking him and the banker he shook his head and said of course anyone can testify to the authenticity of the signature. No answer from me—it isn't signed. Good God dont they know it's Gertrude by Picasso. Of course that's just a banker. There's one thing I'm grateful for—they've insured it.

Yours ever
Alice

To Louise Taylor, England/MS Taylor

20 February 1947 — 5 rue Christine, Paris VI

Louise dear—

The Metropolitan is taking the Picasso portrait early next week —it will be more of a wrench to see it go than I had thought possible. It isnt so much because of its being a portrait—indeed the portrait of Gertrude—but because of there being so much of her in it. You know it was painted while she was writing *Three Lives* and she walked up to the Place Ravignan in Montmartre two or three times a week for months and months thinking out her work the way she had—so that it would all be clear to her before she commenced to write. It was a mutual influence—the painter and his model saw things differently after that winter—so I hate to see it go. At first I was quite indifferent—it didn't seem as if it made the least difference—in fact I kept urging the lawyer to see that they should take it—and now I just dread their coming for it—my courage doesnt fill a thimble.

You must tell me about D.D.T.—when we came back the carpet in two rooms was completely eaten up by moths and several spots in all the others—but there were so many people in and out that we postponed having them taken up. It was too naive to suppose carpets could be taken up—cleaned—and put back again. Oh dear no—nothing as useful as that is done any more. And D.D.T. was not on the market yet—it was still exclusively army—but since it is purchasable I've ruined myself by putting down a heavy white coat everywhere. Of course when one walks on it or the dog rolls upon it a great white cloud rises and hits you in the face. Now I'm ruined—for a week there has been no powder in the quarter and the results—*quien sabe?* What do you advise—should I take it up into a bogus vacuum cleaner and start over again. Would you dare to put down the remaining three Bokhara's on it. Give me some advice—whatever it is it will be better than my present state of utter confusion. If they only would content themselves with the carpet I'd let them alone but there are precious blankets and combies that must not oh but most definitely not be eaten.

And I'm very relieved that Red didnt go abstract—the world is queer enough without that—please dont let him—you give him a sweet pat from me. All my love to you both—and dont catch cold in this awful winter.

Ever affectionately
Alice

combies: Combinations, the one-piece woolen undergarment Alice wore.

To Donald Gallup, New Haven/MS Gallup

11 March 1947 5 rue Christine, Paris VI

Dear Donald—

It is hard for me to say how deeply grateful I am to you for all you are doing. You realize surely that Gertrude's memory is all my life—just as she herself was before and surely you will understand if sometimes I ask too much it is because there are some things that must be done before my end. Carl of course will do his work beautifully—Gertrude had every kind of confidence in him. But there are loose ends in other things that you will help me to accomplish.

Gertrude in her will bequeathed the mss. the correspondence she had received—*books*—photographs that might have an artistic value (in speaking of the books to me she said—this was in May when we began to put together for Mademoiselle Droz)—They would like to have the dedicated volumes I suppose—nothing was said about other books. For many reasons that you will appreciate it distresses me to think of their being dispersed over the landscape —Allan Stein will have everything for his life and then it gets divided amongst his three children—the oldest of nineteen years old shows no appreciation of the intellectual life and the two little ones even less—this just for you—so that you understand. So that if Mr. Babb can be induced to write to Allan Stein and to me asking for the books Allan would not make the slightest objection (he leaves me to decide such things but it would be easier if Mr. Poe gets into the game for which there is no reason to have had Allan's acquiescence)—is this too involved for us to handle—I think not. If they—the books—could only get to Yale and the sooner the easier I'd be. You know what they are—considerable eighteenth century—a few amusing Americans and the things every one reads and a miscellaneous collection which shows Gertrude's interest in everything—you know how the shelves were double stacked. It is my dream that they will be on the way to you before the end of next month. Please don't let me make you feel that I am pressing you—but you will let me know how this all strikes you wont you. By the way would they remain together once at the library?

Then I must tell you that the portrait has gone to the Metropolitan—they took it a week ago tomorrow—it was an awful wrench—I'd supposed the preparation *m'endurcie* but it wasn't so at the last moment. Then I put the large cubist picture that had been on the mirror between the two windows where the portrait had been and to take its place the Francis Rose that had [been] between the fire-place and the door. The cubist picture has gained immensely—but the room is emptier than ever.

About the letters of Gertrude to Lindley Hubbell they wont be found to have any particular interest for it was not a friendship just letters to a nice young man—acknowledging his poems etcetera—not for example like her letters to Donald Sutherland to whom she wrote not only more frequently and at greater length but of his work and of hers. His letters to her you will find very interesting indeed. The first one from Princeton when he [Sutherland] was under twenty—did you perhaps meet him here—it certainly does no harm to be baptised Donald—though nothing could be more unlike than the two of you. Poor Kitty Buss having to sell the letters from Ezra—they had quite a flirtation in the late twenties before Ezra left France to go to Italy. By the way it was Kitty Buss who found the Four Seas Company who printed *Geography and Plays.*

Love from
Alice

Mr. Babb: James T. Babb, Librarian at the Yale University Library.

Mr. Poe: In her will Gertrude Stein had declared herself a citizen of the United States, "legally domiciled in Baltimore, Maryland, but residing at 5 rue Christine, Paris." She also instructed that her will be probated in Maryland, where her affairs were handled by Edgar Allan Poe of Bartlett, Poe & Claggett. From the outset Mr. Poe proved difficult when it came to releasing money for the payment of certain outstanding debts and in arranging the money needed to publish Stein's unpublished writings.

large cubist picture: In the salon at the rue Christine there were large Louis XVI mirrors. The larger pictures would be hung from the molding above the mirrors thus all but covering them. When the Picasso portrait was sent to the Metropolitan, Toklas hung in its place Picasso's *Man With a Guitar* (Paris, 1913), now in the collection of André Meyer. Francis Rose's *Portrait of a Young Boy* hung over the other mirror.

Kitty Buss: Kate Buss, a New England journalist and poet had interviewed Stein in 1922. At her urging, the Four Seas Company in Boston published Stein's *Geography and Plays* (1922). Stein's portrait, "To Kitty or Kate Buss" (1932) appeared in *Portraits and Prayers* (1934).

To Louise Taylor, England/MS Taylor

14 March 1947 5 rue Christine, Paris VI

Dearest Louise—

Having a dentist appointment [near] Raspail and Montparnasse yesterday afternoon I went to the Hôtel de Versailles after it was over. The proprietress says there is no heat. Mr. Louis is still there and they prefer transients to people who stay. It is true in all the smaller hotels—indeed it is true of garages—a friend bought a car and he spends all morning hunting a garage for that night—when he doesnt succeed he leaves it in front of his apartment—which is illegal and risky. I don't know what to suggest because the hotels who are more adaptable are too expensive—the small ones around here are *pas convenable* and Gertrude wouldnt when the mattress was being mended let our *bonne* sleep in any of them for fear—well for fear. I will see a man tomorrow who may know something—if he does it would be what you want because he has taste and not too much money—but you'll understand this—we're all possessed of more taste than shekels.

Please bring me nothing but absolutely nothing—it would be

doing me a great disservice. I can explain when you come over and you will not only understand but agree with me. I know I can trust you Louise dear so you must trust me blindly only once. Oh by the way Red had better bring shaving material—I can help you out easily on other things.

Lots of love to you both.

Alice

To Henry Rago, Chicago/MS Indiana

16 March 1947 5 rue Christine, Paris VI

Dear Rago—

For weeks I've had your article in *Poetry* that you so kindly sent me—unfortunately I've been forced to wait until now to tell you how very much I liked it. You have explained clearly and quite completely why time was Gertrude's preoccupation and your reference to A. N. Whitehead would have pleased her. Then your using as your only quotation the blurb for George John was an excellent idea. I was very touched with the way you wrote of the spontaneity Gertrude always had in expressing thoughts and ideas that she had had over the years—it was that freshness of vision that made it possible for her to recreate what she used to call the less than a dozen fundamental truths. You have said all this and more so very well. And I thank you.

They took the Picasso portrait for the Metropolitan ten days ago. It was another parting and completely undid me. Picasso came over to say good bye to it and said sadly—*ni vous—ni moi le reverra jamais.* It was all there was left of their youth.

Thanks again for *Poetry* and your article.

Always cordially
Alice Toklas

GERTRUDE STEIN WITH PICASSO'S PORTRAIT OF HER, PARIS, 1922

Photograph by Man Ray

They took the Picasso portrait for the Metropolitan. It was another parting and completely undid me.

Poetry: "Gertrude Stein," an article Rago wrote for *Poetry* (November 1946).

George John: One of the many G.I.'s who sought Stein's advice on their manuscripts. Stein was impressed by his poems and before he left Paris gave him a statement about his work to be used as an introduction or a blurb: "A great many soldiers came and one day unexpectedly a poet. He had come and left many little pieces of paper and on each piece of paper was a poem. He like all the soldiers had been in many places, Italy France Belgium Holland Germany England and then later India, as he was a field service man, and everywhere there were landscapes and all the landscapes were poems. He was the only one to whom that happened and he was a poet. I was excited and thought I would never see him again and only have the little pieces of paper with the poems on them and the name George John. At the end of a long week he came again, tall gentle thin and young, and then I told him he was a poet but he knew that and I knew it, and now I am telling it here where the poems are printed. George John." When his first book, *A Garland About Me,* appeared in 1951, it bore the dedication, "In memory of Gertrude Stein: my friend too briefly but my teacher forever."

To W. G. Rogers, New York/MS Rogers

21 March 1947 — 5 rue Christine, Paris VI

Dearest Kiddie—

Yesterday morning when I was cooking an extra company meatless lunch—(because the butchers have been on a strike for a week)—for a Belley friend your letter came. The lunch can curdle and burn for all of me while I read what the Kiddie has to say. And what did the Kiddie have to say—why that he was as nervous as a witch or a *toute jeune fille* about the trip and hadnt I received the parcel yet. Doesnt he know he's expected at the Récamier—doesnt he know that parcels take months if they come at all. So I went on being a cook and then when every one had gone late in the afternoon (more Belleysians for tea) I went into the bed room and there was the package—I was so excited I forgot my exhaustion and boredom and opened it feverishly (but carefully undoing the string). And there were all the treasures—no I just couldn't believe my eyes—the wonderful towels—the warm combies (not a darn—*new new new*) the lavender soap (sweet but naughty Mildred Kiddie) and then oh then the utterly lovely scarf. I never thought to see anything like it again—to say nothing of having it for my own. It's a royal gift and it's overwhelmingly beautiful. In the evening I had a visit from my young Turkish painter and I gave him a long lecture on the simplicity and at the same time subtlety of the American gift—the unerring taste—the appreciation of métier and quality that no European realises or will accept. It's true you know—from Edgar Allan Poe to the scarf. And as for no longer needing it—little do you know the Parisian climate. It suitably turned cold overnight and I'm going to wear it not only with joy but with the greatest comfort when I go out this afternoon. And to both of the Kiddies my warmest thanks.

Virgil's music will be alright. I've had a tremendous quarrel with him about something else—and he hasnt answered me. I told him that I believed in his music but not in him and so I wont hear from him but when he turns up here in summer he'll let me hear the music alright. He just has enough integrity to cover his gift. He spoke well of me to you because he is superstitious. But he will have made good music to Gertrude's opera—and her libretto rises to a wonderful heroic tragic end. You'll be seeing the performance of it and you'll tell me all about it.

Much love from
Alice

Turkish painter: Néjad Bey.

Virgil's music: The score for *The Mother of Us All.*

To Ralph W. Church, Santa Barbara, California
MS Bancroft

9 April 1947 5 rue Christine, Paris VI

Dear Ralph—

You are I hope convalescing satisfactorily—otherwise I will regret writing to you as I am going to. It is about the pictures that finally I was able to get off to you and which the shipper who sent them told me several weeks ago you had safely received. At the time he told me it was very satisfactory to learn that after so many delays the pictures were in your hands. Since then there have been unexpected complications in the settlement of Gertrude's estate and it now would be of the greatest convenience to me if you could without inconvenience to yourself deposit the thousand dollars to my account at the American Express Company Inc.—65 Broadway—New York—attention of Mr. E. Lager. I dont know if you knew that Gertrude left me a life interest in her estate—after me it goes to Allan Stein—the only son of her oldest brother Michael—and finally to be divided by his three children. Allen and I were named executors. It is at his suggestion that I am writing to you—for the inheritance taxes must be paid in two countries.

The Yale University Press is bringing out in the fall *Four in America* with preface by T. Wilder—and Carl Van Vechten was appointed by Gertrude to publish her unedited work—some nine volumes or possibly ten—two later ones—the rest from the twenties when no one would publish her work. There are five translations into Italian—three into French and one into Danish arranged for —she knew about these—except the Danish. The *Picasso* in French is to go into print again. I am telling you because I think it will interest you to know how the appreciation increased—so different from those early days when you first knew Gertrude.

Ever cordially
Alice Toklas

Church: Ralph Withington Church and his mother had met Stein and Toklas through Sherwood Anderson. Church was a philosopher who was working on his doctorate at Oxford. Toklas claimed that his success in the examinations was due to the intervention of Sainte Geneviève to whom she had prayed. Church wrote "A Note on the Writing of Gertrude Stein" for *transition* (Fall 1928). Toklas, with the consent of Allan Stein, had sold Church three pictures: Tchelitchew's *Portrait of Alice Toklas* (1927), now at UCLA, his still life *Grapes* (1927), and a Kristians Tonny, *Le Bateau Ivre* (1927).

Picasso: Stein's long essay on Picasso (1938).

To Donald Gallup, New Haven/MS Gallup

19 April 1947 — 5 rue Christine, Paris VI

Dear Donald—

I am so thrilled with your description of the exhibition of the letters. What a variety there is of human nature in them. And your including the rejections—the refusals—how Gertrude would have appreciated that. You must know how those refusals hurt at the time they were received but one day Blanche Knopf outdid even all Knopf's Knopfishness and then Gertrude forgot our hopes and bitter disappointment and burst into that loud laughter. By the time you knew her—I only realise it now—there was so much less of it—and it hadnt its enormous contagious vitality any more. Have you come across some amusing disgruntled bitter letters signed Emma Erving. She was at Johns Hopkins in the same class I think as Gertrude. There are still here a quantity of letters from Gertrude's sister-in-law Sarah—Mike's wife and the devoted friend of Matisse—from Mike and Leo Stein. They are likely to be fairly personal and intimate. I'll be sending them with the books without looking at them. I've neither the time nor the heart to—I suppose they ought not to be made accessible until after the death of Sarah and Leo. Mike died about eight years ago.

Which brings one to a question you ask—What became of the first novel Gertrude wrote (1904–1905). I have the manuscript. It is a subject I havent known how to handle nor known from what point to act upon. It was something I knew I'd have to meet some day and not too long hence and to cover my cowardice I kept saying—well when every thing else is accomplished. But you are the *only* person who ever asked. Gertrude gave me the manuscript in '33 after she had shown it to Louis Bromfield—Bernard Faÿ—and W. A. Bradley (her literary agent here). Bradley thought it had the hand of the master but advised not to publish—at least not then. Then Gertrude gave it to me and it was never mentioned again. Now what shall I do about it? I am asking you and Carl—who never asked about it and so doesnt know the little I have told you. But you two must decide. The only thing I know is I wouldnt want it read—that is therefore not published—during my life. Gertrude would have understood this perfectly though of course it was never mentioned. Is there not some way of sending it to you or Carl or both of you under this condition. Of course it must not be found here someday when Allan comes and takes over.

About the man who stole William James' copy of *Three Lives* from Harvard—you'll find his letter amongst the collection some day. I dont remember his name but he wrote on paper with a law firm's letter head from Boston I think and he was I think a member of the firm. Some one has just written me that they bought in a second hand shop in New York a copy of *Three Lives* with a dedication to Paul Robeson. Virgil Thomson has a lot of letters from Gertrude—should I speak of his giving them to you. He's bigotty about Harvard but they never wanted her or them—he might—as a *geste*—do it. The end of my page has come but not—never not—of my gratitude and affection always.

Alice

Basket has worms! Until Monday when he goes to the vet.

exhibition of letters: A selection from the manuscripts, books, letters, and photographs bequeathed by Stein to the Yale University Library was shown in the spring of 1947.

Blanche Knopf: Wife and colleague of the publisher Alfred Knopf.

Emma Erving: Emma Lootz Erving was Stein's roommate for two years at Johns Hopkins.

first novel: Stein's first completed novel, *Q.E.D.*, was written in 1903. It is a fictionalized account of Stein's love affair with a fellow student at Hopkins and the complicated and desperate course the affair took because of a rival and because of Stein's frustration in trying to fathom the woman she loved. It was printed in 1950 under the title *Things As They Are* with a number of minor changes in the text made by Carl Van Vechten. It was republished in 1971 by Liveright under its original title and in a corrected edition (*Fernhurst, Q.E.D., and other early writings*).

Louis Bromfield: An American writer who lived with his family in Senlis. When the manuscript for *Q.E.D.* was found in 1933 (Stein had long since forgotten its existence), she gave it to Bromfield to see what he thought about publishing it. Bromfield thought it suitable for publication, but Stein, realizing how painful its publication might be for Alice, gave her the manuscript to do with as she wished.

To W. G. and Mildred Rogers, New York/MS Rogers

13 May 1947 5 rue Christine, Paris VI

Dearest Kiddies—

Any morning now you'll be flying in and I'm doing all the household darning and letter writing and all the back work so as to be free when you want to see me. I'm even getting the English friends off my mind so that if by any mistake they stay on after you come I'll have done my whole duty by them before then. Gertrude's books go off this week with a few things I've found. The flat is emptier than ever. Well here is your second letter with the news of the opera [*The Mother of Us All*] and the clippings. I so longed to be there. It seems to have gone off very well. And it evidently ends as Gertrude wanted it to—a controlled but grandiose finale—that was what worried me the most. And you were dear to write me at once and to send me the clippings. I'm sending the *Herald Tribune* with the reproduction of the photograph of Jo the Loiterer to the original—there's a curious physical resemblance to him—which he wont like. Is it only thirteen years ago you came over that first time we saw you—sometimes it seems a hundred or a thousand or not at all. I will be glad to see you—bless you.

Oh about the Whidney's Hoover—not for the world—nothing would induce me to have it. It's a new one I want (Gertrude and I always had the deepest distaste for second hand mechanical toys) and it's not now that I'd want to try out an aged second hand anything—so please tell Mrs. Kiddie to persuade them to give her one. Virgil's judgement is rotten—he's thoroughly unreliable except on music and so please dont listen to him about our lovely Hoover.

Yes there are three more books projected but not only will yours be the first but—oh just lots of things.

Maillol and Masson are having shows and there will be others—usually the municipality or the government stages some tremendous affair for June. We are no longer afraid of communism—we have forgotten the Russians—we are looking forward—no not to De Gaulle but to a stable government as if it were an entirely new idea. Wait till you read the newspapers—they are a scream. Now I must really get to bed so that I can climb up and get the books down from where they have been since '38 when we moved here. They've been vacuumed endlessly but not with a Hoover.

Dearest love to you both always.

Alice

To Mildred Weston Rogers, New York/MS Rogers

6 June 1947 5 rue Christine, Paris VI

Dearest Mrs. Kiddie—

You don't know my interest—curiosity—and pleasure in kitchen gadgets—so the colored measuring spoons are a toy and more and the paper that replaces silver polish a wonder—the lovely pale mulberry colored cloth—what can it be? The dish cloth I am using as a dining room table mat. And the darning cotton—which does not fall apart when you open the tube is a marvel. I've used it in sheer self-indulgence. The golden safety pins to be worn on the outside are a nine day's wonder and the cook book is so very gay. I made a pudding for the Kiddie from it but as it didnt turn out quite right I didnt tell the Kiddie that it was from the book. I am enclosing a quick way to prepare eggs in advance—i.e. to be eaten cold.

Endless love from
Alice

Jellied eggs

Poach 5 eggs—as little as possible.

Soak 1 tbsp. powered gelatine in ½ cup water.

Heat 1½ cups water—dissolve 3 boullion cubes in it.

Pour over the gelatine—add 1 glass of cognac. When it *begins* to stiffen pour into 5 small molds—drop in the egg and put in ice-chest. Take out of molds—place on dish but keep in ice-chest until time for serving. A little finely chopped ham at the bottom of mold is pretty and tasty—or finely chopped chevril and parsley. Very small tomatoes stuffed with hard boiled eggs or chicken (!!!) is another variation.

To Sir Francis Rose, England/MS Texas

11 June 1947 5 rue Christine, Paris VI

Dearest Francis—

Because W. G. Rogers has been here for over two weeks everything has been a bit topsy turvy—as he came over expressly to see me I can do no less than give him all my time. He is you know the Kiddie of *The Autobiography*—he is quite as sweet as ever—and of course it has been ever so nice having him in Paris—though it leaves me little free time. It has taken me out of my quiet routine—we have gone to picture shows—nothing of any particular interest—except all the French pictures from the Louvre at the Petit Palais—and the impressionists at the Orangerie. The Braque show is feeble—the Poulenc ballet's presentation very vulgar—the weather abominable—Basket adorable—so much for my news.

You dont know what pleasure I have in the pictures you paint even when I've not yet seen them—an anticipatory pleasure you will say—but it is a little more than that—to know your work continues and develops is very actual to me my faith in your work is one of the few sustaining things in my life—and a great comfort to me. I am keeping all of your drawings together and will speak to you about them when you come over because I want them to go back to you—naturally with the water colors of yours that Gertrude had. You do know how much your pictures mean to me beside Gertrude's appreciation of them. Love to you both always.

Alice

Poulenc's ballet: Later it is spoken of as an opera. Toklas is referring to Poulenc's opéra-bouffe *Les Mamelles de Tirésias* (c. 1944, libretto by Guillaume Apollinaire).

SIR FRANCIS ROSE AND GERTRUDE STEIN, BILIGNIN, 1933

. . . you do know how much your pictures mean to me beside Gertrude's appreciation of them.

To Julian Sawyer, New York/MS Unknown

12 June 1947 [5 rue Christine, Paris VI]

You will understand I hope my objection to your repeated references to the subject of sexuality as an approach to the understanding of Gertrude's work. She would have emphatically denied it—she considered it the least characteristic of all expressions of character—her actual references to sexuality are so rare—as one of Gertrude's staunchest defenders it should not lead to other errors. Gertrude always said she did not like private judgements.

Julian Sawyer: Sawyer was an enthusiast of Stein's work. In February–April 1947 he had given a series of seven lectures, "Gertrude Stein: Her Words and Her Ideas," at the Galerie Neuf in New York. This series was repeated in the spring of 1949 at the New School for Social Research.

To Donald Gallup, New Haven/MS Gallup

23 June 1947 5 rue Christine, Paris VI

Dear Donald—

Your idea of publishing the letters is a wonderful one—if I'd not known them what pleasure to discover such a book—nothing would have been half so exciting. Carl feels it would be wrong to publish it before at least one volume of Gertrude's unpublished work has appeared. I suppose he has not written to me about it —but I can see the point as well taken. If later anyone does 80 volumes—your selection would remain the cream of them—and 80 volumes would only be done a century hence when as Gertrude said when I objected to including the concierge and servants' letters—Who knows if in the end they wont be found to be the most interesting. But the selection would be fascinating reading —but what work for you—you would have to ask everyone's permission wouldnt you? Do please speak to Carl further about it.

You must type your letters—your time is too precious for long hand—Carl always types—always has as you've seen—Gertrude at first (years and years ago) was shocked but afterwards only minded it from people she hadnt met. She thought a first letter should have been by hand. So please always type—it would make your pretty new paper go so much further. Did I tell you that Jean Cocteau did the cover to the French translation of *Brewsie and Willie*. Yours—Y.U.L. and Carl's go off tomorrow. What a relief to know that Thornton Wilder is going on with his work for *Four in America*. The Kiddie tells me that though the book was announced for publication in autumn—winter would be equally good—the serious reading public is through to Easter.

You know Thornton isn't really unapproachable but untouchable —just the opposite of Picasso—no not really only half the way for Picasso is unapproachable—but so very easily touched—by a few. Amongst the many places we—the Kiddie and I—have gone to is Darantière's—he lives down in the Marais near the Place des Vosges in Mansard's home—two stories all completely of the period —woodwork and frescoes—quite incredible. He did the original *Making of Americans* with its perfect title page. About twenty years ago he left Dijon to devote himself to hand printed books in limited editions. Now he is working—with the consent of course of the government—with François I and Louis XV type from the Bibliothèque Nationale. He has a mad passion to visit U.S.—to take over some of his books and to show them and to give three or four lectures covering his work and fine printing in France of the past. I wondered if Yale would be interested—he would want about twenty five meters by a little less than a meter of space in which to show the books and he would like to go in autumn. I am sending you two pages of his printing to show you what he does. If you are interested his name is Maurice Darantière and his address is 28 rue des Tournelles—Gertrude was very much interested in his work and eventually he is to do two of her books. Now I must let Basket out and then turn in. I send you all my gratitude and love.

Alice

publishing the letters: Gallup's proposal emerged as *The Flowers of Friendship: Letters Written to Gertrude Stein* (1953), a selection of almost 450 letters written to Stein from 1895 to 1946.

Mansard: Jules Hardouin Mansard, seventeenth-century French architect.

To W. G. and Mildred Rogers, New York/MS Rogers

2 July 1947 — 5 rue Christine, Paris VI

Dearest Kiddies—

In the written testimony of Gertrude for Bernard Faÿ I found this phrase—"he tended to the right and I tended to the radical —so that will help you see the point of being bourgeois and being a radical"—as Picasso said all artists (not American!) do. And please dont forget your word of honor to cut out all remarks which are not literature—put an impartial cool New England eye to this and they will *sautant aux yeux.* Last night I went with Olga Picasso and Marie Laurencin to a rehearsal of Stravinsky's *Le Baiser de la Feé* with very dull décor and costumes by Hellika and Balanchine choreography. His wife is a sturdy American ballerina—whom you probably know. This is not what I started to tell you. It was that Poulenc came to speak to Marie Laurencin and she was enthusiastic about the presentation of *Les Mamelles [de Tirésias]*—not a word about his music—he too was enthusiastic about the presentation so when they had calmed down I told him (in a corner where we could offend no one) what we had thought of the music—he was as pleased as he could allow himself to be. You see how the ballet is the thing still in Paris.

Thanks for having come over. Love to you both always

Alice

testimony of Gertrude: As a foreigner Stein was not permitted to give testimony in court in support of Faÿ. She was, however, permitted to submit a written statement, which she did.

To Sir Francis Rose, England/MS Texas

11 July 1947 — 5 rue Christine, Paris VI

Dearest Francis—

My first thought this morning on awaking was that I'd be writing to you at once. I've been wanting to for over a week—for Rogers and I went out to Père Lachaise to see the tombstone which was just put up. It is so perfectly what it should be—you will find your plan not miscarried—the only disappointment is its size but there was nothing to do about that alas. The marble cutter went at once to the Bibliothèque Nationale and came here with the lettering the following day—he understands the relation of the letters for the name and for the dates below and they will be ready any day now. Dear Francis—you know how deeply grateful I am to you—we have so much to still say to each other that I look forward to seeing you impatiently.

Dearest love to you both.

Alice

tombstone: Rose had designed the tombstone. The lettering was incised (not *en relief*) and was copied directly from Trajan's Arch at Benevento.

To Samuel Steward, Chicago/MS Bancroft

31 July 1947 5 rue Christine, Paris VI

Sammie dear—

I am ashamed to think that you have no better souvenirs than the thorns from Bilignin—you who gave so continuously—so generously. But I can make amends—there will be someone going back sometime who will take the real souvenir to you. I'll manage so that you wont have to wait until you come over. And how I wish you'd make it soon—it would mean so much to have you in Paris—do be a really good boy and save your pennies. I dont think you'd have any trouble to get a position at the American school by applying well in advance. They dont pay handsomely but probably enough to live on quietly. If you dont like the idea dont hate me. I'll try to think of something else. But if you want to teach you'd have to be awfully good which might be a bore. Living conditions are quite possible—everything except keeping warm—heating adequately just doesnt exist. But do make your plans to come. The horrid administrator in Baltimore—his name is Edgar Allan Poe—is doing everything he can to retard Carl Van Vechten's work of the unpublished manuscripts—Carl and I want to see the work started at once—naturally—and he goes on delaying with one excuse and another. It's unbearable—unthinkable that what Gertrude wanted is not being done. I've been trying to find the money here but how to get it over to U.S. in dollars with all the French *office d'échange* is more than anyone is ready to undertake. My last hope here has vanished and I'm sick with it all—there is nothing to do now but wait until October which is the earliest the horrid creature puts as his earliest date. I'm really telling you my worries but you will please forget that I have done so and dont mention it to me or anyone. It's so hot I get foolish in the head.

I havent told you that Francis Rose designed a very simple but beautifully proportioned headstone for Gertrude's grave. I've had some photos taken and will send you one as soon as I get them. Precious—precious Gertrude out there alone—she who was always so surrounded. Sammie are you still *pratiquant*—what a consolation it must be. Forget this weakness it's fatigue and the heat—and I never tear up or censor my letters so I'll let it go *telle quelle.*

Your ever affectionate
Alice

To Louise and Redvers Taylor, England/MS Taylor

18 August 1947 — 5 rue Christine, Paris VI

My dears—

My efforts to get Gertrude's unpublished work published become more risky—more hazardous and less successful. When the last project—fantastic beyond any normal conception—failed I was in despair but the next morning I menaced the administrator in Baltimore and it worked—he immediately sent half the sum to Carl Van Vechten—the other half for the first of October. After so much anxiety and seeing so many people in the intense heat (always over 95°) like a fool I caved in—the doctor said it was nothing but fatigue and heat—said I shouldnt do anything until my energy returned—which it's doing—and of course the relief is enormous. Carl has already commenced work. There are one or two things to straighten out here and there during the winter. I'll probably complain at having nothing to do—which will be the first time since '14.

Do you remember Harriet Levy—well she's eighty years old and has just published her first *two* books and she sent them to me. It has been my exceedingly difficult task to write to her about them because oh dear she should have restrained herself just a little longer. And the worst is she *can* write. It's that she has nothing to say which is a thousand pities as it's nearly always the other way round. Do let me have news of you soon and tell me you forgive my silence. Endless love to you both always.

Alice

Harriet Levy: Harriet Lane Levy was the San Francisco friend with whom Toklas had come to France in September 1907. When Harriet returned to America in 1910 Alice went to live with Gertrude and Leo Stein at 27 rue de Fleurus. Harriet Levy became a newspaper woman in San Francisco and wrote two books: *920 O'Farrell Street* (1947) and *I Love to Talk About Myself & Other Verses Concerning God & Man & Me* (1947).

To The Curator of Paintings,
Metropolitan Museum of Art, New York
MS Metropolitan

15 September 1947 — 5 rue Christine, Paris VI

Dear Sir,

In your release to the press of August twenty-second, concerning the *Portrait of Gertrude Stein* by Pablo Picasso, there are several inaccuracies.

The shipment of the picture was not delayed for several months in deference to my wish to keep it in its place here in the apartment as long as possible. On the contrary I instructed my lawyer to see that the museum take possession of the picture as soon as possible. After some delay the museum's representative telephoned to make arrangements for its removal. The following day when he called he said he was prepared to take the picture away with him at once. I asked him to give me a week's time to permit Picasso and some of Gertrude Stein's friends to see it for the last time. This was graciously immediately accorded. The picture was commenced in 1905 and finished during the late summer of 1906. The picture was not loaned to the Museum of Modern Art's comprehensive show of Picasso in 1939. It has never left France until shipped this spring to the Metropolitan Museum of Art.

When the picture was commenced Gertrude Stein had been living in Paris a little over a year.

Gertrude Stein's first book was completed several months before the portrait was.

Gertrude Stein never supported Braque.

Sincerely
Alice Toklas

To W. G. Rogers, New York/MS Rogers

27 September 1947 5 rue Christine, Paris VI

Dearest Kiddie—

Well—Basket and I did get our vacation and it was wonderful. Georges Maratier and Ed Livergood took us out in their car to Dreux where they've had a little house on the hills above the town and where we had two marvellous days of long walks (without a leash) and drives to the lovely Chateau d'Anet and to the church at Nonancourt. It did us a world of good and we're fit and dandy—which has given Gabrielle the opportunity of not feeling so well—so there we are.

The first thing I want to write to you about was the titles you sent—at first I liked them both and then I cooled to one and then the other—but I'm no judge because I dont at all know the taste of the American public so you'll decide and it will be wonderful and the important thing is the book after all—isnt it. In the end I wrote to the curator of painting at the Metropolitan gently but firmly correcting his inaccuracies and thought that was closed when this morning I got a clipping from the *N.Y. Times* of Sept. 22nd that Carl sent me. It has completely upset me. Gertrude—as you will remember by my having told you several times always with an increasing violence—loathed and despised The Museum of Modern Art and all its little ways. And to think that they have acquired the portrait. It is unbearable—but that isnt the worst—in the same agreement between the two museums which gives the portrait to the Modern the Metropolitan buys two Picassos from the Modern and furthermore the Modern has the right to sell their acquisitions so the portrait may be acquired by Barnes or Chrysler or God knows who. It's unthinkable and I'm very upset and sad that such a thing can be. I'm writing to Carl to find out what can be done. If the *Times* has reported this correctly I'll certainly protest—Allan of course with me.

Virgil leaves in a week—he's in very good form and is become a V.I.P. which is very nice for him. He has just lent me his book *The State of Music* (1939) which I'd never seen. It's witty and brilliant (I've read but the first three chapters) but he is wrong —very wrong about the painters and I've told him so over the telephone and will tell him so in detail when he lunches with me Tuesday. He's been to London to visit almost the Queen —the Beechams.

Everyone says it is going to be a cold winter but Gabrielle says—No—not when the onions peel as they do this year. And how do they peel this year—I asked. And she said—Easily!! In New York you cant predict winter weather by peeling onions because your onions are peeled when you first see them. Since I learned that eggs with two yolks are bought by the dozen—why shouldnt onions grow peeled. Which brings me to the question of the cook book. It was a coincidence your letter and the weekend near Dreux. Georges had as guests not only me but the Sherry Mangans—do you remember or rather did you ever hear of *larus*—a literary review—you probably were still wearing dresses at that time. Well

Gertrude had several things in it. Apparently he's [Mangan] been living in France for some time before the war but we never met him and he's no longer a beautiful young poet but quite a gross middle-aged newspaper man but with a very fine head. He seems to eat and drink too well.

However in speaking of the American commissary which you may remember I've been trying to maneuver to be admitted to and Georges [Maratier] mentioning the food at Bilignin—suddenly it came to me if I could get recipes printed in some magazine I'd be as eligible as Richard Wright—so why not gather my recipes—make the cook book and get a job. Then I took up next with S. Mangan—what would one do with such 18th & 19th century recipes as I have—reduce the measurements to exact American cup measurements and experiment with substitutes. He said Americans *never* read foreign recipes—they hunt for new ones. Is this true.

Please send me a copy of a magazine called the *Gourmet*.

I've gotten beyond the end of daylight—and no artificial light—yet—and to the end of my paper but not the end of the love I send you both.

Alice

Georges Maratier: A picture dealer who first knew Stein and Toklas in the late twenties. Livergood was an American living in Paris.

Gabrielle: Toklas' *femme de ménage.*

agreement between the two museums: An agreement between the Metropolitan Museum of Art and the Museum of Modern Art (it originally included the Whitney Museum of American Art) by which the scope of each collection was defined and the Metropolitan's area limited to "classical art" and the Modern to "European and American visual art of the present and recent past." As part of the agreement the Metropolitan agreed to "deposit" with the Modern those paintings, prints, drawings, and sculpture that could more appropriately be exhibited at the Modern. In addition the Modern agreed to sell to the Metropolitan, for $191,000, some forty works of art which were deemed more appropriate to the Metropolitan. Picasso's *Portrait of Gertrude Stein* was one of the works placed on "deposit."

Sherry Mangan: An American writer who edited *larus,* a literary review which had published two pieces by Stein, "Waterpipe" in February 1927 and "Elie Nadelman" in July 1927.

To Donald Gallup, New Haven/MS Gallup

6 October 1947 — 5 rue Christine, Paris VI

Dear Donald–

The delay in answering you is caused by the miserable affair of the transfer of the portrait from and by the Metropolitan to the Museum of Modern Art–I've written to two or three people appealing for aid to prevent such disregard of Gertrude's wishes. The lawyer here sent a wire registering Allan's and my protest to which the director (Mr. Redmond)–who made the original statement to the press–answered with the information that it was loaned to the Modern and would return to the Metropolitan in due course. The whole thing doesnt make sense as the Metropolitan has bought from the Modern two Picassos (earlier period and later than the portrait) and give as reason for <u>lending</u> the portrait–because they are not yet ready to exhibit art of the period of the portrait. It makes me very unhappy because they have legally the right–bad faith and stupidity are not illegal–so I'm not very hopeful. Would you and Carl advise a public statement from Allan and me in case the small influence I've appealed to fails. Another burden I ask you to share. [Roger] Shattuck says the Met is "snide"–so sweetly 1900.

There is a small reproduction in lead–about 10 inches high–which Jo Davidson had especially made for Gertrude of his portrait of her which I'll send to you for the Y.U.L. About Francis' portrait of me–of course you may have [it] if I can find one of Gertrude's to send at the same time. Francis did one of her–it wasnt very good as portrait or as painting [as the one] which

Gertrude gave to Allan (did you ever see it?). Allan definitely refuses to give it to Y.U.L. There were two Picabia portraits—one hangs in the gallery over the fireplace—I dont at all like it as portrait or presentation but I think I could easily get Allan's consent to giving that. Let me know if you want it please. The Riba [-Rovira] portrait that Bob Sweet has you'll remember—Bob wont give it to you now but will bequeathe it (fifty years hence) to Y.U.L. if I write a very careful letter to him which I will. Did I warn you about his letters. They are terrific! I dont think Etta Cone would give any picture away—particularly if she thought it was important enough for Y.U.L. to want it—but if you could flatter her (and she accepts what would be for any one else an enormously indigestible quantity) she might bequeathe the letters if she has kept them. Could you say that they would become part of the correspondence but known as the Etta Cone bequest or something equally grossly publicising herself you'd have a fair chance of getting them. No the row about Biarritz production of *Yes* wasnt about the mode of transport—that was merely a minor irritation. Col (Mac?) of Fordham College accepted it enthusiastically as a result of his request for a play for Biarritz and after hearing it read aloud here. Then he brought a charming General Paul Thompson—newly appointed E.O.T. (?)—and they were enthusiastic. He asked to meet Paco [Riba-Rovira] to arrange for a décor and accepted his décor. Then the colonel went back to Biarritz having told us the precise dates of the ten performances they were to give and made the arrangements for Gertrude's being there for the rehearsals. Then silence and more silence and about ten days before the rehearsals were to commence I commenced telephoning three times a day for three days without being able to get the Col.—finally he wired that a major would call on Gertrude the next day. The major was a captain and he came accompanied by Mr. McClintoc the husband of Katharine Cornell who hadnt liked the play when he'd heard it read here—and said they'd decided to give it experimental performances without costume or décor just simply readings. Gertrude refused and asked for the immediate return of the ms. More violent telephoning and finally the ms. was returned after I'd gotten into conversation by error of course with another general. Later a sergeant turned up—he'd made a décor (horrible—symbolic and God knows what) and that fell through *before* the change of plan. He said that the colonel was not in command at Biarritz—he'd only been interim director—when his chief turned up he wouldnt hear of *Yes* having regular Biarritz performances but he would consent to "experimental" ones. Isnt it a typical army story?

Leo [Stein] was never interested in Marsden Hartley—Gertrude had one drawing and it hasnt turned up. I dont seem to remember seeing it since our return. Can it have been the only one that was taken in August '44? Yes I'll make you an inventory of the pictures and drawings of Gertrude's collection—do you want titles because most of the pictures havent titles—would for example "cubist period still life" be sufficient? Janet Flanner isnt very accurate. Gertrude said not to send bills (doing over the studio rue de Fleurus—preparing the flat here '38 etcetera—so that period was destroyed)—there may be a few here still from other times—there never are receipts for pictures in France—you pay the artist cash—the dealer by cheque. If you had receipts for your pictures it was probably because of passing them at the customs. Please ask any questions you like on the *typewriter*—because they are about Gertrude or her activities and what in the else is there for me but that. Fondest love to you always and gratitude and blessings.

Alice

two Picassos: As part of the agreement the Metropolitan bought Picasso's *La Coiffure* (1906) and *The Woman in White* (1923). They did not actually take possession of the pictures until 1952 when the museum agreement expired.

Riba portrait: Francisco Riba-Rovira (nicknamed Paco), a Spanish artist living in Paris, met Stein in 1945 while he was painting along one of the quais and she was walking Basket. Stein bought a number of drawings from him. Riba-Rovira did three portraits of Stein.

Etta Cone: Etta Cone and her sister Dr. Claribel Cone were friends of Stein's in Baltimore. It was under the tutelage of Leo and Gertrude that they acquired many of the finest of the works of modern art that are now the Cone Collection in the Baltimore Museum of Art. Etta Cone in 1906 typed the manuscript of *Three Lives.* In 1912 Stein wrote "Two Women," a portrait of the sisters whom Gertrude named Martha (Claribel) and Ada (Etta). (See *Contact Collection of Contemporary Writers* [Paris: Contact Editions, 1925].)

Marsden Hartley: Stein was, for a time, an admirer of Hartley's paintings and wrote a foreword for a 1914 exhibition of his work at gallery "291."

To Roland L. Redmond, Esq., President, Metropolitan Museum of Art, New York
MS Metropolitan

6 October 1947 — 5 rue Christine, Paris VI

Dear Sir,

C. D. Morgan, Esquire has suggested that I should give you some details concerning Miss Gertrude Stein's bequest to the Metropolitan Museum of Art of her portrait by Picasso.

Miss Gertrude Stein very deliberately chose the Metropolitan Museum—having decided to leave the picture to a museum in her mind there was no choice—if there had been one—the Museum of Modern Art would not have been an alternative.

Miss Gertrude Stein was not interested in the Museum of Modern Art—indeed she thoroughly disapproved of its policy and aims—of its choice of pictures for its permanent collection—of its interest in subjects unconnected with modern art. This was not a hastily formed judgement but one that grew over the years. She had followed the career of the museum over the years.

It is now very sad to see her wishes so disregarded—so miscarried. It is an ethical question. And I appeal to you to reconsider your decision to lend the picture to the Museum of Modern Art taking into account her opinions and feelings and to make these clear to the other trustees of the Metropolitan Museum and to ask them to change their decision so that the painting remains at the Metropolitan Museum.

Yours very sincerely
Alice Toklas

To Donald Sutherland, Boulder, Colorado
MS Sutherland

8 October 1947 5 rue Christine, Paris VI

Dear Sutherland—

I am so sorry to have left your letter unanswered for so long—and now your kindness in writing to me again makes me realise how much and how often I think of you. The last three months have been a nightmare trying to find means to get the money and then get it to New York for the printing of Gertrude's unpublished work. There were endless projects—fantastic and risky—which all failed—finally the administrator in Baltimore was bluffed into doing his duty and he has sent the necessary check to Carl Van Vechten. Now he's [Van Vechten] commenced having the manuscript typed. But before it was over I was so completely exhausted —anxiety and the heat—that for the first time in fifty-three years I'd to see the doctor. Now I'm alright again.

Your book on Gertrude interests me passionately—there is no one else that I know of who is capable of doing what you will do—who could go so far—so deep and so directly. I hang on to see the first of Gertrude's books and your book about her published. But you mustnt speak again please of showing me the manuscript when you and Gilberte come over in March for any other reason than the pleasure and satisfaction it will give me. It would have meant an awful lot to Gertrude.

No dont take on Julian Sawyer—he is ignorant—unintelligent insensitive and pretentious. He gave a series of five lectures on Gertrude's complete works—with interpretations that angered one. In the synopsis he innocently sent me there was amongst a mad jumble of topics—Gertrude Stein and sex—so that a word seemed necessary.

About Proust and Joyce and James—wouldnt Proust come off better in comparison with James—as for Joyce wouldnt he be better off without a comparison. Of course James was the precursor alright. But in rereading *The Wings of the Dove* there were suddenly some very direct connections between Kate Croy and Melanctha—between Gertrude's dialectic and his. It fascinated me. It was the only one of his books I remember her having reread several times. I'm not indelicate in asking you to send me what you have done because you suggest doing so—you would if you knew how much it will mean to me—the need to have Gertrude presented as you will seems more important every day and seeing it would be the encouragement one needs—you know the Yale University Press is publishing a short thing of Gertrude's —*Four in America* (G. Washington—Wilbur Wright—James—and General Grant) with a long introduction by Thornton Wilder which I've not seen and which I a little dread—without your warning "too much psychology"—because any is already poisonous as well as hopelessly the *bas fond* of the last century's approach. The book is to be out next month and I'll be sending you a copy.

The situation here politically is less of a mess than usual so perhaps more critical—economically it's hopeless—but the serious end is the inability of any government they may have to vote any laws to bring the farmers and the middle men under its control. One used to reproach the French because they had no imagination about money but they have learned that there is so much to do with money beside hoarding and spending it. God only knows how they are going to crawl out from under but they will finally—to everybody's surprise but their own.

To both of you my love.

Alice Toklas

Donald Sutherland: Sutherland was a student at Princeton when Stein came to lecture there in November 1934. She was impressed by the excitement and diligence he brought to his study of her work. Sutherland was for many years Professor of Classics at the University of Colorado in Boulder.

book on Gertrude: Sutherland had begun his book, *Gertrude Stein: A Biography of Her Work,* which Yale University Press published in 1951.

To Donald Sutherland, Boulder, Colorado
MS Sutherland

19 October 1947 — 5 rue Christine, Paris VI

Dear Sutherland—

The first chapter came ten days ago and I've been reading it over and over again. I cant thank you enough for it—for having written it exactly as you have. It is deeply satisfying and a great comfort to me to know that the important—the authoritative thing for this generation will be said in my time and by you.

It is all very clear from the Radcliffe of 1895 to Gertrude's leaving it—with character and present thinking as her only but most precious possessions. You have so perfectly defined the steps between that any one reading it attentively can see with what and why she started off to write. Your definitions are perfect—there are long sentences that would seem ready to become classic. At the same time you are so completely in the other camp—(felicitations and alas sympathy)—in other words in the same boat that

Gertrude was from your presently acquired thirty-two years and for many after. It wasnt until later that I meant to speak of it but as it's apropos now—very likely no magazine will take your manuscript but I've an idea that something might be done. Would you allow me to send copies of the first chapter to Carl Van Vechten and to Donald Gallup (he's the librarian of the American section of the Yale University Library and a very nice person and completely devoted to Gertrude's memory). It would be no bother to copy. (It would be best—would it not—that it came from me rather than from you?) The way you have made the difference between the work of Proust—Joyce—and the work of "the English ladies" and Gertrude's—is admirable. It is beautifully concise and clear—"differing conception of time" etc. Then "whether language is going to look in the future like a dialect or like a diction." About the extreme attention to abstraction Gertrude repeatedly said it was American—she thought it was as an American that cubism—natural to Spaniards—had meant so much to her and ought to be natural to Americans too. She never much believed that her being a Jewess had made any difference in her work—she didnt think Jews were necessarily interested in abstraction. (*Please* dont take my saying this as having any importance —because it is in what you have said not even a side issue.) About Henry James it must have been when she was at Johns Hopkins that she read the last two long novels because in 1903 in a novelette (which was the point of departure for "Melanctha"—the three characters were white) she quotes Kate Croy. When I came along in '07 with an undiminished chronically young enthusiasm for H.J. we subscribed to the N.Y. Scribner's edition of H.J. and Gertrude reread the two last and the two or three later novels. She always liked to use his word—the *precursor*—in speaking of him. It was his paragraphs that finally enthused her. There are some pure Gertrude phrases in *The Wings of the Dove*—perhaps I've already written you this. Then all you say about character —projecting it into time—leading to repetition—is immensely helpful. And from there on to the end everything you say—so filled with light and air—warms me and makes me happy as I never expected to be again.

Oh yes I've forgotten to say how right you are about science and history not being able to serve life—literature—or criticism. Gertrude would have been so pleased with the excitement that your program brings you. If from Princeton your knowing what *The Makings* was about gave her so much satisfaction what pleasure she would have had in what you are doing. Very definitely you are able to formulate what was largely dimmed by the large lacunae in my head. Mabel Dodge wouldnt be able to help you —though she has a good memory when she is telling the truth one can never know when she has commenced to invent—she does things so diabolically well "in the manner of."

Always affectionately
Alice Toklas

in a novelette: For the relationship of *Q.E.D.* to "Melanctha," see Leon Katz' introduction to *Fernhurst, Q.E.D. and other early writings* (1971).

Mabel Dodge: Mabel (Ganson) Dodge Luhan, the subject of Stein's *Portrait of Mabel Dodge at the Villa Curonia* (1912), which begins, "The days are wonderful and the nights are wonderful and the life is pleasant." While married to Edwin Dodge, a wealthy Boston architect, she lived in the Villa Curonia near Florence. In 1913 she returned to America. Her salon at 23 Fifth Avenue attracted such figures as John Reed, Edwin Arlington Robinson, Margaret Sanger, Emma Goldman, Walter Lippmann, Lincoln Steffens, and Carl Van Vechten. Divorced from Dodge in 1916, she married the painter Maurice Sterne and in 1918 settled in an adobe house in Taos. In 1924 she divorced Sterne and married Antonio Luhan, a full-blooded Pueblo Indian. Her memoirs (3 volumes) were published collectively as *Intimate Memories* (1936). Volume 3, *Movers and Shakers,* contains ten letters from Stein to Mabel Dodge written between 1912 and 1913. It also reprints her article on Stein, "Speculations, or Post-impressions in Prose," which had appeared in 1913. *Lorenzo in Taos* (1932) is the story of her friendship with D. H. Lawrence.

To W. G. Rogers, New York/MS Rogers

28 October 1947 5 rue Christine, Paris VI

Dearest Kiddie—

Isnt *Four in America* perfect. It has given me such pleasure. Thornton is remarkably good—very clear and helpful to the half initiate about audience and recognition. I'm sorry he didnt tackle Gertrude's theory of the double time sense. And the *Four*—isnt it a moving picture of our American characteristics—isnt Gertrude the essence of U.S. How I wish she could have seen the book—it was always the happiest day of the year (way back it was of the decade) when a new book of hers came in the post and she spent the morning or the whole day reading it. And then when it was read she would say *oui c'est cela.* I wish to God we had gone together as I always so fatuously thought we would—a bomb—a shipwreck—just anything but this.

Do you remember *larus* and Sherry Mangan? He and his wife were on a visit to Georges Maratier. He is a great gourmet and they are all lunching with me tomorrow. It would be a worry if I cared—but Georges in his friendly exaggeration made the whole thing so absurd that I'm indifferent to the point of only not wanting anything burned or *a travers* on its dish. As the wine is just ordinary the cooking shouldnt be too much better—that is the way I encourage myself. *Assez de cuisine.*

I send you both much love.

Alice

GERTRUDE STEIN AND ALICE B. TOKLAS IN THE COURTYARD OF 27 RUE DE FLEURUS, 1914

I wish to God we had gone together as I always fatuously thought we would—a bomb—a shipwreck—just anything but this.

To Donald Sutherland, Boulder, Colorado
MS Sutherland

30 November 1947 5 rue Christine, Paris VI

Dear Sutherland—

Asking you to excuse me for not answering your letters more promptly has become a *banalité*—it merely indicates the degree to which my mind and habits have become disorderly—disfused and disgusting. This is not the case—*je vous jure*—concerning you and your first chapter. You and it clear the general befuddlement —so that there is an added reason to my gratitude to you. Perhaps you have heard my theory that you cant appreciate the form of an object—its proportions or its volume—nor of a piece of furniture—until you have dusted it many times. Well then one day I discovered that typing a manuscript gave you a greater intimacy with it—or at least more quickly—than reading it did. So that when I typed the first chapter it was not a surprise to me to find new treasures in it. For example before I typed it what you had to say and the clarity with which you said it was what impressed me. Now the actual writing in it has become a pleasure. There are paragraphs that Gertrude would have loved. The three first paragraphs on the consciousness have a flow and a rise and fall that illustrate perfectly her diagrams before and during the writing of *The Makings* and that she insisted she always thereafter used— even when not only the paragraph counted less and the sentences were broken up. In a kind of way it was all there and that—she used to say—doesnt change. Change and progress bored her— indeed she used to say there werent any such animals.

After the new pleasure from typing the first chapter one copy to C. Van Vechten and one to Gallup at Yale got off before the annoying postal strike commenced—but now for over a week there is no delivery of mail—so the answers are somewhere—will they ever come out of their corner and be delivered. The strikes are futile—they arent at all achieving their purpose—the wages of certain categories of workers are always being raised—and with the liveliness of the French the prices go up correspondingly in advance—in anticipation. Then the workers who touch very closely the chosen categories are told to go home and shut up—which they dont do—but they are never chosen even so. The garbage workers are trying to break up the combine and have done something—everyone is pleased with them. Life is considerably more difficult and much more expensive but one manages to do without some new thing. The only thing that bothers me is cold and the trouble of finding food for the dog—but the first snowfall is melting and an American who is in the U.S. commissary is giving me flour—so there'll be vermicelli for the dog—and none of it (the difficulties) can last long—we'll be having something else by the time this gets out of the post-box.

Bye the way there's a word on Hawthorne's democracy that struck me was an excellent description of Gertrude's [democracy]. Henry James however would probably not have known it. No word of his about Gertrude ever came to us—though it is probable that William James spoke to him of her. It is too cold to fetch the typewriter so if you'll excuse the longhand—I'll copy and enclose it.

About Joyce and his work. The paragraph in *The Autobiography* is what she felt about him—written because I insisted it should be said. He was for several years a grievous thorn in her side—his success came before the thousand copies of the original French edition of *The Makings* had been published and those years were a nightmare—Gertrude so desperately wanted the endless manuscripts published. Of *Ulysses* she thought very little—she once said it was rather more than she could manage of the Irish fairies—that Irish fairies were even less palatable than German fairies. She met Joyce much later at Jo Davidson's one afternoon. Sylvia Beach asked her if she would come across the room and speak to him—his eyes were very bad—which of course she did. (By that time he wasnt an Irish fairy to her any more—he was just an Irish legend.) She told me that she said to him—After all these years.

He said—Yes and our names are always linked together. She said —We live in the same *arrondisement.* And he said nothing so she went back to talk to a Californian. We once discovered a second influence he'd undergone and how he came by it—but by that time Gertrude *s'est désintéressée de lui.*

Thanks for the Mabel Dodge–Mrs. Jeffer's story. Is that recent? It's Mabel's inevitable end because the only way she can convince the people around her that she's won the man—sometimes it convinces him too—is to have some one—she or he or his wife or an ex-lover—try to commit suicide. When we knew her best—in '12 to '14—there were then attempts and no victims. John Reed she said was one of them. Later she claimed Mrs. Lawrence as another. Mabel was not what Gertrude said repetition was—repeating with a slight difference. It was in Mabel just the same repetition with nothing added or taken away and she was deadly dull. But she did have a pretty old-fashioned coquetry.

Apropos of William James' remark after looking at the Picassos and Matisses about keeping an open mind—Henry James after looking at the first exhibition of the same painters and others —in '10 I think—when pressed by Clive Bell had nothing to say. He preserved an enormous silence. Clive Bell irritated but persistent said—But Mr. James you have impressions of the pictures you've just seen. Finally James let out—And what impressions.

Ever affectionately
Alice Toklas

Hawthorne's democracy: Toklas enclosed (typed) a section from Henry James' *Hawthorne* (1879). "Like almost all people who possess in a strong degree the story-telling faculty, Hawthorne had a democratic strain in his composition, and a relish for the commoner stuff of human nature. Thoroughly American in all ways, he was in none more so than in the vagueness of his sense of social distinctions, and his readiness to forget them if a moral or intellectual sensation were to be gained by it. He liked to fraternise with plain people, to take them on their own terms, and put himself, if possible, into their shoes. His Note-Books, and even his tales, are full of evidence of this easy and natural feeling about all his unconventional fellow-mortals—this imaginative interest and contemplative curiosity; and it sometimes takes the most charming and graceful forms. Commingled as it is with his own subtlety and delicacy, his complete exemption from vulgarity, it is one of the points in his character which his reader comes most to appreciate—that reader I mean for whom he is not, as for some few, a dusky and malarious genius."

Joyce and his work: The paragraph referred to is: "Picasso never wished Braque away. Picasso said once when he and Gertrude Stein were talking together, yes Braque and James Joyce, they are the incomprehensibles whom anybody can understand. *Les incompréhensibles que tout le monde peut comprendre.*" (*Autobiography of Alice B. Toklas* [*AABT*], p. 260.)

To Donald Gallup, New Haven/MS Gallup

2 December 1947 — 5 rue Christine, Paris VI

Dear Donald—

When I first came back here alone it seemed as if it wasnt going to be possible to go on with all the small souvenirs there were in drawers and cupboards and in boxes so constantly I kept hiding them—hence the present confusion and uncertainty. The last *envoi* has finally gotten off to Y.U.L. Hereafter there will just be the letters that are a continuation of those you have or that are about Gertrude which could be sent at the end of each month by boat post. Already there are quite a few—nearly all of Carl's and others. Speaking of letters I've had such a very kind one from Thornton—he writes of spending the winter in Portugal—of possibly coming up here in spring—but I dont count on that. (The lights have just gone off—electricity is fitful.) But it was nice to know that Thornton was satisfied with my pleasure in his introduction. It really is very complete and clear—I am looking forward immensely to his new book. He says that he has taken the character of Caesar from the point of view that Gertrude and he had discussed after she wrote *Ida*. Thornton has enormous technical facility—it interests him passionately and he was one of the few people—perhaps the only writer—who prodded Gertrude with questions about method and technique and got the answers. It

MRS. CHARLES B. GOODSPEED, ALICE B. TOKLAS,
AND THORNTON WILDER, CHICAGO, 1935

*. . . he was one of the few people—
perhaps the only writer—who prodded Gertrude
with questions about method and
technique and got the answers.*

isnt for me to tell you that his were the only letters to her that could possibly be called literary. Sherwood and even poor dear Hemingway never wrote any thing but friendly letters—in which they would casually remark they were working or that they had commenced or finished a book.

Lloyd Lewis wrote me to ask for Sherwood's letters to Gertrude for the Newberry Library where he is working on the material they have there for a life of Grant he is doing. Gertrude would have been deeply interested in this book because she had wanted to collaborate with him on a life of Grant whom she always considered our greatest man—not second to Lincoln but first.

I am so pleased you liked Sutherland's first chapter—he is sound and though he wont be able to finish the book on Gertrude until late into next year because of his work at the university and at what he says is a revolutionary book on Homer—he is constant and will finish it. The second chapter is well on the way he writes. When the package reaches Y.U.L. I hope you'll find time to read his letters—they will give you a precise picture of the man he is—he has a pure direct intelligence and sensibility. The lights have gone off again and the candle flickers so I'm saying good night to you rather hastily but so gratefully.

Affectionately
Alice

new book: Wilder's *Ides of March* (1948).

Ida: Ida A Novel (New York: Random House, 1941) is concerned with the effect of publicity on people. Stein had discussed the problems she was encountering with the novel when Wilder visited Bilignin in the summer of 1937.

Lloyd Lewis: In 1935, through Sherwood Anderson, Stein met Lewis, with whom she shared a passionate interest in Ulysses S. Grant. Stein lent Lewis the then unpublished *Four in America* (George Washington, Ulysses S. Grant, Henry James, and Wilbur Wright). Writing to Lewis in 1937 she suggested that they collaborate on a life of Grant. Enthusiastic about the plan, Lewis wrote: "You see into Grant more clearly than anyone, and you have already collaborated far more than you know in my concept of the man." Because of the war the collaboration never occurred. Lewis died in 1949; his *Captain Sam Grant* appeared in 1950.

Sherwood's letters: Anderson's letters to Stein are in the Yale Collection of American Literature, hers to Anderson are in the Newberry Library, Chicago. The entire correspondence was published in *Sherwood Anderson/Gertrude Stein: Correspondence and Personal Essays* (Chapel Hill: University of North Carolina Press, 1972).

To W. G. and Mildred Rogers, New York/MS Rogers

27 December 1947 — 5 rue Christine, Paris VI

Dearest Kiddies—

I've seen Katherine Anne Porter's article. If that is what you call not being unfriendly to the person—*je n'y suis plus.* I consider it a violent attack against the person. The only reason that I'm not violent about is because the arguments or rather her deductions dont hold water—paraphrasing colored by anger is not sound reasoning. Could you possibly find the letter in the contributors column. I want to write (inspired by Whistler's remark when he removed a hair from a brush that was on the canvas that he'd been asked to criticise—You want to be careful) to Katherine Anne Porter—You want to be careful—the French poet was named Max Jacob not Max Jacobs.

What's the matter with the photograph of Virgil in *The Mother of Us All*—did Carl take it. Virgil can snap his mouth closed but it rarely stays so for more than a second. You know the old joke of the photographer who says—Look pleasant please—thank you—now you may resume your natural expression.

I'd just written to Thornton telling him that I didnt expect he'd get to Portugal and even if he did he wouldnt make Paris—but as he's going to Portugal who knows he may get to Paris. His sister's name is Isabel—not Isobel or Isabelle—careful there—very careful indeed.

Francis Rose came over for three days with a manufacturer for whom he's making textile designs. He brought the gouache studies for the *Hommage* and placed them together on the floor so I could see them as a picture. It's very beautiful—holds together—some beautiful draped figures and a lovely portrait of Gertrude. We dont know how we are going to manage that I can see the picture when it's finished—as Francis will have difficulty in getting it out of England—it's a tighter little island than ever.

Mrs. Kiddie is an angel to get the cigs off to me—I was getting perilously low—now there's a comfortable feeling that I wont have to face morning coffee with only coffee sugar and cream. Please tell Mrs. Kiddie to pay Virgil for the Pall Malls if he has found a way to send them. French cigarette prices have gone up terrifically. I hope taxes on imported tobacco wont jump still higher. The new income tax doesnt touch me. Beside they may not pass it. And as for barricades you are too romantic. And even if there were we wouldnt know anything about it in the rue Christine—no one expects the General [De Gaulle] to act before spring and he would prefer it to be bloodless. Seriously every one is so relieved that the strikes are over and worried because people have refused to buy any of the merchandise the shops are filled with that they are not thinking of violence but are more normal than they've been for a long time. You can buy all the lemons you want and still more bananas—the first in eight years. I'm trying one tomorrow to see what it will do to me. Gabrielle who just had one said it was alright.

Happy New Year to the Kiddies and much much love.

Alice

Katherine Anne Porter: Porter had, at one time, been an enthusiastic admirer of Stein's work. In 1927, writing about *The Making of Americans,* she said, "I doubt if all the people who should read it will read it for a great while yet . . . and reading it is anyhow a sort of permanent occupation. Yet to shorten it would be to mutilate its vitals, and it is a very necessary book." Toklas felt that Porter became antagonistic toward Stein because she and Stein had made some disparaging remarks about Katherine Anne

Porter's work when her nephew came to see them at one of their G.I. salons. The critical article referred to in the letter is "Gertrude Stein: A Self Portrait," in *Harper's,* December 1947.

To Louise Taylor, England/MS Taylor

28 December 1947 5 rue Christine, Paris VI

Dearest Louise—

Here I am for over a week in possession of the most elegant—the most fleecy—the warmest at the same time lightest—pale pink *matinée*—when my room is all clean in the morning I take it out of its tissue paper and careless-like throw it over the chair and oh dear it is a beauty—and you're a dear to have sent it to me. You overwhelm me as well as keep me warm. But about sending me wool dont you dare—give it away quickly to some one who really needs it now—for I absolutely dont and wont for the rest of my days with all you've already bestowed upon me. As for the breakfast-in-bed wooley—"coffee in the kitchen" is its name and it isnt the pale pink or the apricot colored one but the black and grey. The others I wear elegantly in the afternoon—my advanced age permits eccentricity!

I'm going up to the shrine of Sainte-Geneviève to light the biggest candle for the success of [Red's] show—the last time it was for Ralph Church's doctorate at Oxford—they told him they didnt want to give any more doctorates in philosophy—they hadnt given any for eleven years—but they couldnt refuse to bring the five or six examiners from Edinburgh and Paris to help Oxford ones to refuse him. But I started Sainte-Geneviève to work and by Jove she did do the trick and he was accepted. So I'm going to get the good saint working for Red and his show. It's a good moment—the seventeenth—just before her own fête two days later—she will naturally be more than usually well disposed. Red musnt be anything but calm—dont pay the *slightest* attention to critics—even if they're favorable they wont know what the pictures really are —just trust to the enthusiastic amateur (French meaning of the word) who is discerning because he is risking his money—whereas the fool critic isnt even risking his reputation because he will or has already hedged.

Endless love always
Alice

1948

To Claude Fredericks and Milton Saul,
Pawlet, Vermont/MS Fredericks

11 January 1948 5 rue Christine, Paris VI

Dear Banyan Press and Banyan Tots—

How beautifully you do it. *Kisses Can* came yesterday and it gave me so much pleasure—it's perfectly dispersed and designed and it moved me deeply that you should have thought of doing it and I was going to write to thank you when just now the John Donne Prayer has come—and I've completely lost my heart to it and so to the Banyan Press and consequently to the Banyan Tots. It is beautiful and I'm showing it to Maurice Darantière—one of France's great printers. It's a proud moment when one can show him something like that.

Ever cordially
Alice Toklas

Banyan Press and Banyan Tots: In 1947 Fredericks and Saul founded The Banyan Press in a basement butcher-shop on East 29 Street, New York. Early in 1948 they moved the press to a farmhouse near Pawlet, Vermont. Stein's poem *Kisses Can* was published by them in December 1947.

To Donald Gallup, New Haven/MS Gallup

18 January 1948 — 5 rue Christine, Paris VI

No—I really must see all of what you wrote about *Three Lives* for the *Colophon*—you've found a lot of things I'm sure I dont know—for example the extra sum payed to the Grafton Press—I wonder what it was for—not possibly for changes after reading the proof—I never knew her to change a word. I did the proof reading for a little more than the last half commencing with about the last two thirds of "Melanctha." What I propose is that you should have your article *professionally* typed at *my* expense—none of your sitting up nights to do it. You will let me know how much I owe you and Mrs. Kiddie will send you a check—she has some money of mine from California. Yes you *may* pay the postage by *boat* mail. (I'm underlining like an eighteenth century Englishwoman—but it does translate one's emphasis.)

Bye the way have you read [Lincoln] Kirstein's introduction to a catalogue of P. [Tchelitchew] drawings. It is passionately interesting—has nothing to do with the Pavlik or the drawings. If the Y.U.L. hasnt it I'll send you the copy he sent me—let me know.

About *In Savoy* or *Yes* did I write you how the "Yes" title was chosen. Everybody said *In Savoy* wouldnt possibly do for U.S.—that to Americans it suggested a hotel or a Negro dance hall—and if it didnt a great many wouldnt at all know what it was. One day Norma Chambers—a charming creature—an actress—one of the first to read the play (long before the Biarritz group or the Montie Johnsons) and whom Gertrude hoped would someday play Constance—said she agreed and Gertrude said—Then we must find it in the play itself—and it was Norma Chambers who found it—we were all delighted.

I met the Lascauxs at Olga Picasso's last week but hadnt much chance to speak to them. Marie Laurencin was there—*très grande dame* simply and naturally. Germaine was there with an early Manet headdress which suited her charmingly and Marie asked her if she had time to pose for her portrait—which Germaine of course accepted. It should be a perfectly delightful picture.

It is wet and a little colder but much much warmer for the time of year than is normal—below freezing only twice. We cant have Jerusalem artichokes yet—which would be no particular deprivation—if they werent nourishing comparatively inexpensive and a change.

I was taken to see a frightful performance of an equally frightful modern version of *Oedipus Rex* with an even more frightful back drop after a beautiful drawing of Picasso. It's incredible to what degree of stupidity and vulgarity the French can go—they who shouldnt ever be either. It was a consolation to see a very large audience receive it coldly.

Deep gratitude and fondest love to you always.

Alice

Colophon: Gallup's article "A Book is a Book is a Book: A History of the Writing and Publication of Gertrude Stein's *Three Lives,*" published in *New Colophon* I (January 1948). Stein's *Three Lives,* written 1904–5, had been published in 1909 by the Grafton Press.

Kirstein: Lincoln Kirstein, a writer and a promoter of ballet, had written an introduction for *Pavel Tchelitchew Drawings* (1947). Kirstein founded the literary periodical *Hound & Horn* in 1927, and in 1932 (July/September) published in it Stein's "Scenery and George Washington, a novel or a play."

Lascauxs: The French painter Élie Lascaux, his wife Béro (sister-in-law of Daniel-Henry Kahnweiler), and their daughter Germaine.

Marie Laurencin: Gertrude Stein bought the first picture Marie Laurencin ever sold, *Group of Artists* (1908), now in the Cone Collection of the Baltimore Museum of Art.

1948

To Mildred Weston Rogers, New York/MS Rogers

20 January 1948 5 rue Christine, Paris VI

Dear Mrs. Kiddie—

You are indeed a very sweet but a very naughty Mrs. Kiddie—you know very well if you go on like this you'll have spent all your royalties—instead of saving every penny to come over as you should be doing. It was all so unheard of what you call and so literally "out of this world"—candied fruits (pineapple unknown here for over eight years) and chicken and—well I'm going to splurge when Thornton comes—and he will be told whence it all came. And as the dining room is permanently closed and we will have to eat from trays here in the salon I'm refurbishing it—even to the extent of possibly having chairs recovered—you'll have heard when the Kiddie reported to what extent their elbows if not their arms—and their knees if not their legs—were worn to the bone making very unseemly exposures. Thornton has such a seeing eye and then what he doesnt see he has felt and the combination has always made me a little afraid of him.

Love to you both always
Alice

To Fania Marinoff Van Vechten, New York/MS Yale

21 February 1948 5 rue Christine, Paris VI

Fania dearest—

You dont know how your sweet letter touched me—everything you say brings you still nearer and warms me—for now you are my only woman friend—there was Baby—and from my extreme youth—she was eight and I ten when we vowed eternal friendship—there was Clare de Gruchy. Baby and she liked each other so much when they got to know each other in S. Francisco in '35. The two weeks in S.F. were all I saw of Clare for forty years and now she is no more. So lovely Fania you are my unique woman friend. And when you tell me you are religious it makes me rejoice for you and it does explain so much—for faith is so much more to be preferred to anything else. It was a G.I. who said—Now I ask you what is the impulse that comes from the possession of even the kindest heart compared to real faith in God and a hereafter. Without it one just plods on and now without Baby there is no direction to anything—it's just milling around in the dark—back to where one was before one was grown up. So it's your faith that has worked your miracle—I kiss you.

How to tell you of my disappointment that the hideously careless Mary Anne Graves went and lost Baby's brooch that was for you. It isnt pleasant to think of it possibly in stranger's hands now—but we musnt think of that. Pierre Balmain is going over next month and he's not careless and will take you another brooch of Baby's. It's perhaps one that will suit your dark flashing eyes better. It's dark red and cream colored enamel with a miniature of Saint Joseph. The other one you would perhaps have remembered—I think Baby wore it in one of P.W.'s [Papa Woojum's] photographs. It was backed topazes in the form of a conventionalised flower. But the Saint Joseph the more I think of it is really made for you—so you'll be having it soon after Easter. Pierre is going over for only three weeks and I'm trying to help to have him lecture in some of the colleges—not on clothes but on French art and civilization for in spite of his being a gay and charming and very spontaneously frank young man *au fond* he's quite a cultivated person. His lecturing was Baby's idea and so it isnt hard for me to push it—as you can easily understand.

Now I must tell you how delighted I am going to be to have the challis. It is just as I remember it only the little palm pattern is ever so much prettier than mine were sixty years ago—I'll love

FANIA MARINOFF VAN VECHTEN AND GERTRUDE STEIN,
NEW YORK, 1935

Photograph by Carl Van Vechten

So lovely Fania you are my unique woman friend.

to have it and and I'm so grateful to you but you do spoil me. It's to you and dearest P.W. I owe *everything.*

Of course I know Joseph Brewer. We met him first at Oxford when he was a Rhodes scholar—then here—then he published a book of Baby's when he was an editor—then we met him when we lunched with you at a restaurant one day and then we spent two days with him when he was prex at Olivet [College]. And now what is he doing. When you see him remember me warmly to him please—I always had a *faiblesse* for him.

Things here are not as bad as they seemed in the U.S. papers—there may be new strikes but there may not. There are some hopeful signs. The really serious thing is the rise in the cost of living—it is beyond the beyond—doubled since Xmas and every day new rises. If it hadnt been a mild winter there would have been serious trouble. Perhaps I am like Baby always believing the worst couldnt happen—that the near-best at least would and that soon. Well for me that would mean seeing you both. We will meet wont we. Oh say yes. And until then and always all my love. Your grateful devoted—

M.W.

Baby's brooch: This is not the coral brooch which Stein is wearing in the Picasso portrait and which she was wearing when Toklas met her for the first time. That brooch, made for Gertrude by her brother Leo, was given by Alice to Louise Taylor who has subsequently presented it and other pieces of Stein's jewlery to the Fitzwilliam Museum, Cambridge University.

Joseph Brewer: Brewer was with the firm of Payson & Clarke Ltd., New York, which published Stein's *Useful Knowledge* (1928). In 1935 Brewer was president of Olivet College.

To Dudley T. Easby, Jr., Secretary
Metropolitan Museum of Art, New York
MS Metropolitan

22 March 1948 5 rue Christine, Paris VI

Dear Mr Easby—

Thank you so much for sending me the official certificate declaring Gertrude Stein a benefactor of the museum. May I ask you to convey to the trustees my deep appreciation. I wish to also ask you to kindly say to them how much this recognition of her bequest touches me.

I have still the hope of seeing the portrait returned to the museum—though I fear it will require a considerable connection before that can be achieved.

I thank you for your good wishes. Pray accept mine for yourself and for the museum.

Cordially
Alice Toklas

To Donald Gallup, New Haven/MS Gallup

23 March 1948 5 rue Christine, Paris VI

Dear Donald—

Things were very messy indeed—and though they're clearer they're not much brighter. There's no intention to be vague or mysterious but in trying to tell you all I wish you to know I must not let my feelings get the better of me. There is no hope of having the pictures go to Yale as a collection. What I most feared will probably happen—after my day they will probably not be dispersed but just disappear. It has upset me but now whatever can be done must be accomplished with as little delay as possible. Allan Stein refuses not only to cooperate but will make everything as difficult as possible—he has commenced to assert himself with cold aggression. After a severe illness he has made it evident that he will definitely obstruct wherever he can. Now I have his consent to sell a picture and if your museum is prepared—as I think you once said they might be—will you please tell me what is the next step for me to take. I want to sell the latest Picasso here—the brightly colored cubist in the little salon. Picasso told me that it was worth 10,000. When I wanted to sell it last summer I had an offer for it for that price in francs—but then I wanted dollars for Carl's publishing. There will be a way of getting the picture over. It is eighty-one centimetres by one metre. I will have a photograph of it by the end of the week. Now further—I will want an answer to this as soon as convenient—and I will want the money within two months. This all sounds hateful but I trust to your understanding and to your kindness as always—and you will please tell me what to do.

Now I can commence over again and answer your letter which came this morning just as I was about to write to you. First—please dont think that the state in which the Davidson bust arrived disturbed me—it is regrettable and I will speak to the packer about it and see if he will pay you any damages you are having to have repaired but Gertrude and I never considered it a portrait of her—*entre nous*—aside from not liking sculptures—she didnt like it. I dont remember if she even ever showed it to you. I'm glad you liked the Picabia—I did originally and then lost the early impression. It is in any case a much better picture and portrait than Francis Rose's of Gertrude. You must show them if you wish to but please do not mention my name because of Allan.

Now I have a small gift for Yale. Do you remember the little early Picasso—the *Café Scene*—under the influence of Toulouse-Lautrec—that is in the dining room—you may remember that it is mine (Pierre Loeb—knowing this—said to me once—You know whenever you are ready to sell your collection I am ready to buy it). And there are two lovely drawings that belong to me—a nude on a horse—and two nudes—one with a fan—do you remember them. Well I want Yale to have them and if I can get them over the sooner the better.

Do forgive this despicable letter and next time and soon it will be better. Until then and always my love to you.

Alice

Something nice has happened—a Mr. Sulzberger who is the European correspondent of the *N.Y. Times*—who interviewed Gertrude and whom she liked very much—months ago sent me a photograph of a picture belonging to a friend of his who had bought it as a Picasso in Barcelona in '36. Picasso has just sent me word that it is. A very early one indeed—'03 probably—perhaps earlier.

pictures to Yale as a collection: Toklas' plan to have some alumni friends of Yale purchase the collection and present it to the Yale University Art Gallery as the Gertrude Stein Collection did not succeed. When the pictures were sold after Toklas' death, they were bought by a group of Trustees of the Museum of Modern Art and a Patron of the Museum Collections. Each member of the group pledged to bequeath at least one of the most important paintings he had acquired to the museum. In tribute to the role the Steins played in the history of modern art, the Modern undertook an exhibition, under the direction of its then associate curator of painting and sculpture, Margaret Potter, which brought together a large number of the works of art once owned by Leo, Gertrude, and Michael and Sarah Stein.

latest Picasso here: Calligraphic Still Life (1922), now in The Art Institute of Chicago.

Davidson bust: Gertrude Stein (*ca.* 1923). A 7¾ inch high miniature version of the almost life size original.

Picabia: Gertrude Stein (1933). Now at YCAL.

Café Scene: Only this 1900 oil on panel picture went to Yale; the two drawings were sold privately.

To John Breon, Rockford, Illinois/MS Yale

8 April 1948 5 rue Christine, Paris VI

Dear John—

What you say about Sartre interested me because immediately after the liberation the young writers were talking of nothing but existentialism—and I read what the literary magazines were publishing of him and found it not important and later saw no reason to change my mind. Just lately I read his *Baudelaire*—it is really nothing and his *Literature*—also nothing. And his choice of Dos Passos as the great modern writer is merely proof that he is mistaken. On the other hand his new play is generally considered interesting but the French write plays and paint as naturally as we play jazz—it's just a national gift. A man came to see me the other day to get some information about Christian Bérard for an article he is doing about C.B. for *Life*. And he was surprised that one should think of the French as painters and dramatists—rather than musicians and architects. It's so evident to me. As soon as it is returned to me I am going to send you a book [*Marcel*] *Proust* by Madame de Clermont-Tonnerre. It is interesting as a personal memoir—she knew him when he was young. She was the model for his Duchesse de Guermantes—(which I have suspected for over twenty years!) and she gives the key to many of his characters. It will amuse you. The winter thank goodness was mild—March was balmy—but this month is abnormally cold. Yesterday the sun came out for half an hour and the Luxembourg was incredibly maddeningly fairylike in its fresh spring green. In forty years I've never seen it anything like it was yesterday. Like the *Midsummer Night's Dream* when one is young. It was the realest pleasure I've had in a long long time.

Always yours affectionately.

Alice Toklas

John Breon: In 1945 Breon, then in the army, wrote Stein a fan letter. When he came to Paris he brought Stein some of his manuscripts.

Sartre: Jean-Paul Sartre's *Baudelaire* and his *Qu'est ce que la littérature?* were both published in 1948. His new play was *Les mains sales.*

Christian Bérard: Bérard (nicknamed Bébé) was a painter and designer. He created the settings for many operas, ballets, and dramas. He did a number of portraits of Stein, two of which are in YCAL.

To W. G. Rogers, New York/MS Rogers

18 April 1948 5 rue Christine, Paris VI

Dearest Kiddie—

I suppose that this very moment you know the result of the Italian elections—which is more than I will until I go across town to have my hair cut tomorrow afternoon—for there are no papers on Monday as you may remember—how very inconvenient and difficult the French do make one's daily life. And I would like to know. Well I'll do without knowing and I've rung up everybody I know and they are all out and not reading the returns at the newspaper offices because there are none. How unlike the life of our dear queen as an English woman is supposed to have said when she saw *Anthony and Cleopatra.* Which reminds me I have just seen *The New Yorker* with the review of Thornton's *Ides* [*of March*]—how little they like him—I was quite aghast—when it's so much easier to like him than not.

What do you think [Alfred] Barr's done—he wrote me that the San Francisco Museum wanted the Portrait [of Gertrude] for their Picasso Gris Miro show—that the Metropolitan approved of lending it but *he would like my approval*—can you imagine anything more insolent—in worst taste—more provocative of bad feeling. I answered that my connection with the picture ceased when Gertrude Stein's intentions would be realised and that I trusted that would be in my lifetime. Good night—as we said after the other war.

Oh dear I've forgotten to thank you for the cook books you're sending—you know how much I enjoy them. By the way the Katish Russian cook book which reads so badly has excellent recipes and Mrs. Laverty's—which reads so gayly—recipes are really unpardonably vile. I suspected them but said dont trust your readings try them so I went to it. Gabrielle who knows nothing about food and doesnt propose learning was overjoyed with the results and after eating herself to a standstill was in a liver temper for 48 hours! Yes the money was wired and I took Basket over to the [Place] Madeleine twice to make the demand for permission to sell dollars—and the *office d'échange* kindly consented and the bank sold them at 305 and then I took Basket over to the [Place] Madeleine again and they gave me the money and then we came here by way of the Place Vendôme where I deposited it—and then home—all this on foot—and then I had to go to another bank where I left my *carte d'identité*—and Basket was not so overjoyed—he thought this all day promenade was too much of a good thing—and he doesnt dance for joy when he sees me put on my hat anymore.

Now this is for the May package—

Cigs as usual
2 of the summer underwear—already written about
1 lb. cube sugar
1 lb. confectioners sugar
2 dustless dusters white or beige
Kleenex or something that can be used as handkerchiefs
1 caddy polishing cloth (marvellous)
1 pink cloth for woodwork (does not polish—label lost) also marvellous

No floor polishing cloths—the flat is completely carpeted and nearly completely eaten by moths

Oh the washers came but not the plumber. The Paris one *non plus.*

Picasso Gris Miro show: The exhibition *Picasso, Gris, Miro: The Spanish Masters of Twentieth Century Painting* and its catalogue were "Dedicated to Gertrude Stein."

To Claude Fredericks and Milton Saul, Pawlet, Vermont/MS Fredericks

19 April 1948 5 rue Christine, Paris VI

Dear Banyan Tots—

Your perfect book has arrived and I am completely sharing your delight—what indescribable pleasure it would have given to Gertrude Stein—she would have said that the text and its presentation were equally good—as she said years ago of the purely commercial printing of the Contact edition of *The Making of Americans.* She really longed for publication of her books in commercial editions because she didnt consider her work either rare or precious but as editors didnt agree with her she was forced to accept an assorted collection of limited editions—some of them deplorable indeed. Well—she would have liked your book because anyone with clean hands can read it without spoiling it—however beautiful your printing and paper are they dont cry for attention but make reading easier and pleasanter—there is not one thing that interferes. And it is beautiful—really beautiful. About forty years ago when there were dozens of Matisses at Gertrude Stein's—some one seeing [them] for the first time said that a picture begging for attention could not be a work of art. So you see in how you have fulfilled one requisite—and how many others. It amused me to know that the *h*'s were worn out while the rest of the alphabet was still standing up. As a matter of fact Gertrude Stein when she commenced to write had a conscious preference for the letter *M*—then I noticed it cropping up about fifteen years ago—there was presently an epidemic—in her manuscripts that I typed *N* became *M*—and then it was gradually over. Jane Heap years ago said you couldnt possibly appreciate the work to the utmost until you corrected proof.

I thank you many many times for your precious gift.
With warmest greetings—always cordially.

Alice Toklas

perfect book: The Banyan Press had just printed Stein's detective story about a hotel-keeper and a horticulturist, *Blood on the Dining-Room Floor.*

To L. Elizabeth Hansen, Pasadena, California/MS Yale

19 April 1948 — 5 rue Christine, Paris VI

Dear Lilyana—

Finally I have run down some of Jean Cocteau's plays and the one of Picasso in paper bindings of course—but as they are all out of print—they are about to become what one may call collector's items. Now I'm not sending you the books immediately because I want them dedicated and as Jean Cocteau is out of town some one must be found who will take them to him and bring them back—otherwise we'd never see them again.

And as for Picasso—it's the devil and all to get anything away from him again but we will try—it's worth waiting for isnt it. Picasso's play is what is now called surrealist but it is really a descendant of *Ubu Roi** but not half so amusing. And I havent sent you Gertrude's *Operas and Plays* yet (the volume Carl Van Vechten is preparing and which will come out in autumn is all the unpublished operas and plays) but I will any day now. This is not a threat but a promise as Harriet Levy used to say. Do you remember her—she is eighty-one years old and published her two first books last year—a pity to have waited until then—for them—and not to have resisted the temptation to do so a little longer.

Ah yes Bach was our geometry—for which we can be eternally grateful to Otto Bendix—for everything else I learned was a waste of time—experience does just as well if not better. How is the story of your school getting on—is it finished.

No I'm not ever pained that you can write. You may have been timid but you were never inarticulate. Love to you always—with a greeting to Agnes.

Alice

* What's this about my not having liked it. For over forty years I've been the butt of everybody's humor apropos of my faithfulness to an old enthusiasm. The copy Gertrude sent me in '06 (1st edition unfortunately went to Yale not more than a month before I received your letter about wanting a copy—they've just received it.)

Lilyana: A name Alice bestowed upon Elizabeth Hansen in their youth after learning that she had been christened Lily Anna Elizabeth Hansen. Lilyana, her sister Agnes, and their brother Frederick were all California friends of Alice's. Alice and Lilyana both studied piano with Otto Bendix (who had been a pupil of Liszt) and harmony with Oscar Weil. For many years Hansen was a librarian with a special interest in modern theatre; Toklas helped her collect important European editions.

Picasso's play: Desire Caught by the Tail (1941) was given its first reading in the Paris apartment of Michel and Louise Leiris. The cast included Simone de Beauvoir, Raymond Queneau, Jean-Paul Sartre, Dora Maar, Germaine Hugnet, Jean Aubier, Zeanie Aubier, and Jacques-Laurent Bost. Georges Hugnet supplied the music, and Albert Camus directed.

Operas and Plays: Published by Toklas in her Plain Edition (1932). Van Vechten was preparing *Last Operas and Plays* (New York: Rinehart & Co., 1949).

Ubu Roi: When Michael and Sarah Stein returned to San Francisco in 1906 to inspect the damage done to the Stein property by the San Francisco earthquake, they brought with them souvenirs of the artistic and intellectual life they were leading in Paris. Among these was a copy of Alfred Jarry's play *Ubu Roi.* Gertrude had signed a number of these books not knowing who the recipient would be. When Alice came to Paris in 1907 she brought this book with her; later Gertrude signed it twice again on the cover.

To Donald Gallup, New Haven/MS Gallup

30 April 1948 5 rue Christine, Paris VI

Dear Donald—

A very nice intelligent Italian (female) turned up—she is doing the translation for Mondadori of one of Gertrude's books and hopes to do *The Makings* in its entirety if she can persuade them to undertake so much. She is a wildly enthusiastic admirer and lectures about Gertrude's work—which she said was secretly passed and largely read by the resistance during the occupation. She seems to have gathered together quite a number of books but what she declares she can't get on without is "The Life and Death of Juan Gris" and this she has been unable to get at. She asked me if I would lend her a copy but of course I havent one but as she was so bitterly disappointed (she had seen it before the war and had considered it so moving she wanted to quote from it in her lectures)—I told her I would have it copied for her. So that now I must ask you if it isn't going to take too much of your time to have it typed and sent by air mail to Dott. Fernanda Pivano. And Carl will pay for this (all inclusive—typing paper envelope and stamps) from some money he has left over.

Now my second request is less pleasant—more work for you and the whole thing goes completely against all my feelings—but there is no saying no—unless by a sudden decision on your part to be able to do so and I'd be grateful and no one would know because I would truthfully say the [Yale University] Library regrets but it is not possible. And the more I think of it the better I like the idea of your refusing—so I beg of you to do so. But I suppose you have to know what you are refusing. Did you ever know Jaime Sabartés—the aged protégé of Picasso—he's a dreary hanger-on kind of a person whom Picasso supports and who in return pays the taxes and answers the telephone etcetera and who has written a lamentable book or two. Now he proposes to write another book about P. or rather to write a very short text to many photographs of Picasso which will be a sort of biography. Picasso if not encouraging in any case is not discouraging him. The other morning he rang me up and wanted all the little early photographs. When he heard they were at Yale he said please have them photographed for me—Picasso wishes the early ones particularly and Gertrude's are the only ones we know of. It is once more an endless nuisance and loss of time for you but it involves my friendship for Olga. I know that she will hate seeing all Pablo's past with Fernande and Eva (and these as you will soon see are what Sabartés particularly wants dragged before the eyes of everybody—she will feel that it all dishonors her and Paulot—she is after all his wife and the mother of his only legitimate child. As if the present wasn't bad enough Sabartés will revive an irregular past. It reduces her to an episode of respectability which he has repudiated. This is her point of view—I know it—and still here I am backing every thing that she loathes—largely because I'm fond of Pablo too—but weak before him but more particularly because I'm not sure that Gertrude would have refused. It would have depended with Gertrude a little on the mood of the moment. And as Sabartés talked endlessly there was time for all this to go through my head and finally I said yes. Now if you don't refuse—which I devoutly hope you will—S. wants copies of them all up to the period and including the one of P. with his arm outstretched with Paulot—but *not* the Man Ray photograph. He also wants the one with Fernande and the dog and the small one of Eva alone in a kimono looking as much like a geisha as a French petite bourgeoise could. These will be paid for by Mrs. Kiddie—

Sabartés editor will eventually repay me. They can go by ordinary mail (*all* expenses paid by Mrs. Kiddie).

News here has been mostly coming and going of Americans. Sutherland and his wife are here—except for short visits to Belgium and Holland—for over a month—they stay for two months more. He is at work on the third chapter—the second is admirable. His being here has meant a great great deal to me—in every way he is sympathetic—one always finds oneself in agreement with him. Then W. [William] Raney of Rinehart—Carl's friend—who is a dear and very sound. Then a friend of Virgil's and Carl's—a Mrs. [Mina] Curtiss—who is doing the correspondence of Proust who is extremely entertaining. And a *tas des jeunes gens assortis.* It has kept me busy—but not as much so as I do you. Forgive me please—let us hope there will be no demands upon you—at least from me. All my thanks always and my love.

Alice

Jaime Sabartés: Sabartés, a close friend of Picasso since their youth in Barcelona, was then preparing *Picasso: documents iconographiques* (1954). He wanted photographs of Fernande Olivier, Picasso's first mistress, and her successor Marcelle Humbert (called Eva).

The Life and Death of Juan Gris: One of Stein's most moving short pieces, it was written just after the death of Gris. It first appeared in *transition* (July 1927).

To William Whitehead, New York/MS Yale

5 May 1948 — 5 rue Christine, Paris VI

Dear Mr. Whitehead—

From all sides there comes the same story that you tell of the depression in the theatrical affairs in New York. There was an announcement by the experimental theatre people that Gertrude Stein's play *Yes Is For A Very Young Man* was one of the six plays they were to produce. It had been played with considerable success in Pasadena—where a Mr. Lewis—the producer of *Brigadoon*—saw it and was enthusiastic. Miss Cheryl Crawford liked it too. In spite of their support it was not done. It is evident that U.S. only wants best sellers—in any field. In books a hundred thousand copies sold was in the old days the dream of a publisher—now it's a million five hundred thousand. So what succeeds is not of the quality that interests the average intelligence—unless the average intelligence has lamentably *dégringolée* as it is probably natural to suppose it should have—nourished as it has been for many years now on the third rate—as best. It is a deplorable sign of the times. Do you ever read Henry James. I came upon some astonishing predictions of what is happening *chez nous* in a story hc wrote in seventy-nine. He would have enjoyed it but not its reason. All this is far from cheerful—but neither are the times we are living in.

Though the general situation in France is improved—very definitely—the morale—in spite of a métro strike and the possibility of other sympathetic ones to follow—is much better than it was—which means here that they'll commence to work with more enthusiasm and that of course is what they've not been doing. It is the most important condition for a possible renaissance for France. There seem to be small signs pointing that way. It would be pleasant to once more live in a country that was rising.

Better and then best luck to you. Warm remembrances always.

Alice Toklas

To W. G. and Mildred Rogers, New York/MS Rogers

1 June 1948 5 rue Christine, Paris VI

Dearest Kiddies—

Send your friends or acquaintances the Foldes—I'll see them from nine to ten p.m.—that's my new trick—if they are amusing they can stay on—it works very well—it's a bit pretentious but saves time.

What's the book Rinehart's doing on Ford. If it's Ford Madox etc. I *must* see it. If it's only Detroit Ford dont bother. I can eat Ford M. with a spoon—but I can see it isnt he possibly. Bill Raney sent me Mrs. [Mary Roberts] Rinehart's novel because Gertrude used to read her before the other war—she doesnt suggest her age—like Matisse's paintings—now that he is eighty he's getting back to the youth he never had.

There's a number of *Verve* with hundreds of reproductions of Picasso's—his line is incredible—there never never was anything like it—but otherwise there's not much to be said—but the line is more beautiful than anything ever was—it is so sensitive that it makes one quiver—it's a long time since there's been anything so perfect around the art center of the world.

We have extra bread rations—Basket's is already ample—the supplement will mean sandwich bread for tea. Gabrielle will have enough not to have to buy black market—butter is supposed to go free shortly at 900 [francs] the kilo which is less than the black price—so you see the market is getting freer but terrifically high. People accustom themselves too quickly to the new prices. People dont expect to receive two or three francs change any more than they expect to pay it. Having learned the value of *petites économies* in '15 it leaves me flabbergasted—how can one save *sous* (that is present francs) if they arent returned to one—it's very confusing if not immoral.

Alice

Bill Raney: William Raney, an editor at Rinehart. The book referred to was about "the Detroit Ford"—Keith Sward's *Legend of Henry Ford* (1948).

To W. G. Rogers, New York/MS Yale

22 June 48 5 rue Christine, Paris VI

Dearest Kiddie—

The book came a week ago and I've not written before because I wanted to be sure what several readings would do to my first impression. I've read it three times through and many pieces many times and here are my mixed feelings about it. All of the manuscript that I read last year I like even more than last year—it has more sweetness—more of your quality than I had realised and so for that I can wholeheartedly congratulate you and thank you—and for the analysis of "a bell within me rang" and for *Tender Buttons* too. And now for what I would rather not have to say because you wont like it being said any more than I like having you having written it. You couldnt expect me to subscribe to Gertrude's being described as aloof (she was the most approachable person I ever knew—ask any working man or G.I. of the hundreds she knew) or to accept the implication of snobbishness because a warm friend happened to be a duchesse as well as a writer or a kind neighbor was a count—nor the fact that one of her early 1911 friends who understood what G.S. was writing was an H.R.H. There are several inaccuracies: I didnt discover *"rose is a rose"* etc. on a scrap of paper. It was in a manuscript. Gertrude did not know she was to die the day the operation was finally decided upon nor even after. She did not have the copies of *Brewsie and Willie* in her hands—that was three or four days before the end. If I've brought myself to saying these things be assured—Kiddie dear—it is because I care so much for you—you will know that it is not easy. There are—to continue—mistakes about *The Makings*—it is one long description of individuals

—she was not creating the mass—perish the thought. The Croix de Feu were *not* Vichyites. She did *not* regard a man out of work as lazy—she certainly did not believe in looking to the community (state!) for aid but the path of success was *never* what she chose—you are woefully wrong there—nor did she turn in her conceit to you for confirmation of her gift—she was confident from the beginning. And now to end.

Are Ryder and Cézanne commonly spoken of in the same breath in N.Y.

Days later. So many many interruptions—and I've ended with my objections and now for the *revers de la médaille.* It is a fascinating book—lively gay and holds one interested all the time. It should have a *great* success and I suspect if it had been written about some one else (which it couldnt have been of course—but why dont you do one about some one else—I have one in mind but you would *never* do it and despise me if I told you which I'm not going to—but she too had a tremendous personality) it would be a book club selection. And you have unqualified enthusiastic praise from Virgil—Carl and Donald Gallup—and please tell Virgil to send me a copy of his review—Carl will send his without our asking for it. I hope the A.P. gives you clippings—otherwise it would cost a fortune to receive them from a press clipper. And how you and Mrs. Kiddie are running around and being fêted—make sure to write me everything.

Endless love to you both.

Alice

rose is a rose: The phrase "Rose is a rose is a rose is a rose" first appears in Stein's "Sacred Emily" (1913), a poem about Madame Amélie Matisse, the wife of the painter. It was André Derain who said of Madame Matisse, "Sainte Amélie, la plus grande martyre de nôtre siècle." This comment was celebrated as a joke, but it was serious though exaggerated. Stein, remembering Derain's phrase, named her portrait of Madame Matisse "Sacred Emily." See *Geography and Plays* (1922).

Brewsie and Willie: Rogers got this story from Van Vechten; in later editions of Rogers' *When This You See Remember Me* it was deleted.

To Christopher Rambo, Berkeley, California
MS Bancroft

30 June 1948 5 rue Christine, Paris VI

My dear Mr. Rambo—

How very kind you are to send me the very lively little drawing of 2300 California Street. It does revive many old memories—very old ones indeed for I lived there with my parents and brother from '95 to '99—when my mother died and then we went to live with my grandfather in the house where I was born. It was at 2300 that I became intimate with Miss [Annette] Rosenshine—it was there that she told me that she was leaving school to go to the Mark Hopkins [Institute of Art]. It is indeed a pleasure to have your drawing and I am very grateful to you for sending it to me. When Gertrude Stein and I were in San Francisco in thirty-five I tried to find the house and failing to do so stupidly took it for granted that it had been demolished. So to see it again was a double surprise.

Cordially
A. B. Toklas

To Annette Rosenshine, Berkeley, California
MS Bancroft

30 June 1948 5 rue Christine, Paris VI

Dear Annette—

For weeks I've been wanting to write to you but there has been a veritable invasion of compatriots and other foreigners and they—friends and acquaintances and correspondents—fill the flat and my time. But as they come because of Gertrude there seemed to be nothing else to do. Do you remember [Patrick] Bruce (with a gold beard and a son named Tim). After Blériot flew the channel he said one day—Mark my words—we'll live to see them flying to Paris to spend the week end. And a few literally do. But now the rush is over and I am free to sit down and write to you—though with a wretched pen. It was sweet of you to remember the date of my birthday and I do thank you for your good wishes. We all need them so I return mine most heartily though the fourteenth of April is long since passed. And I've also to thank you for Christopher Rambo's drawing of 2300 [California Street]. It was hard to believe my eyes—so exactly like my memory of it—though considerably tumbled down and so typically San Francisco. We moved into it over fifty years ago—in ninety five. Do you remember the sitting room—into which I introduced an illustration from *The Gibson Girl* framed with a dull green border to Mama's astonishment and my father's horror. And then after four years Mama died and we moved to O'Farrell Street which was much less amusing than 2300 in spite of Mama's illness. You probably remember what an old fashioned tyrant Grandpa was. And here we are old enough now to be great grandmothers—but you're three years less than I. Perhaps if we had those grandchildren they'd have found us so much of a bore and as annoying as we did ours. As Mike used to say—Dont let's go into that.

The other day when I saw in the newspaper that Mrs. [Gertrude] Atherton had died it was quite a shock—for though she was very very old one thought of her as going on forever. We had known her a little years ago and then again in S. Francisco in '35 when she was most hospitable to Gertrude—she was then well over seventy and very beautiful in an outrageously pale blue dress. Do you remember our enthusiasm for her novels. During the occupation I reread quite a few of them and was surprised and delighted to find how successfully she wrote. Though markedly dated they held one's attention to the end—she had something of the grand manner.

Has Picasso's portrait of Gertrude gotten to S.F. yet—it was to go for a show of his—Miro's and Juan Gris. When it was to leave here I phoned P. and asked him if he wanted to see it before it left. He came over at once—he lives only three blocks from here. He talked with me a while (I see him rarely) and then in his brusque way jumped up suddenly and stepped before the picture a few minutes drinking it in and then quite simply saluted it. Oh my dear—he said—neither you nor I will ever see it again. Then he kissed my hand and flew out of the flat. Now I've only room to send you my love.

Always
Alice

Annette Rosenshine: She was introduced to Michael and Sarah Stein during their visit to San Francisco in 1906. Sarah Stein wanted to take Alice under her wing and bring her back to Paris with them, but Alice successfully maneuvered them into taking Annette instead. Annette Rosenshine, together with Sarah Stein, Patrick Bruce, Max Weber, Olga Merson, Hans Purrmann, and others, was one of the first students in the school that Matisse had started.

To John Breon, Rockford, Illinois/MS Yale

6 July 1948 — 5 rue Christine, Paris VI

My dear John—

You have done a unique thing—you have described the returned soldier without one stroke of false drama or sentiment—will they see or understand or like it. If I saw the book just casually in a bookshop—I'd buy it and take it home to read because any page I might have glanced at would have told me something I wanted to know more about—something that arrested my attention and held it. But do the editors these days see that. I am cynical about them—largely because of the books they choose to publish. And I must not delay to tell you how moved I am by your dedication. It was natural that you should have thought of dedicating it to Gertrude Stein—but to have included me is very sweet and brings the three of us together again as we were in those happy happy days—when you would come to see us bringing the most exquisite but quite too extravagant flowers. I do hope I hang on to see you again. The very best always.

Alice Toklas

the book: Breon had sent Toklas the manuscript of a novel, *The Sorrows of Travel*. When the book eventually was published in 1955 it bore the dedication, "In memory of Miss Stein and for Alice B. Toklas."

To L. Elizabeth Hansen, Pasadena, California/MS Yale

21 July 1948 5 rue Christine, Paris VI

Dearest Lilyana—

Your letter was a great relief and if it hasnt been answered before now it was because I was waiting for the books to come back dedicated. I know Jean Cocteau—it's an old acquaintance—he was Gertrude's friend and when I was able to gather in all of his plays—all of them out of print now—I asked a friend to take them to Jean Cocteau—when he brought them back to me I was breathless with surprise and pleasure at his generosity. I hope you will be too. I've shown them to everyone because of the lovely pages he has made and to have everyone appreciate what he had done. If you care to you might write him a few words—in English for he knows it well—better than we know his tongue—and if you wish you might mention how much his work is appreciated at the university. He's a wonderful person—beside films and books and plays and drawings he's the most astounding conversationalist. Three or four times I've heard him burst forth—it's quite incredible and at such a velocity that you [are] carried up and on and end exhausted while he's composed and starting another explosion. He's French at its best.

Gertrude's nephew Allan has completely collapsed—suddenly discovered everything was wrong with him and now wanders around disconsolately—having no inner resource—he only cared for business and horses and of course they're not for him again. He was the natural reaction of an exaggeratedly cultivated home—quite an abnormal atmosphere for a child who had no proper childhood. Now he's unhappy and embittered. Do tell me about the arthritis—has it left everything but the knees—that is really a cure. Mine is less bad but has found new places—it's very annoying. No I havent seen the doctor since last year and then not for arthritis. What are you supposed not to eat. I have given up wine—no deprivation.

Now good night to you and much love always.

Alice

To W. G. and Mildred Rogers, New York/MS Rogers

22 July 1948 5 rue Christine, Paris VI

Dearest Kiddies—

Do you remember Harriet Levy's book you brought me last year. She has written to me about one Doubleday has asked her to write about her life in Paris—'07–'10. She wants me to suggest names and episodes. She has some extraordinary material but she'll never use it. It's not for me to say what she should or shouldnt do—but oh but what a book if she dared. And then again she may—who knows. And will she get it done. It quite fascinates me. Probably it will peter out into a feeble journalese of the beginning of the century when she and Frank Norris were O'Hara Cosgrave's bright hopes.

The other day at Natalie Barney's Mrs. Bradley was full of the new young Parisian hero—Truman Capote—Gallimard is launching his novel with immense publicity and as Mrs. Bradley is his agent she has every interest to make the most of the sensation he is causing. Not having seen the youth I'm not a fair judge but I prefer Mrs. Bradley herself to any mere Capote. She was wearing a quill in her hat larger and longer than any dropped by a monster prehistoric bird so that you were convinced that the quill was mightier than—well—any atomic bomb.

So good night my dear Kiddies.

Alice

Harriet Levy's book: 920 O'Farrell Street (1947), a memoir of her childhood in a well-to-do Jewish home in San Francisco in the days before the earthquake. She never completed the memoir of her Paris experiences, but a set of "Recollections" is deposited in the Bancroft Library of the University of California at Berkeley. Harriet had two important visits to Paris—one in 1904–5 when she stayed with the Michael Steins, and the second with Alice Toklas from 1907 to 1910.

Truman Capote: Gallimard was preparing an edition of *Other Voices Other Rooms* (1948).

Mrs. Bradley: Jennie Bradley, wife of the Paris literary agent William A. Bradley.

To Samuel Steward, Chicago/MS Bancroft

22 July 1948 — 5 rue Christine, Paris VI

Sam dear—

It's not possible to describe to you the way I've been shoved about—just like the G.I.s and not liking it any more than they did. There have been a lot of things to straighten out—and most of them still look very crooked—and an avalanche of Americans—friends—children of friends—grandchildren of friends—acquaintances and their descendants—friends of friends and their—but no you can see the effort and the futility. Now they are in Sweden or Switzerland and in September Basket and I may be in the country. An inn in the Dordogne has been recommended—the patron is an ex-chef—there is a woods not far away and a hot bath daily—the three requisites—and very cheap—perhaps it is dirty. *Tant pis.* Basket needs some country runs and a change. To leave here will be a wrench and it will be lonesome down there but it's all but arranged—just a letter from the patron.

Now enough about myself—let's talk about you. It is not for me to tell you for you know it by now that it's all one to me how you achieve your salvation as long as you do—whatever makes you happy—the Church or Alcoholics Anonymous or anything else. I'm a good Jesuit—any means that suits you—why even what Francis [Rose] chose—a strong wife. It was difficult to accustom oneself to her at first but in spite of obvious and hidden faults—it's because she's not so simple as she first seemed that one likes her—she gradually impresses herself on you as being altogether respectable. So if a good looking female a very few years older than you are says she wants to marry you and you think she really is in love with you—why just let her have her way. Francis is really happy and it's she who has induced this. And dont talk about the loss of a good woman—for though she may not be bad she's certainly not what one would call good. Is there anything like her in the offing for you. For you and Francis are not so awfully unlike. And she would give you every chance to work and the way you want to.

Here there have been many shows—the painters paint stupid abstractions that dont achieve becoming pictures and are too pretentious for decorations. Picasso is in the south avoiding an issue by making or rather designing and decorating pottery. The only person who keeps his early energy is Jean Cocteau—who is ageless and agile. He has kept the unfashionable virtues of generosity and loyalty and makes they say good films.

They are translating into Italian *The Making of Americans* unabridged. If Gertrude could only have known this—and they are doing four others—they propose doing all of them eventually. Mondadori the editor is an enthusiastic admirer. *The Makings* was passed about amongst the resistance—they considered it liberation literature—how much Gertrude would have loved all this. It was the translator [Fernanda Pivano] who was here for a few days who told me all this—such a nice warm sympathetic person. The French translations are continuing—the last *Three Lives* is just being placed. The book of *inédits Last Operas and Plays* that Carl Van Vechten has arranged with Rinehart is postponed from October to January. The Kiddie's book is out. It is not the manuscript I saw—*n'en parlons pas* [*plus?*]. Père Bernardet from Hautecombe is now at L'Hay la Rose and gets into Paris lately more frequently than before. He came to see me the other day.

Did I tell you that the Daniel Rops have bought a *domaine* on the lac de Bourget. His *Life of Christ*—for adults—for young people—for children—illustrated—unillustrated—with notes—without notes—*de luxe*—without luxe—has sold a million copies. He says he will write no more novels not even the lives of the saints—nor the martyrs—nor the mystics—there never was a more enterprising salesman than he—and Madeleine [Rops] remains an enigma to me—of how much is she conscious—does she know all or nothing—she's a fascinating subject.

Do you remember Cecil Beaton—he's desperately in love with Greta Garbo and the Duchess of Kent equally so with him. Do you like my gossip—everybody tells me a little—eventually I hear it all—none of it holds my attention long enough for me to follow the plot. Do you remember Madame Giraud—she is living at a convent near here—she is having a sad end for she does not at all like living with the *bons secours*—but her grandchild has married (she has three children) and there is no room in the flat anymore for her.

The sentence of Bernard Faÿ has been reduced from life to twenty years so that when there is an amnesty for political prisoners—

he will be freed. If De Gaulle comes in—and he may—he'll declare an amnesty before the end of the year. If not perhaps someone else may—but not so likely.

I have just learned a delicious French usage. On wedding invitations when they say the mass is at noon they mean one o'clock—when they say at noon precise they mean half after twelve—and when they say at very precisely noon they mean noon. Are they not the most delightful children. It's their aged childhood that makes them so surprisingly naive later.

Well now to the kitchen. You know Wendell Wilcox taunted me once with cowardice because I was afraid to use yeast—so here I am off to it now. *Nous verrons ce que nous verrons.* My love to you always—my dear. Do forgive me and write to me again soon.

Alice

Daniel Rops: It was customary for Stein and Toklas to take American guests visiting Bilignin to meet their neighbors in Bugey (the neighborhood around Belley). In particular, they would often visit the French writer Daniel Rops and his wife Madeleine; at Béon they would visit the Baronne Pierlot (who once tried to arrange a marriage for W. G. Rogers), and others.

To William Whitehead, New York/MS Yale

31 July 1948 — 5 rue Christine, Paris VI

My dear ~~Mr. Whitehead~~—Bill—

The great news of your marriage which you so gently *glisse* into the end of your letter left me so astonished and happy that it seemed as if I must tell you of my pleasure and here it is over a month since then before I've found a moment to write you. Gertrude Stein and I so often wondered how it was that some girl nice or otherwise hadnt long ago secured you—and then we concluded that your instinct to resist and make your own choice later would save you from a possible mistake. And here you are now having so happily accomplished it and you will accept my very warm fond good wishes to you both. And though it is definitely not done my felicitations to Lucienne (she will allow me to call her by her lovely Christian name I hope) because I'm sure you've made no mistake and because G.S. and I not only liked you so much but appreciated you. And you must tell your wife that when I was young I very much liked the pictures of her grandfather and that when I first went to Florence there were people there who knew him and talked about him and it is now a romantic memory and you both now make my youth realer than it has been for a long time. And so bless you both.

Really really really you must not send me a package again. We get along very well indeed—more than one needs. The only things that are either non-existent or rare are the things that one has no longer at all the habit of. There never was quite such a bag as you sent because of the quality of each thing. How Switzerland manages to still do such things puzzles me—for goodness knows of all the neutral countries she suffered the most and paid the highest and behaved the best. We were right near the Swiss frontier through the occupation and the stories of Swiss protection and generosity told by the escaped prisoners were beyond imagination—they gave them food—some one to put them on the road into France and French money to wire to their family. Isnt it a lovely story and they came over by way of Annecy about seven a day from the spring of '42 until the liberation. And there was the Swiss radio which was the only one to give us all the news and unbiased news at that—it was the only thing that gave us any comfort—though the news was unbiased their feelings were really not neutral and how we loved them for that. And so I am grateful to your wife's country—particularly now when there's enough *recul*—and the memory of G.S. at the radio at a quarter of twelve and a quarter of seven saying—Hush here it comes. She was never down for the early morning one—so I wrote it down and slipped the paper under the door for when she woke up.

RENÉ REULOZ, MADAME CHABOUX, GERTRUDE STEIN,
DOCTOR CHABOUX, ALICE B. TOKLAS,
AND PIERRE REULOZ, BILIGNIN, 1939

We were right near the
Swiss frontier through the occupation.

The H. James I wrote you of—the one in which I found him so wonderfully foreseeing our present attitude to Europe—was "A Bundle of Letters"—only interesting for this and some characterisations. I'd planned a few weeks in the Dordogne near Périgueux in a village with the incredible name of Excideux—but finally renounced going there because of a nine hour train trip with three changes. And the trains are now even worse than you remember them to have been. And so though I expect to leave within the week I dont know where—everything is now full up.

Once more I send you both my affectionate good wishes.

Alice ~~Toklas~~

her grandfather: William Whitehead was married to the granddaughter of the painter Arnold Böcklin.

To L. Elizabeth Hansen, Pasadena, California/MS Yale

14 August 1948

Hôtel du Cheval Blanc,
Thouars, Deux-Sèvres

Dear Lilyana—

Yes finally taking all my courage in my hand I brought the poodle and myself down here four days ago—the first time in four years that I'm in the country and in forty years alone in it. And it's going to be a successful effort since as you see I'm already taking up a large neglected correspondence. Thouars is a wonderful very old but clean little town with no one even from Paris at the hotel. The inhabitants are intelligent amiable and polite—the air delicious—not far from the Atlantic with enough wind to make it resemble San Francisco and I'm staying on until the beginning of next month.

Now we will talk of other things—if you havent already you

will soon receive—by boat mail to be sure—three little volumes of Voltaire's play—1824—in their original bindings printed by Didot. If you will not think me abominably pretentious I'll tell you about Didot—if I know it's because his father invented the type which the little books are printed in during the French revolution (which pleased Gertrude as an example of the way the French go about this business no matter what's going on about them. Didot *père* was the father-in-law of Bernardin de Saint-Pierre who wrote *Paul et Virginie*. During the occupation I found his letters to his wife in the library of the house we were living in at Culoz after we had to leave Bilignin. And those letters described how you lived in the country during the revolution and it was exactly as we were living then—the first struggle was to keep warm—the rest was to find food—apples to be traded for bread—bread for potatoes and they in turn for wood—Little Daisy's endless chain. And when I had Gertrude's books printed in '32 I got one done in Didot type and in the format of the period but the work was badly done.

Now in spite of all this talky talk I hope you'll like the little books. I found them quite by accident one day when it was blisteringly hot and I was exhausted from running about. It was a nice surprise for they were cheap (at once I got a man I know who knows old books to look at them and he said okay in the American language) and I sat down in the shop and had a conversation with the shop keeper who is an expert (at the Hôtel Druot) and a cigarette and came away with the possibility of another find—only it doesnt seem to me you should spend so much money for old books when the collection you are making is the modern theatre. In any case I'll tell you and you can decide. 10 volumes of Corneille (1758) original leather bindings beautifully illustrated (engravings) for 9500 francs. The Voltaires were 1400 so that I have about 1000 francs left from your cheque. Of course they may have been sold by the time I get back.

Only room now for my love to you and remembrances to Agnes and Freddie.

Alice

we had to leave Bilignin: In August 1924, while on their way to Nice to spend the summer visiting Picasso, Stein and Toklas stopped to spend a few days at the Hôtel Pernollet in Belley, a hotel noted for the excellence of its cuisine. When after a number of letters they had no reply from the hotel in Nice that they had expected to stay in, Stein and Toklas decided to spend the summer in Belley. They fell in love with the region and returned for the next few summers. In 1926 they saw from the valley below the manor house in Bilignin. The occupant was an army officer who sublet it from its owner. With no prospect that he would leave the regiment at Belley, Stein and Toklas spent two years maneuvering with French friends for a promotion for the officer. It came through, he was transferred, and in the summer of 1928 they moved into the house where they lived for six months of each year until World War II was declared. They then remained all year until 1942 when the owner, by then a married woman with children of her own, reclaimed the house and Stein and Toklas moved to Le Columbier, a house in nearby Culoz.

To W. G. and Mildred Rogers, New York/MS Rogers

14 August 1948

Hôtel du Cheval Blanc,
Thouars, Deux-Sèvres

Dearest Kiddies—

If you're enjoying a vacation in the mountains of Pennsylvania Basket and I are trying to do as much here in this very charming clean very old town. We are still surprised to find ourselves here. The plan to go to the Dordogne was abandoned—the train trip of eight hours and two changes seemed too much of an undertaking with three indispensable hand bags and the more than indispensable Basket. But by the end of July there wasnt a room with two windows free anywhere—at least not at any place I could afford—until some one recommended this place as a pleasant village with agreeable walks and good food. Well it isnt a village but a town bigger than Belley. The weather has been too abominable for any real walks—and the food is not good—and for all this it's really extremely satisfactory. The air is delicious (we're less than three hundred kilometers from the Atlantic with no mountains between it and us)—the hotel comfortable—the little town filled with fine old architecture (you cant throw a stone without hitting a romanesque—Basket and I've had—as a result—to abandon what might have become a favorite sport—we dont know as we've never tried)—and the population is clean orderly polite and amiable—as only survives (less the cleanliness of course which we've taught them during two wars) in the provençal town far away from big cities. And there's an excellent book shop were I can find all I need to keep me going—so we'll stay on at least to the end of the month if not longer. So continue to address me here until then—that is five days before the time it has taken for air mail from N.Y. forwarded from Paris.

The last days in Paris were hectic. Basket went and got an abscess—his vet was vacationing—the only decent one any one could recommend had not proven satisfactory with Basket I but experience has made a better vet out of him than he was twenty years ago and he fixed up poor Baskie so that I could travel with him on the day I engaged a seat in the train for and he's alright now—though as a good bourgeois he's completely *dépaysé* and very capricious about all his daily habits.

And thanks and thanks again for everything and good vacation and lots of love to the Kiddies always.

Alice

To Fernanda Pivano, Milan/MS Pivano

16 August 1948

Hôtel du Cheval Blanc,
Thouars, Deux-Sèvres

Dear Miss Pivano—

G. S. had *Everybody's Autobiography* translated into French as *L'Autobiographie de tout le monde. Chacun* is more in the spirit of *The Making of Americans* and of the portraits that followed. I leave the choice entirely to you and above all—dear Miss Pivano—do not ask my advice—I know Italian not at all—many many years ago I pattered it and I can only read it with the greatest difficulty. I trust you—your understanding of G.S.'s work. Your enthusiasm—may it not be better called respect—will guide you in your work. You know G.S. always said that the force of the original always came through in translation—even in a faulty one—and that yours will not be. But if there is anything within my ability to do then you must not hesitate—it would be a rare pleasure for me to be able to show you my appreciation and gratitude for what you are doing—G.S. would have been so very very pleased about *The Making of Americans*. It is a very precious gift that you offer.

The copy of *Rassegna* was forwarded to me here yesterday from Paris and it reads very well indeed—a very impressive exposition of G.S.'s work—and clearly and logically explaining the development. May I tell you that I think you have a special and happy instinct in the choice of your illustrations and the introduction of your backgrounds. There is one typographical error—*Yes Is For A Very Young Man* should not have a comma between the first two words. And the other—an omission—is my fault in not having spoken of them and not having provided you with copies—G.S. had started to write some meditations and an article on the atomic bomb—neither of them were completed. They were written during the first two weeks of July—that is they were not written after that—and the meditations were commenced a little before the last half of June. As soon as I get back to Paris I'll send you copies.

And all my warmest grateful thanks to you always.

Alice Toklas

Fernanda Pivano: From the time the Italian novelist Cesare Pavese had introduced her to Stein's work (he translated *The Autobiography of Alice B. Toklas* in 1938), Fernanda Pivano, a leader in the Italian anti-fascist movement, had one ambition—to go to Paris and meet Gertrude Stein. Not until just after Stein's death was she able to get to Paris and meet Toklas. Pivano had translated Stein's *Everybody's Autobiography* for the Italian publisher Arnoldo Mondadori; when Mondadori decided not to publish it, Pivano published parts of her long introductory essay in *Rassegna d'Italia*. The complete essay, "Gertrude Stein, Pioniera Di Un Secolo," is collected in a volume of Pivano's pieces on American literature and civilization, *La Balena Bianca E Altri Miti* (1961). Her essay "Alice B. Toklas a Roma" recalls Pivano's visits to Alice in Rome. The essay is collected in *America Rossa E Nera* (1964). In addition to translating Stein, Pivano is the translator of Hemingway, Fitzgerald, Wilder, and the "beat generation," Kerouac, Ginsberg, Corso, and Burroughs.

To John Breon, Rockford, Illinois/MS Yale

24 August 1948

Hôtel du Cheval Blanc,
Thouars, Deux-Sèvres

Dear John—

Bravo for Macmillan's. Gertrude Stein several times recommended (before the war) first novels to her publisher Bennett Cerf of Random House but one after the other they turned them down. If they didnt consider her recommendation sufficient what attention would they pay to me. It wasnt a pleasant feeling not to be at all helpful to you. But now with a warm word from one of their own editors Macmillan is an excellent hope. In case they dont accept it you musnt be discouraged—really not the least little bit—but try some one else and settle down at once to work on the next one. *Continuez.*

The story of [Robert] Hutchins and the [Chicago] police wasnt quite that—we were dining with them and there were other guests—Professor Mortimer Adler amongst them. G.S. and he didnt agree about anything and finally G.S. with her usual energy commenced to tell him how and why and where he was mistaken. (You know how she would do that.) Well—at that moment the maid came in and announced—The police—Professor Adler turned quite white and rose. And then G.S. explained it was the suicidal squad (I think that was its name)—a newspaper friend had arranged to take us with them on their nightly ride. Poor Professor Adler!

Love to you always—John dear—

Alice Toklas

To Louise Taylor, England/MS Taylor

4 September 1948

Hôtel du Cheval Blanc,
Thouars, Deux-Sèvres

Dearest Louise—

I'd hoped to be writing to you just casually as a lady of leisure but that comfortable state is now nearly over for I go back to Paris shortly. Bobsie Goodspeed who was so awfully nice to us when we were in Chicago is in Paris and will lunch with me before she leaves—so I'm praying this will reach you so that Red's recipe for Circassian (one or two "s"?) chicken will reach me in time. From here I'll take up a fowl—(neither a young pullet or *une poularde de Bresse)* just a cock or a hen—which needs something to make it appear to B.G. sophisticated *un plat!* And surely Persian chickens were hens and cocks and not *poulardes et capons* even in the days before Hitler meddled everything up. So that if Red mailed [the recipe] at once my lunch would have the *pièce de résistance* it needs.

My dear—when you want news of me dont apply to Sarah Stein—you'd get yourself in for a Christian Science lecture probably if she deigned to answer you at all—she'd probably get Gabrielle de Monzie to type you two lines to say she knew nothing about my present whereabouts. She doesnt answer my letters—that is two I wrote her two years ago when Allan was ill. She spared me her answers—of course the letters were written at Allan's request! He's a horror—we dont meet any more frequently than necessary—and then I dont listen to him. I made my last effort a year ago—now that's over. Please dont write to Sarah anything but that I propose being a lady of leisure in Paris—why not.

Endless love to you both always from

Alice

dont apply to Sarah Stein: The Taylors had not heard from Alice in almost three months, an unusually long silence. Fearing that something might be wrong and not knowing whom to write, Louise sent a note to Sarah Stein. When Alice heard of this she was furious. Ever since 1906, when she first met Michael and Sarah Stein, she had had a strong affection for Michael and an equally strong dislike of Sarah. The Michael Steins moved back to San Francisco in 1935 and Michael died three years later. Sarah was then living with her friend Gabrielle de Monzie, and both were practicing Christian Scientists.

To Louise and Redvers Taylor, England/MS Taylor

15 September 1948 — 5 rue Christine, Paris VI

My dears—

But you were sweet to get that recipe off to me so promptly but dont you remember there are no walnuts (any more than there are dates or prunes during the summer—we are waiting for the new ones to be gathered) now and as for half a loaf of bread—could it possibly be made with such bread as we have now. But we'll talk of this when we meet. The hen was quite presentable with an *estragon* sauce—which I'll be making for you soon.

I got back last Friday after a frightful trip—Basket and I in the corridor of the train trying to sit on my bags—no way of reserving seats—as it is always full up long before I get on. Not unless there's a possibility of a reserved seat will I go on a train again—not I. But it didnt seem to do either of us the least harm—on the contrary it just affected my temper!

If there is anything new in Paris it isnt I who have heard it. The flat has to be put in order and winter has to be arranged—not for—but against. Francis and Frederica [Rose] are coming through next week on their way from Corsica—they have done the island for the book she's to write—roughing it it would seem as one evidently must if one goes inland and even on some of the coast. Alas alas in my effort to clear things up before I left I gave two small bottles of perfume away (scarcely know how to use it any more) but I've some very nice *eau de Cologne* for you—much more useful!!

All my thanks and love always.

Alice

To Donald Gallup, New Haven/MS Gallup

12 October 1948 — 5 rue Christine, Paris VI

Dear Donald—

There is a Picasso show at [Galerie] Louise Leiris and I went over for the *vernissage* and saw Kahnweiler—looking older but very well—in spite of his sadness he is having a rather charming life—going to new countries to lecture—being very much appreciated (his book on Gris has amongst the young become the authoritative work on cubism). He plans to go to U.S. in early spring and is looking forward to it with almost a romantic sense of adventure. I do hope he wont be disappointed. Then I saw Madame Lascaux and she asked for news of you and told me that Germaine was working at the gallery and I didnt see her because there were too many people but I had seen the pictures quietly—'45–'48—all smallish and many drawings. Incredible as it may sound to you his line is finer than ever—more moving—sensitive and inconceivably beautiful. There are four landscapes that I wish you could see. Strange that no one has considered him as a great landscape painter. In the twenties he made a series of very small pictures—each perfection in itself—we saw them at Boisgeloup—his place in Normandy—and then never again. I imagine they are still there. Picasso never moves his belongings with him. When the home no longer pleases him (on account of its memories) he moves on and wants no souvenirs—as soon as he is through with a thing it belongs to his past and that naturally he refuses to accept—as even having been his. But the landscapes haunt me—no new pictures—even of his—have been as revealing as they are.

Austerity has gone so far that the population has become submissive through lack of physical resistance. Here there is always more and more to buy but at such prices that very few can afford to buy half of what is offered them. There are some of us who dont do badly on the minimum. The strikes in the mines have already cut two days electricity a week—which is a bore—but if that is all one can manage.

Riba [-Rovira] has moved back to the quarter. An affair with a married woman has just ended—fortunately for him for she was very possessive and left him no liberty for she was jealous of every one. He had an order to do the portrait of the minister of Cuba and his daughter but she objected so he renounced doing the daughter's but she forbade his going to do the father's for fear he'd meet the daughter—whom she had never seen but suspected of having designs upon Riba. Now he is free and independent again but a little *désorienté*. I've found some Americans who are buying one of Riba's and one of Francis Rose's pictures.

There are a great many Americans still in Paris—not residents just tourists but nothing compared to Rome they say—which is livelier—more cheerful and cheaper than Paris. Now I've told you all I know—except about all your kindness to me—for which I am so very grateful. Without Carl and you where would I have been today—to know that you are both there taking care of Gertrude's future is my comfort—the one consolation in the general bleakness. Bless you and thank you—love to you always.

Alice

To W. G. Rogers, New York/MS Rogers

20 October 1948 5 rue Christine, Paris VI

Dearest Kiddie—

No the Steins didnt care for Gertrude's work. The Ford car—Aunt Pauline—on whose step you sat was named after Fred Stein's mother for reasons you know and that could not have pleased her sentimental children. Madame Giraud from Ceyzerieu—who remembers you well enough to make it thoroughly impolite for you not to return the compliment—was here yesterday afternoon and said she had heard *La Voix d'Amérique* about Gertrude—that she was more pleased with its being about Gertrude than she was with what was said—that she could have done it more interestingly.

Picasso has unexpectedly returned for the winter to Paris—perhaps the pottery had commenced to pall—and he is my neighbor again. I havent seen him yet.

Allan Stein has had another *crise* and was desperately ill but with a new specialist and at a nursing home he is now out of pain and is sleeping normally—so there is more hope than there was.

Thornton and his sister took me last night to a Berlioz oratorio at Notre Dame flood lighted full force on the outside and discreetly within—just enough to bring out the flags suspended on either side—the flags of the U.N. for whose delegates the show was put on. The stars and stripes on one side nearest the altar—the red flag with the sickle and hammer opposite! Notre Dame flood lighted is incomparable—for daylight Chartres and for moonlight Rheims.

For this evening this is all and best love to you both always.

Alice

1949

To W. G. and Mildred Rogers, New York/MS Rogers

12 March 1949 5 rue Christine, Paris VI

Dearest Kiddies—

If it has been weeks and weeks if not months and months since I've written to you it isnt because I havent tried to find time. First Basket was desperately sick—for a while it was nip and tuck if he'd ever be really well again. Finally he came back from the vet all bandaged and pitifully thin. Now he's much much better but not completely healed but he is allowed to walk as much as I do. And we're both more cheerful naturally. Then Gabrielle cant do as much as formerly—she has more things the matter with her than are necessary to enumerate. Then Bébé's [Christian Bérard] death was a shock—though I didnt see him often I was very very fond of him and there were a great many people I hadnt seen for years and that is always painful. And then a friend who is to have a show in the autumn brought his pictures here and everybody came to see them and that kept me busy for several weeks. And—and—and.

But here we are today and the first thing to say is all my thanks for all the wonderful things the Kiddies sent me in such a Christmas box as never was (and as never must be again for reasons to follow)—all the purest luxuries—things one has ceased to dream about—one doesnt remember their names—and cant remember when one saw them last—was it in '14 or in California before '07 or '49 or what. Mrs. Kiddie when she puts her mind to it can completely lose it and just run amuck. So my dears I send you belated but warmest thanks for the last Christmas box you must send me because 1. we're to go off ration tickets after the elections (you get the implication—yes?) which are within the month—2. I've given up all luxuries—the frugal life in all directions suits me best. The only thing that is a temptation is heat—as the winter has been unusually mild and the electrical company mysteriously lenient to me the room here has been comfortable except the two days the current is cut. I'm better off than many and am properly grateful—though a friend from N.Y. for whom I preheated the room ruinously wrote to another friend in N.Y.—What will she do when it gets cold (!!!!).

Thornton W. and his sister were here in November and December and then again for a week lately before sailing. Finally it came to me why Mrs. Kiddie had so scandalously lost her heart to him on sight. They have the same high spirits and gaiety—just irresistibly wrecklessly unashamedly gay—and what a blessing that is—well who am I to tell it to you—I ask you. Have you seen reproductions of Picasso's pottery—pottery such as one never dreamed of—and still I prefer drawings to it. I went to see him the other day—he's in very good form and very sweet and happily less irritable than half of the people who see him describe him and less hilariously gay than the other half say—*enfin* much more like himself than any of these extremes though as usual extremely Picasso. Have you seen the Matisse collages (and to remember what he used to say about others when they used it)—and have you seen *La Folle de Chaillot*—Bébé's last décor for *Les Fourberies* was incredibly beautiful—quite perfect—the *générale* was the evening of the day after [Bébé's] funeral and everyone was in black and it was all very sad. But it didn't change the clowning of Jean-Louis Barrault—nothing can—it is useless to hope for that.

Arent the records of *4 Saints* beautiful—and have you read Faulkner's new novel (which is interesting for the godparents it has)—

and do you have the new novel of Elizabeth Bowen (and how is it)—and do you know a Mrs. Harvey who is doing a book on the writers of the Mississippi valley.

The vacuum after months of well bred Hoovering went on the blink in all of its essential parts—but a half hour of the expert's efforts (and God be praised there is such a thing)—also found a perfect electrician—what more does U.S. offer—except climate and the affection for which Disraeli's duchess only lived.

Wasnt it nice the Sitwells had such a good time. Didnt you think Edith beautiful—we always did—and what's this about not understanding her—she's quite the most comprehensible English woman ever. I have a new young painter—have had indeed for some time—he was in Italy when you were here—who has just had a successful show in London—and what is still a wonder to me is that his mother is even a better painter. They are Turks and under strong Byzantine influence and both of them are delightfully fertile. Do you know an American female painter named Buffie Johnson—a pest to us all but very clever—she's having a show. And Picabia is having a fifty year retrospective—*50 ans de plaisir*—originally called *de joie!* And there's to be a retrospective of Bébé's in the autumn and in the meantime a show next week of his gouaches. But of course the best of them are the pictures from the Pinacothèque—do you know Altdorfer—I didnt! And am mad about him—if you ever get to the Metropolitan will you get me a *p.c. (not* a *photograph)* of it or of them. Such a precursor—foresaw—well—2 centuries.

Many many thanks to you both and love.

Alice

4 Saints: An abridged version of *Four Saints,* made for the recording, June 1947, by Virgil Thomson. It included about one-half of the complete score; the cast was substantially that of the original production.

Faulkner's new novel: Intruder in the Dust (1948).

new novel of Elizabeth Bowen: The Heat of the Day (1949).

new young painter: Néjad. His mother was the Princess Zeid.

To Thornton Wilder, Hamden, Connecticut/MS Wilder

5 April 1949 5 rue Christine, Paris VI

Dear Thornton—

Do I commence by telling you at once or do I wait for the end or would it be best not to put myself amongst what Gertrude used to call the undistinguished majority—no you havent heard how tremendously I miss you because you musnt be so bored that you'll become deaf indifferent cold and only come to rue Christine in the autumn from a sense of duty—no you wont have to do that—not even as prettily as you only could. Anyway it is too late to tell you now and I didn't earlier because I've had Basket sick—very sick—ever since you left—here and at the vet—where he is now—every Tuesday or Wednesday or some other horrid day the vet is to tell me what we can expect—but now it doesnt seem to be reasonable to suppose he'll be well again—not easy to accustom oneself to—he has filled the corners of the room and the minutes and me so sweetly these last years.

Other wise there isnt much news. Natalie Barney has gone to Italy. Francis and Frederica [Rose] and the [Joseph] Barrys are not getting the flat they wanted. Marie Laurencin has been made an *officier de la Légion d'honneur*. The government is studying the plan for a general amnesty which would free Bernard Faÿ. I've seen Picasso—his girl is pregnant again. It is warm—the chestnuts all green and the peach trees in blossom. The rents are being raised according to a new law which is filled with coefficients and articles and titles and which requires an expert to convince even the most amiable of landladies that the stairs are not carpeted—that seven windows never see the sun—that a carpenter and a bookbinder are not bourgeois so that the rent can not be increased to what she hopes for—and oh yes H.R.H. the Princess Zeid is visiting her daughter in New Haven who unexpectedly married a Yale student and who longs to meet you and Isabel—to whom I've written that neither of you should bother to do anything about it unless it amused you.

You describe Ezra [Pound] exactly as he was when we knew him here in the middle or was it early twenties when he'd discovered [T.S.] Eliot and wanted everyone to subscribe five dollars to get him [Eliot] out of the bank and believed in some English political economist who was to save Europe who wasnt Keynes and believed in Japanese prints and didnt know Cézanne from Derain or the other way around and was only quieted by falling out of a low chair on to the ground. If the war had only lasted longer he would have turned against Italy—the way he did against France twice and England—and he'd be free now to find a more varied audience —which is what one always most wished for him.

Your resigning from the fragrance of the artificial flowers of the P.E.N. club was a most hopeful sign. I'm still smiling about it first thing in the morning. If all the old men of the sea would become artificial flowers how unencumbered one would be. *La veille de la rue Christine*—is it the concierge or I—misses you very very much and sends you love.

Alice

Remember everything about the Goethe festival in Aspen Colorado to tell me.

To Samuel Steward, Chicago/MS Bancroft

8 April 1949 5 rue Christine, Paris VI

Dearest Sam—

I've never written to you to tell you so many things but first of all to thank you for the beautiful beautiful basket and all the treasures it holds. You cant fancy what the fragrance of the sweet grass did to me as I undid the package—it's one—indeed the most precious—of my perfume memories—sweet grass and heliotrope are more my mother to me except the smile in her eyes. When I was a little girl we spent a summer at Lake George—where I fell off a log & into the river and was promptly taught Our Father—and my mother bought endless baskets made of sweet grass for her friends and herself. And when she died there was one in which she kept her best handkerchiefs which I kept until I left San Francisco and always wondered afterwards why I had. And only you would have answered and understood the need now to have something to connect me with my childhood.

Do you read Capote—his success [is] a bit overdone—excellent climate and good landscape—too many butterflies—his and his characters' sexual life boresome. Faulkner's last interesting but mistaken. Is there no one writing better than these two. Here they're mad about Steinbeck and Dos Passos—Sartre discovered them and though he's beginning to be old fashioned his Americans continue popular.

I've kept off the subject of your teaching again—fearful that you had once more thrown it over. I do hope not. You always made one feel that you were exceptionally good at it—making things come alive to the dullest of impossible boys—they are of course no duller than girls—who know how to make themselves look so. Dont you find subjects galore amongst their strange relationships—you ought to be able to do a smashing novel about them and no one has in U.S. They do it all the time still in England—so try it.

Oh by the way about brilliant conversations when under the influence of . . . —Jo Davidson used to say the same thing—in fact used it as an excuse—it made him brilliant and gave him courage. Gertrude used to tell him it was just the contrary—he lost his usual easy native wit. Well one afternoon we went to see the Davidsons and a friend of Jo's was there completely *parti* and quite a bit maudlin. Jo took Gertrude aside and excused his friend and Gertrude said she didn't much care for it and added—You see Jo why I say what I do when you are like that. Like that—never—said Jo

ALICE B. TOKLAS AND TWO UNIDENTIFIED CHILDREN

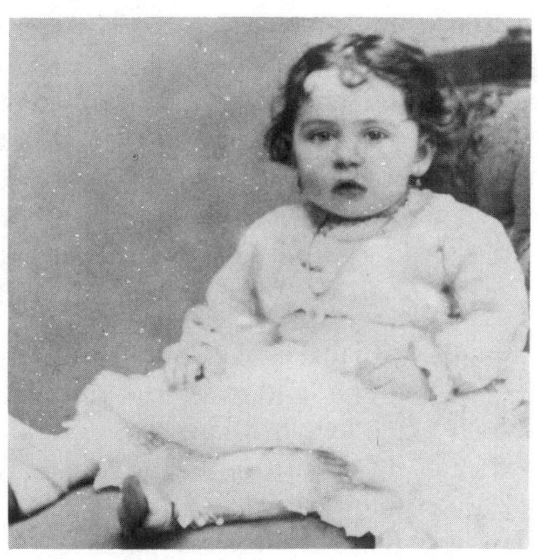

ALICE AS AN INFANT

indignantly and wouldn't believe her. So Gertrude said—Why not let me be the judge—you see how little your friend is capable of weighing his wit. Gertrude always said that liquor only improved the *deséquilibrés*—and my dear we do hope you are not that.

Always yours
Alice

To L. Elizabeth Hansen, Pasadena, California/MS Yale

14 April 1949 — 5 rue Christine, Paris VI

Lilyana dear—

First of all I must acknowledge the check. It has gone for an Easter [present] (yes it came just after Xmas and we're in Holy Week now) to a family of eleven—father mother grandmother and eight children—of whom only two are old enough to partly earn their living. They will write to you—of course twenty dollars makes more than even a festive dinner for working people—but it is understood that they are to have *cochon*—a good portion of meat—a vegetable—not potatoes or cabbage—and an orange and a banana—a glass of wine and a cup of coffee. Thank you for them dear Lily.

The moment that I have time and money I'll see the doctor for the arthritis which has become a nuisance—it fatigues one so—walking with one's head always a little nearer the ground is a bore. To prove I'm a good American I'm going to get myself cured.

There are rarely any Gris for sale—his output wasnt like Matisse's and Picasso's—I mean per year—he only painted for fifteen years—that is devoting himself exclusively to painting—from 1912 to 1927—he died the following year when he was forty. I have a lithograph he gave me—something I think that is called the first state and I would like you to have it. It is so suitable—it was to illustrate a limited edition of Salacrou's play *Le Casseur d'Assiettes*—done when they were both young. I'll try to see how I can get it to you and by what I can replace it on the wall—but it will get to you soon—by hook or by crook. My dear I've just gone in and looked at it and it's a pen and ink drawing! *Tant pis* only would you think it horrid of me if I asked you to leave it to Yale University Library for the G.S. collection. I've promised them my few treasures. But I'd like you to have the pleasure of it for your time. How about it. Yes Juan was wonderful. I used to tease him and say he was Andrea del Sarto the perfect painter. He understood and knew everything—you had only to ask Juan why and how and he made everything crystal clear—and not at all only about painting—he understood people and human relationships and he was the most honorable man I ever knew—inflexible though not unappreciative of weakness. He had been weak—corrupted he said as only Spaniards could be—he hated that. He was absolutely *dépouillé* of all that—such a very human saint. And he loved to laugh and make merry and dance (none too well). He was handsome—slightly Arab or nigger or both looking—he had a son who has his beautiful and so intelligent eyes—who is a chemist. Do you know Gertrude's short piece "The Life and Death of Juan Gris." He was the first friend I had who died and it was dreadful.* I can still hear them telling us that it was over—he had suffered so long and so greatly—and he knew his work wasnt completed. That's the way Juan was—so serious and so almost sillily merry—he laughed easily and looked almost solemn—dear dear Juan.

I learned a lot about the Russians from knowing very intimately a Russian brother and sister—émigrés of the early '20ies. He was the painter Pavel Tchelitchew. He was absolutely cannibal—he devoured everything—men women children—flats—furniture—everything except the original Russian ballet which he caressed. His sister as one of his victims I took an immense fancy to—she was like one of the sisters of a Turgenev heroine—appearing with a basket of flowers or fruit in a doorway—no word—scarcely a gesture—but full of mystery portent and tragedy. Now they say she has said she never wants to see her brother again—she doesn't want

JUAN GRIS, PARIS, 1922

Photograph by Man Ray

He understood and knew everything—you had only to ask Juan why and how and he made everything crystal clear.

to see me because she thinks I treated her brother badly. They—the Russians—are cannibals—you have to be of hard metal to resist them. A word soon and my love always.

Alice

*Dead is dead but that is why memory is all and all the immortality there is.

Gris: Gris had arrived in Paris in 1906. At that time he made his living drawing for such newspapers as *L'Assiette au Beurre, Le Charivari,* and others. He soon broke away from this work, but it was only in 1910, with a series of drawings and gouaches, that the true work of Gris began. Gris first exhibited his work in 1912 at the Salon des Indépendants to which he sent *Hommage à Picasso.* In 1926 he illustrated Stein's *A Book Concluding With As A Wife Has A Cow* which was published by Kahnweiler under the imprint of Galerie Simon.

To Annette Rosenshine, Berkeley, California
MS Bancroft

17 April 1949 — 5 rue Christine, Paris VI

Dear Annette—

It was Papa who said that I'd been born a day too late and had never found a way to catch up. Indeed it isn't a day too late that I am this time but three days. I had thought to write to you on your birthday hoping you would excuse the months too late an answer would come to you for your nice kind warm letter—to thank you for it and for your gay Christmas card of the California Street dummy mounting the hill of a very respectablised Chinatown. When for the briefest moment we saw it in '35 Gertrude and I were terribly disappointed—it looked like the Chinese quarter of any town.

One has to scamper about to make ends meet. It keeps one active and lively but it takes a great deal of time. During the occupation *forcément* I became a fairly good and economical cook—we had one who couldn't cook the plainest meal without a pint of dry white wine a pint of cream and the yolks of at least six eggs—so I got the habit then. The cook went with the house and was frightfully underpaid and I learned more from her (her cooking was famous in the region) than she cared to learn from me—she despised economy and saving in detail. But when the Americans came in '44 she was wonderful. She had fresh trout—we were just 15 minutes from the Rhone—and enormous apple pies fresh from the oven from early morning to late at night. She was a great person. But why should you have to hear about Clothilde from me—a pen can run away from one just as easily as a tongue.

About Roubina and Allan [Stein]—I see them rarely—but as a matter of fact Roubina asked me to lunch with her the day before yesterday and took me to a nice Chinese restaurant—nice but not like in S.F. oh dear no—no Chinese bowls greenlined—no bird's nests—no water chestnuts—but soya and pork with transparent vermicelli etcetera. Roubina looks better than she did—not so thin and wan and worn. Allan has been seriously ill—with crises from time to time. You will please not speak to any one of this and what further I'll be telling you because I dont think Sarah has been told anything. Allan believes somewhat in the Christian Science practices but when I went to see him some time ago he spent two hours describing his illnesses—for alas he has more than one—his symptoms and what the specialists say. It was an incredible story and before leaving it was I not he who said a word for mind over matter—when he allowed me to talk! Poor Allan—he is so little disciplined that a cure doesn't seem possible. Roubina with her calm and good judgment has carried on alone—not only sick Allan and the household with the two children at Garches but the shop as well and very successfully at that. She has been admirable in every way and Allan is an impossible patient—for he is only interested in a cure for a very short while and as part of the cure is diet and he's always breaking it—it's a hopelessly discouraging situation. This is just for you as I've already said but it justifies your appreciation of Roubina so you should know how admirably she has come up to scratch.

People are beginning to shake their rugs out of the window above me so I've closed the windows—do you remember the French way of cleaning. I'm the only person on the whole rue Christine—to be sure it [is] only one long block—who has a vacuum cleaner—and a Hoover at that—to protect the pictures.

A friend has lately seen Matisse in the south—he rarely goes out to walk any more but under his direction is [a] Russian model who takes care of him—pins colored paper on a board—and they are to be the mural decorations of a chapel at Vence.

Jane Heap was well for her—she has had diabetes for years when we heard directly from a friend who came to see us three years ago to bring us news of her. She had been one of the heroines of the Blitz in London and had commenced lecturing again afterwards—still Gourchief (?—spelling as usual doubtful). Then a few weeks ago I saw Sylvia Beach and she had news of Jane. Sylvia said she thought the disease was sufficiently under control to be neither painful nor alarming. Brave Jane—how much I like her. Margaret Anderson continues to live on in Normandy—much quieter than formerly but quite as beautiful—a man told me this only a few days ago—he had seen her there not long ago. People who move about bring me news as I stay put—not only a comfortable but [an] economical way of getting older.

I haven't seen Man Ray for years and years now. Picasso said he was a little old man—had seen him last year—which is what Picasso himself is—which is what we all more or less are according to our sex—except you my dear. I hope you are well and you musnt take on the future—especially the world's—only in as far as it can be changed for some one person at a time—large causes seem to have less chance of succeeding than individual cases. Forgive my sententiousness and my long silence and let me hear from you again please.

Always affectionately
Alice

the house: The house at Culoz came with two servants, Clothilde and Olympe. Clothilde was a fine cook who refused to cook when she learned of the scant materials the ration coupons would allow. "She was old, tired and pessimistic," as Toklas remembered her in 1953. Both servants appear as characters in Stein's play *Yes Is For A Very Young Man.*

Garches: Allan Stein, with his second wife Roubina and their two children, was living in Garches on the outskirts of Paris, but not in the Villa Stein (Les Terrasses) which had been designed by Le Corbusier in 1927 for his parents. Allan owned a small perfume business, the management of which was totally in Roubina's hands.

Gourchief: Georgi Ivanovitch Gurdjieff, a Russian mystic who came to Paris in the twenties. Margaret Anderson, editor with Jane Heap of *The Little Review,* had adopted his philosophical teachings. Stein and Toklas met him briefly when they went to see Anderson's two young nephews whom Heap had adopted and left with Gurdjieff. Toklas and Stein were supposed to supplement Gurdjieff's efforts at educating the boys: Stein was to give the boys books and Toklas "creature comforts and do the mending and darning."

Sylvia Beach: In 1919, under the sign "Shakespeare and Company," Sylvia Beach founded an English language bookshop in Paris. (See her memoir *Shakespeare and Company* [1959].)

Man Ray: American painter and photographer who lived in Paris. In the early twenties he took a number of photographs of Stein, Toklas, and Basket I.

To Louise and Redvers Taylor, England/MS Taylor

1 May 1949 — 5 rue Christine, Paris VI

My dears—

Today being May Day I send you all warm wishes *pour le bonheur.* This afternoon I'm going to have the visit of a young English girl who was a near neighbor—though in Savoy—whom we saw a good deal of during the occupation—that is until they were able to get out—Papa was in the hush hush—she will tell me just how one makes out in London—hoping that something more than lollipops have been added to your diet. We do all too well here except rent and taxes and prices generally. But keeping an eye on one's *petites économies* ceaselessly one keeps one's head above water. Very shortly I'm going to earn some money—yes quite possibly—never too late to commence—eight years earlier than Harriet Levy! It appears that she only appears on great occasions and then in the newest of new looks aided by everything that Elizabeth Arden manufactures and that it is worth the price of admission. This was lately told me by a very serious Mrs. Curtiss who knew Harriet four or five years ago—can you believe it.

Best of luck and love.

Alice

Mrs. Curtiss: Mina Curtiss, American writer and editor and sister of Lincoln Kirstein, met Toklas through Virgil Thomson and Carl Van Vechten.

To Allison Delarue, Princeton, New Jersey/MS Princeton

6 May 1949 5 rue Christine, Paris VI

My dear Mr. Delarue—

Your article on [Eugene] Berman interested me a lot—you are quite right in giving him the importance you do in his work for the theatre—his painting—though distinguished—is of interest only as a point of departure for his décors. Subjects and emotions about them do not make pictures—they really do not. But Berman's great gift for the theatre—the many and varied reproductions you send me are ample evidence—is accomplished and original.

I am sending two colored reproductions of Picasso's pictures. If they do not interest you as painting you will enjoy them as souvenirs of Gertrude Stein—the nude was the first Picasso she bought

(1905) and the blue landscape is one of the very few landscapes of that period—if not the only one. If you get to Paris in my time come to see me and you will see them and all the other Picassos here.

Thank you again many times.

Cordially
Alice Toklas

Allison Delarue: A drama historian who was connected with theatre at Princeton University. He had sent Toklas his article "Some American Lithographs of the Romantic Ballet" from the *American Collector* (November 1942).

Picasso's pictures: Girl With a Basket of Flowers (Paris, 1905), now in the collection of Mr. and Mrs. David Rockefeller; *The Blue House* (Barcelona, 1902), now in the collection of André Meyer.

To W. G. and Mildred Rogers, New York/MS Rogers

13 May 1949 — 5 rue Christine, Paris VI

Dearest Kiddies—

There is only the news of the quarter—more particularly the rue Christine—which indulged in a small excitement the other afternoon late. A man whom we knew in the army has returned—with a wife—as one of the big Marshall Plan experts—railroad—and when they came over to have a cup of tea with me they announced they'd to make their way between a cordon of police—another at the other end—one before nos. 5 and 7 and a great many young men a few young women—some of them with mattresses others with blankets—milling about—gesticulating and screaming. When the friends left Gabrielle announced that the students—mostly from the Beaux Arts—wanted to force their way into no. 7—an empty building—because they could no longer afford the continuously rising prices in even the little hotels and that there werent any rooms to let anywhere anymore. Gabrielle who is a great gossip and likes to know what goes on in her quarter rushed to the front door when she first heard the noise and thereafter naturally every quarter of an hour with more regularity than she bastes a roast (on the very rare occasions that she is required to). I must tell you that the building at no. 7 is owned by Hachette who have a monopoly for the distribution of printed matter throughout the country and are enormously rich and powerful. After the war they were accused of collaboration—they had enough influence to have the case dismissed. Some enemy had their whole concern nationalised—they got themselves denationalised—all this with the varied colors of the different parties in power. Gabrielle hates them because they are avowedly communists and because they are undoubtedly capitalists. So siding with the students she conceived a brilliant idea to help them. Choosing two young men who looked capable of executing her plan—she got them into the court—the concierge had closed the door at the beginning of the trouble but could not refuse a tenant and whose fault was it that two others slipped past with her. She then lead them up to the top floor where she has her bedroom and which she has so completely explored that she was able to show them the trap door that leads to the room from which they could walk to the roof of no. 7. (How did she know—is that the way she used to take to visit the concierge of no. 7.) Well they successfully followed her indications but in the dark they werent able to find the trap door of no. 7. *Le projet a échoué*. It undoubtedly did. So later the police took half dozen of the loudest students to the police station for the night. The next day Gabrielle brought an armful of the likeliest newspapers to give an account of the episode. In one of them it said the police had mounted to the roof—this was as near as she was mentioned but the stupidity of the error so enraged [her] that she had all the angry satisfaction—the only kind she knows—she was looking for. She's been in one continuous state of temper ever since and Basket and I avoid her as much as we can contrive to. If she would only retire to the country but no—having achieved Paris—

she clings to it. She exhausts me as I have you. Fondest love to you both.

Alice

To Sir Francis Rose, England/MS Texas

26 May 1949 — 5 rue Christine, Paris VI

Dearest Francis—

First a scant letter from Frederica—then yours and today the photographs have arrived—all to my great delight. The preliminary *hommage* is immensely impressive—there is a mastery of all the means—a beauty of line and an intensity of movement that seem to me far beyond anything you've done. And it's a very real and touching portrait of Gertrude—and it is deeply satisfying. When you come over for your vacation you will explain some of the symbolism which escapes me though it (my ignorance) doesn't worry me or interfere with the direct meaning or beauty of the picture.

But your new idea is ideal if it can materialise—it is in museums that they should be and would have been if it hadnt been for Allan Stein's obstinacy and contrary mindedness. His oldest son out in California has just lost a lot of money raising horses and Allan's mother sold most if not all her Matisses and the small Cézannes she had to pay the debts. So of all the pictures the three of them had there are only Gertrude's left as a collection.

Thanks again for everything—Francis dear.

All my love always
Alice

To Samuel Steward, Chicago, Illinois/MS Bancroft

27 May 1949 5 rue Christine, Paris VI

Sam dear—

Sweet Sammie's basket is more than ever my delight—it has cheered me through some dark days. Basket was desperately sick. The vet didn't think he could cure him—for four days he didn't recognise me and then the treatment commenced to be effective and so at last he came back and we were both pleased. He is as thin as a hound at the feet of his master on a gothic tomb and isnt as gay as he used to be but he's here again and for the moment that is everything. Then I had what one might call a household accident—in an excess of zeal I took the large cover off the radiator to wash the woodwork in the back—it's a tricky operation—having succeeded in lifting it into the sink the radiator fell on me and one foot and ankle were pinned under it. And I had to wait forty minutes to have Gabrielle come and rescue me. As it wasn't possible to walk out came the lovely basket and all my mending and darning done I commenced some fancy sewing—neckerchiefs—and now every day there it is scenting the room and inviting me to what I like most to do—a little fine foolish sewing—one gets so bored with doing useful things—necessary things. *Vive l'inutil—la périssable!* And the lovely sachets are acacia—but definitely—Gertrude's favorite scent—acacia in France and iris in Italy—and saffron in Spain.

And saffron reminds me I'm so glad the allergy has been thrown overboard. Dont you think A. Anonymous has something to do with it. I do. I'm all for it since it has done so handsomely for you. The program is sensible and generous and for God's sake take it as yours and *doucement allez doucement* as they used to say in Bilignin. Painting as a diversion for you is perfect—the trouble with Picasso was that he allowed himself to be flattered into believing that he was a poet too. Gertrude and he had quite a scene about his writing—but she told it in *Everybody's Autobiography.*

The only person who did both—not equally well though equally charmingly—was Max Jacob—do you know either his poetry or his painting.

It is naturally days since I commenced to write to you—interrupted by photographers who came to do a picture or pictures for an illustrated book on Picassso—one a month appears. A Swiss editor came to see what he would choose for his book *Picasso Before Picasso* (!). There's a little café scene he did in '02 or '03 that a friend gave me in '08—one of the rare ones under the influence of Toulouse-Lautrec—which I produced with considerable pride. Ah yes said he looking at it a little cock-eyed—just what I want but unfortunately not the right proportions for the format of the book I envisage. Then there is the lady who is organising a loan show for charity and who wanted the blue nude with the basket of flowers. The title of the show was The Mother and her Child. But—said I—she is not a child and her mother—would she not be just a shocking *fille*. She was ready to overlook the nude's lack of reference. Then there has been a deluge of musicians—executants and composers—and one or two concerts which frankly bore me—I would have preferred *The Marriage of Figaro* by the Vienna opera which unfortunately I didnt hear.

Do you know the Knapiks—she is very refreshing—a strong wind off the lake—and ever so good looking. They have republished Gide's *Oscar Wilde*—did you ever read it. Gide has become a worried Victor Hugo—that's what the French feel. And Sartre is out of fashion—like Dior—the new look is no longer new. Now I must get this to the p.o.—air mail in the pillar boxes it seems goes by boat mail so Basket and I will trot up to get it into the proper box.

Sammie dear I send you my grateful love.

Alice

Knapiks: Harold and Virginia Knapik went to Paris in 1948, he to study music at the École Normale de Musique and she to work at the American Embassy. In the summer of 1948 they were staying in Chantilly with their friends Osborn and Marian Andreas when Toklas and a friend came for

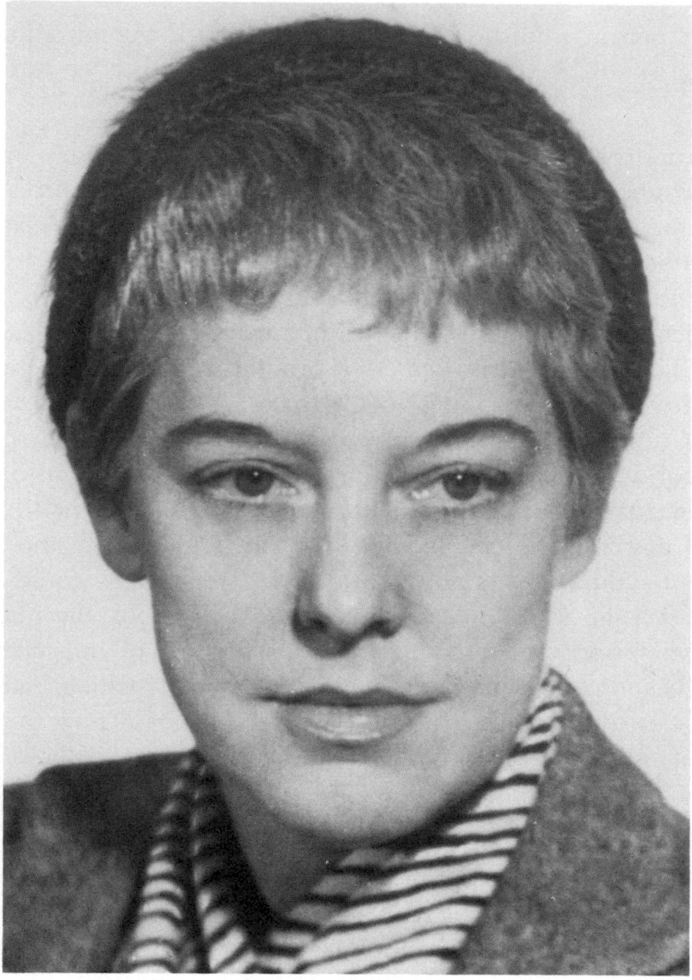

PORTRAIT OF VIRGINIA KNAPIK, PARIS, 1956

Photograph by Man Ray

Do you know the Knapiks—she is very refreshing—a strong wind off the lake—and ever so good looking.

lunch. When the Knapiks met Toklas she was just beginning to come to terms with the wound of Stein's death. From their initial meeting, the Knapiks and Toklas became friends.

To John Breon, Rockford, Illinois/MS Yale

4 June 1949 5 rue Christine, Paris VI

Dear John—

Your plan to come over to work for the Quakers is admirable—they have done very fine work in France—as elsewhere—I have heard nothing but praise of it. We never knew many Quakers. Gertrude Stein was a friend of Logan Pearsall Smith—you may have heard of a little book of his called *Trivia* which had an immense influence many years ago. And then there was Nora Wahl who came to see us after the liberation and she was very impressive as a Quaker. So I do hope the plan goes through. As it is not at all likely that you will be working in Paris would it not be possible for you to say that you have a dear and old—with a double meaning—[friend] with whom you wish to stay if it were only for twenty four hours. Literally perhaps you wouldnt be staying with me for there is no extra bed here but I would have you put up at a small hotel near here and you would have your meals with me and it is a very pleasant hope that this may come true and you will let me know as soon as you know.

There is the first summer influx of visitors but I try [to] keep from seeing too many of them—some are people who were kind to us when we were over and to whom we were greatly obligated—others are friends of friends. Tomorrow—Whitsun—when you are being graduated I'll be taking the daughter of a friend to Fontainebleau—unless it's pouring—which it mostly has been doing for a month now—or threatening to. About being secure of the future—of knowing exactly how your life is to [be] conducted from decade to decade—Gertrude Stein was aghast when a young French friend told her what his life was to be. She said to me afterwards—No elasticity—no spontaneity—no adventure—why not even an interference or obstruction—no John—that wouldn't be natural to you. When I was young I read Nietzsche—my father hated it and for the only time tried to stop me—but it was only a pseudo intellectual pretension on my part. And Pascal only came much later and was a real thing. And he has such concentrated purity that it's bound to penetrate—you'll come out alright—you musnt think anything could take that conviction away.

The best of everything for you always—come soon. And my loving remembrances.

Alice Toklas

To Mina Curtiss, Williamsburg, Massachusetts/MS Yale

18 June 1949 — 5 rue Christine, Paris VI

Dear Mrs. Curtiss—

Your letter compensated for your absence. I miss your visits—they meant a great deal to me—each one has left a sweet memory. *Les jours se suivent et ils se resemblent affreusement*—though the days are warmer and longer and Basket is a bit better—but he is an old dog before his time alas.

Virgil's success and the honors that are so continuously being bestowed upon him are the most encouraging and satisfactory proofs that justice does—at least occasionally—prevail. And it's his rare but adorable naïveté which makes him feel that the Pulitzer award is no more than a Guggenheim fellowship. Virgil has taken his success quietly and gently—which in him is almost unnatural. It is winning and attaching beyond anything one would have expected from the young Virgil who showed sweetness and light only in his music. There have been several American musicians here and they are grateful to Virgil and to the music he writes. I have written to him to tell him so. Leonard Bernstein—in the clipping you sent—is not always sensitive to the real meaning of Gertrude's work and Virgil's music—though intending to convey his appreciation. But it is not to you—who have suffered from blind but well intentioned critics—that one should complain of the critics' misunderstanding of the simplest expression of a belief they've not experienced daily. It is as Gertrude used to say unfamiliarity that breeds contempt.

You cant half fancy how the wind blew the foolishness out of me on that heavenly trip you took me into Normandy. How very good you have been to me—commencing with letting me know you—and with so much between—ending with taking over the trifles to Virgil and Carl—who writes to me that he is now like his old self—but one asks oneself old self of what moment—his illness has worried me a lot.

My fondest remembrances.

Alice Toklas

To Fernanda Pivano, Milan/MS Pivano

18 June 1949 — 5 rue Christine, Paris VI

Dear Nanda—

Unhappily I know no books for you to read for the work you are to do about Fitzgerald except the one of course you know—*The Crack Up* that [Edmund] Wilson edited very shortly after poor lovable unhappy Fitzgerald's death. Surely I told you about Gertrude and him—of her unfailing appreciation of his work and belief in his gift—which he would not believe. I mean he did neither believe in his gift nor believe she meant what she told him

FERNANDA PIVANO AND ALICE B. TOKLAS, PARIS, 1951

Photograph by Ettore Sottsass, Jr.

Your name was my father's. . . . And Nanda is the name of my favorite modern heroine.

about his work. Did I not tell you. And the tragedy of his betrayal by one of his contemporaries—but that of course was a personal story which only added to his miseries—he was the most sensitive—except Thornton—the most distinguished—the most gifted and intelligent of all his contemporaries. And the most lovable—he is one of those great tragic American figures—but you know all this and it is of no help to you if you didnt.

Your name was my father's—isnt that nice—Gertrude always thought baptismal names were important—because they were a kind that the possessor could not escape. And Nanda is the name of my favorite modern heroine. Do you remember her in *The Awkward Age*—only I want you to be happier than she was—perhaps happy is not the right word—neither she nor her creator would have admitted it. I should have said I wish you more fortunate—though she didn't feel herself unfortunate—well I musnt drag on—but get this to the p.o. Get well quickly.

With much fond affection
Alice

my father's: Ferdinand Toklas.

To L. Elizabeth Hansen, Pasadena, California/MS Yale

19 July 1949 | 5 rue Christine, Paris VI

Dearest Lilyana—

The young [Joe] Barrys who have just bought a charming house with a big garden high up in the woods above Montmorency which is just twenty kilometers from Paris asked me stay with them. We have compromised—they accept me as a paying guest. It will be quiet comfortable and agreeable and I go out there quietly without any railroad confusion in their car after Gertrude's anniversary. In the old days anniversaries—other than Christmas and Gertrude's birthday—never meant anything but now they do and everything is one. Do you know what I mean. And I have so many things to do.

Donald Gallup who is curator of American [Literature] at Yale University [Library]—really of all manuscripts—and who has been an angel to me—has been here for ten days and is coming back for two more—so I was busy with him—having him meet Gertrude's friends. He is taking back with him my little early Picasso and the portrait of the poodle by Marie Laurencin and the red tape to get them out of the country—everything has to be passed by something called the *office d'échange* beside having spent two hours at the American embassy for an affidavit—and only because I was Gertrude's friend was I spared a second morning's effort.

And the number of acquaintances and friends of acquaintances who have turned up and filled the flat is tiring to remember. But it has been so hot and dry that the arthritis—if it is that—is dormant for which I'm grateful.

At one moment it was very musical—a violinist—Angel Regus—was here and he gave a concert. Mozart and Bartok—yes why Bartok you may well ask—and then at a friends they played Bach and Bach and Bach and it was heavenly—not the playing but Bach—including the Italian suite—do you remember me pegging away at it—making a mess generally. And then there were some youngish Americans—whom we had known much younger—Paul Bowles and [John] Cage and Aaron Copeland—of whom the first has considerable endowment and more understanding—they did a concerto of his for two pianos—wind—and percussion instruments which interested me for a really American quality, not at all primitive but an approach to the sterner qualities of the Red Indian. Cage annoys me with a "prepared piano"- and a Hindu—Tibetan—Japanese (?) scale. Aaron Copeland isnt amusing—that was my intensive belated musical experience—the first since many years and probably the last. Of course I dont count V. Thomson—he's a continuation.

No you and Clare [de Gruchy] accomplished things. You lived and saw deeply and well and I think of this and you both often. Yes there's Bach in Juan Gris—if you mean supreme discipline and order and no superficial melody or [word?] sensuousness. *Ubu Roi* as puppets. What's this. I've no memory of it as approaching puppets—either in the beginning—middle or end. It was written either when he was still at the *lycée* or immediately after with a boy's—especially a kind of French boy's—exuberance and mockery and of course their great sense of drama. And that's all. Anything more is just read in.

Gertrude didn't like reading aloud because she just couldn't tolerate being read aloud [to]. The French never give you a manuscript to read—they read it aloud to you or make an appointment to do so. This used to be a considerable annoyance to Gertrude. She never heard what was read to her. She thought that there were really two different things—the spoken language and the written prose as well as poetry. When the students used to ask her—Why dont you speak as you write—she used to answer—Do you think Shelley [*sic*] spoke like the "Ode to the Nightingale" or any other author like his written work. More like it perhaps than any one else perhaps but not the same. As for the music which disengages itself more easily from a work when it is read aloud she said that was not intentional with her—music there was—particularly at one period—but that that was a by product. And still if people could enjoy reading aloud or being read aloud to—she was all for everyone's getting their pleasure in their own way. In one of the conversations with Picasso after the liberation she was saying more or less this ending with—I read with my eyes not my ears—ears are inside me. To which Picasso said—Of course writers write with their eyes painters paint with their ears. And further neither painters nor writers have ever been painted with their mouths open. Well I've gotten to the end of the subject—of the page—of your patience and my time. Hurrah for December when Agnes and you will be over.

Fondest love always
Alice

To Annette Rosenshine, Berkeley, California
MS Bancroft

11 August 1949 Montmorency, Seine et Oise

Dear Annette–

The Barrys though young are pleasant companions—Gertrude was very fond of Joe (who is a character in her opera *The Mother of Us All*). Naomi his wife whom Gertrude didn't know is one of those frightfully energetic women who are so gentle and low keyed and nonchalant that one scarcely realises how much she is capable of accomplishing in a day's work. So it is a very pleasant arrangement for me and I hope for them.

Conditions in France are probably much better than your newspapers say—better even than the French newspapers tell! And politics in France are not as despairful as Albert [Rosenshine] has the impression they are. And please do not class me amongst the expatriates or expatriots. Isnt it so that the further one goes the more certain one is that our freedom can not even be submerged—that we have not lost it and that it's only a temporary mistakeness of the people in power that causes us to fear we have. It is the few things that there are still left for me to do for Gertrude and this faith in my country that help to make the daily tasks not too irksome—for counting the *sous* (of course there are no more and when they save five they dont mean five francs or five hundred francs but five thousand) is just a habit and making a choice of what is imperative and what is not is instinctive—and rent and gas and electricity and the dentist are necessities though I resent paying for them. And the poodle who is a luxury and who has been sick and at the vets frequently this winter and spring was Gertrude's and he is my sweet and faithful companion and so he is well cared for.

Picasso now has a daughter Paloma (the dove of peace?) and a grandson—his legitimate's illegitimate son—which is not as confused as it sounds. And Picasso's only wife is pleased that their son has a son but she deeply resents Picasso's bastards—not reasonable but very human.

I don't know who lives at 58 rue Madame—though I occasionally pass there on my way to the cleaners on the rue de Fleurus—faithfully returning to her in spite of poor work. 27 [rue de Flerus] was taken over by the landlord for his son who was to be married—he had otherwise legally no right to put us out and they made it look [like] something that is called *rustique provençale* which is generally used in remodelling inns and small restaurants. I saw it once in '39 and flew from it and I had to go to see the concierge a couple of years ago but I fortunately met him on the street—it was too painful. Do you remember the photographs Mike took of Gertrude and Leo before the atelier door—you must have had copies of them—they were taken in '06 or '07—I think.

My warm affectionate good wishes to you always.

Alice

To W. G. and Mildred Rogers, New York/MS Rogers

17 August 1949 Montmorency, Seine et Oise

Dearest Kiddies—

Yes this is where Basket and I have been since the end of last month and will be—alas no longer than the beginning of the next month staying with the Joe Barrys whom you may remember. They bought this house and Naomi bravely moved her little family —Joe herself and the baby who is a gay blade trying to talk and walk—while the painter the plumber and the paper hanger were still at work and not only that but the next day Joe called for me in his car to come and stay with them. So here I am under one of the magnificent trees of their deserted garden in a California redwood mission garden armchair on rollers! Can you believe it. Do you know Montmorency where Jean Jacques lived—meditated and wrote—only fifteen kilometers from Notre Dame but being (the part the Barrys live in) on a high wooded hill the same altitude as Bilignin—though Joe says higher as is natural he should considering how lately he has become a propriétaire—the air delicious and nothing to be desired except the song of birds—no one seems to be able to explain their absence—no cats about. Or are there too many airplanes—could that be it—I wonder.

Montmorency is so unspoiled because it has no communication with the outside world except by an incredible wee railroad four or five times a day to Enghien. The train is really the sweetest toy and the *gare* a gem of amiability. The railroad I'm convinced is the last souvenir of Louis Napoleon's great improvements. I'm going to hate [to] leave it and the garden and the Barrys but I have to go back to see some people before they leave. It's too bad —otherwise the Barry would have had me on their hands until it commenced to snow.

I had a few lines from delightful Norma Chambers and she said she had such a pleasant meeting with you. Didnt you like her and whatever do you mean by calling her glamor girl.

Or are you of the generation who never did like the very beautiful very long and narrow (face and hair—hands feet and body) Texas girl who came to see me about two years ago—brought as the first example of the "new look." And when I was asked what I thought of it and of her I said but she is a du Maurier. To which she inquired—And so what is that—perhaps some relation of Daphne du Maurier. My generation likes the story. I have returned from gathering apples—such quantities too. In the neglected orchards there are endless apple pear and cherry trees (you know the Montmorency cherry of course—this is its *place d'origine*)—two peach and two apricot trees which bear so much fruit that the branches break. There are no vegetables yet—nor any flowers except roses but next year it should be a charming place.

Have you read the Hopkins–Roosevelt book—what a thoroughly

unlikeable person he makes Hopkins and how carelessly it is written or if not how wretchedly—the reviewers seem to be so pleased with the material that they seem to have not noticed the manner in which it has been presented. I brought it to read here but am not enjoying it—besides I dont like a garden book to be too heavy—one should be able to hold it one hand and smoke or caress Basket with the other.

Love to you both always.

Alice

Hopkins–Roosevelt book: Robert E. Sherwood's *Roosevelt and Hopkins: An Intimate History* (1948).

To W. G. and Mildred Rogers, New York/MS Rogers

7 November 1949 5 rue Christine, Paris VI

Dearest Kiddies—

For weeks I've been trying to thank you for your letters and your clippings—hoping each day that the next would give me the opportunity but no it (life) always grew more complicated. At least during that time I had the intense pleasure and satisfaction of seeing Carl—he looked so much better than I had either hoped or expected and as sprightly as the mouse that is infesting my provision closet. As one of his friends said instead of being a blonde with blue eyes he now has white hair with dark eyes—otherwise he is just as he used to be. He took me to a great many places—to the de Quevas Ballet—which dances ever so much better than the Ballets des Champs Elysées does—but the décors are lamentably inferior both in conception and execution to what we are accustomed to. (Bye the way Cecil Beaton is here for one of his—it is to open tomorrow evening—the costumes were started yesterday morning! He is nervous because it is his first décor and costumes in Paris.) And then we went to Cocteau's adaptation of *A Streetcar* [*Named Desire*]—I am mad about it—not for the longest time has any theatre pleased me and this was captivating. The American subtlety is preserved—almost the idiom. Of course I haven't seen the U.S. performance but the woman was tremendous—quite unforgettable. She has the distinction and delicacy of Mrs. Fiske and of course the beautiful French precision. Well so much for that. Carl took photographs of most of the people he wanted to—Sauguet and Marie Laurencin—Arletty and Julian Green—Cocteau and Jouhandeau—everybody but Picasso who was in the South. and Colette who is very sick. (I've been told notices are being written for when she is dead—with French matter of factness.) And he said he liked his visit and might come again but will he—once back to the movement of New York. He said Paris had not changed since '34 or indeed since '07 except the taxi drivers werent as polite and the telephone service was abominable (of course no one telephoned in '07). Well I have seen him and it was wonderful and it is over and there'll be a long dark winter to know it in.

To the natural dark of Paris we are having two days of electrical cuts from 7 in the morning until 8:30 in the evening—which means already four and a half hours of candle light and still 88 days to go before the day will be as long as today—and we know how much shorter it is. And dark and cold is just a little too much so I'm going to get a petrol lamp and stay in bed! I have plenty of candles but they hurt my eyes—I *hate* winter!

There have been millions of people coming through—from Egyptologists to dancers but the most interesting are the Paul Bowles—Freddie to us—he has written a novel *The Sheltering Sky*—it has just come out in London (Book of the Month Club) and I've a copy and just started it. It commences well. I told him to send you an advance copy when the American edition appears. I hope you see your way to be amiably inclined toward it. Do you know her [Jane Bowles] novel called *Two Serious Ladies* which Knopf published at the beginning of the war—obviously not a propitious moment to present gaiety and insouciance. It is *the* most delightful novel [to] come my way in years and years. Unfortunately she doesn't produce much—since then only a play and short stories. Do you know Edwin Denby. It was he who found a copy for me to read. Mrs. Bowles is spending the winter here which will be nice—for she's—not surprisingly—like her novel.

Did you meet the Père Couturier when he was in N. York. He's the Dominican monk who got Matisse to decorate a chapel near Vence and now he's at work on another that Picasso and Rouault and other disparate painters are working for. And beyond being a friend of painters is a thoroughly delightful person. This is all my news. And thanks again for the clippings and everything. Love to you both always.

Alice

Carl took photographs: Henri Sauguet, French composer; Arletty, celebrated French actress who was then appearing in *A Streetcar Named Desire;* Julian Green, French writer of American parentage; Marcel Jouhandeau, French novelist.

Edwin Denby: American writer and dance critic.

Père Couturier: Father M. A. Couturier, the Dominican entrepreneur of modern religious art. He was the artistic advisor for a number of years in the decoration of the Church of Assy in the Haute-Savoie in which several major French artists participated—among them Bonnard, Braque, Léger, Lipschitz, Lurçat, and Rouault.

To Annette Rosenshine, Berkeley, California
MS Bancroft

24 November 1949 — 5 rue Christine, Paris VI

Dear Annette—

What a tragic story is Sarah's—pursued by the furies it is Greek—but pursued by your grandson it is Jewish—pitiable in any case.

Vaguely rumors had been coming to me of this and of that but the whole story as told by Roubina upon her return surprised and shocked me—one always thought of Sarah as unusually protected against all knocks—and of course she was by Mike. But everything could and a great deal did happen to her since. Roubina seems to have acted capably and with decision but only so late that Sarah is protected from further disaster but with her health a wreck. What a *dégringolade* from the Sarah we first knew. Roubina's own situation is none too brilliant. Allan is the father of Danny—more *rusé* and less adventuresome. It is hard to advise Roubina—the children are in boarding schools for the moment. Allan lives at the American Hospital and Roubina is at Garches recovering from a minor operation—of which I do not know the details (Roubina has an oriental shyness—which is not unattractive but surprises me each time anew). What is to become of them they themselves do not know.

My own news is more cheerful—the poodle and I go our little train train. The young come to see me to talk about Gertrude—some times there is a question I can answer or a deduction I can change. A few come to see the pictures—a very few—and there are a dozen people who come more constantly who are Gertrude's friends and now mine—and with them I occasionally go to a concert or a theatre—in spring and in the autumn—the winter I keep to the radiator.

The shops are full of merchandise at prohibitive prices—only sugar and coffee are on ration coupons and embassy friends have always supplied me with whatever I needed (they have a special commissary with American supplies—all sorts of things I never heard of—soya oil—water chestnuts—salted cocoanut chips). In a half century (since you wrote it it's become a habit) even the food is unrecognisable. How can you gain weight if all the fats are proscribed—are you allowed milk and bread—they are nourishing and fattening—corn meal (puddings or mush) with honey or molasses—milk—vegetable or fish soups too and bread puddings. I've betaken myself to one hearty meal a day—12 or 2 o'clock—a little meat or fish—two vegetables—bread. Coffee when I get up. A plate of cooked fruit in the evening—it does very well for me. When I have guests—as rarely as possible—inhospitable?—yes but no drain physically or well otherwise—why then I cook all day if I dont spend the day before as well—chopping.

Yes the reproductions of the Matisse mural decorations were shown to me some time ago—frankly they didnt touch me at all—nor some recent paintings—he is incredible for he is sick and in pain most of the time—but there were ten or twelve large (flower) drawings of last year that seemed to have more beauty and concentration and certainty of line than anything he has ever done.

Picasso's two enormous interiors—at a big show of his still going on—are quite overwhelming—the only thing that frightens me—is it a good sign—is that they are undoubtedly masterpieces—were Goya or Greco painting masterpieces in their old age that were unquestionably masterpieces to their contemporaries—*on se demande*. His son does nothing—rides a motorbike or drives a car—Picasso would not allow him to earn a living though Paulot proved himself highly capable during the war when he worked with the Red Cross in Switzerland (he is of course a Spanish citizen). His father said when his mother plead for him to be allowed to work—Who ever earned the living of this family. Paulot is not at all mentally deficient but has an unstable character—is easily influenced and above all adores his father—sometimes I fear he will meet a violent death—some horrible accident. His son Pablito is the spitting image of Picasso—who does not seem as happy as he is supposed to be. I see him rarely but he is very sweet to me—as all Gertrude's friends are. By the way Picasso has kept more of his early beauty than his late photographs suggest.

I see Marie Laurencin quite often—she wants me to translate for her some of the poems of Emily Dickinson so that she may do some illustrations—most certainly her dish of tea.

Always affectionately
Alice

poems of Emily Dickinson: Toklas never did the translations.

To Donald Gallup, New Haven / MS Gallup

15 December 1949 5 rue Christine, Paris VI

Dear Donald—

The days have been so filled with unexpected interruptions. Carl may have told you of Allan Stein's latest unpleasant ideas—with the nice lawyers help it looks as if everything was securely arranged. Allan's attitude should of course [have] been foreseen—it's only after proof that my eyes are opened. So complete inventories have been made of each object in the flat separating those belonging to me from Gertrude's. To diminish the horror of Allan a really delightful cousin of Gertrude's from Baltimore has turned up with a sweet wife on some important work for E.C.A.—he has reassured me that Allan is very little Stein—mostly his impossible mother.

Wendell Wilcox—whose letters I send to the collection because Gertrude always enjoyed those he wrote to her—has come to Paris. I'd only seen him once at one of the lectures Gertrude gave at the University of Chicago in '35 and seeing him now has been a pleasure. He is an old friend of Thornton from before then even and it's strange to meet the second literary person—Thornton having been unique—and they both have the same enjoyment in people—though in quite different spheres—so different but so specially chosen. Wendell wrote a short but not uninteresting novel a few years ago—he cant get to work easily though writing is as natural as living to him—he wants to stay a bit and get to work here.

You're quite right—Alfy [Maurer] was interesting as a person—and to what a degree—not as a painter. Over the years I knew him I only saw his pictures once at his studio and occasionally at a salon. He had a lightning quick—very lively wit and his whole little body and face expressed it—and the most dancing eyes and the blackest ever was.

Gabrielle who has been unusually calm and reasonable for two weeks had a rather serious outbreak last night—she is all calm again. Gertrude always treated drunken people as if they were sober—so I use that technique on the unbalanced. However I do think two landladies during the occupation and Allan and Gabrielle now is a little overdoing it.

Did I tell you that I saw Ezra Pound's son Omar Shakespeare—when he was here—a nice boy fleeing from his father's scandal—it's such a frightful situation for him to have had to face when he went to U.S. after his demobilization—he hadn't seen Ezra since he was nine years old.

This is the end of my gossip. A merry merry Christmas to you and all my gratitude and appreciation and love always.

Alice

To Mina Curtiss, Williamsburg, Massachusetts/MS Yale

[25 December 1949] 5 rue Christine, Paris VI
Christmas Day In The Morning

Dear Mrs. Curtiss—

Thank you for what you said of Gertrude's play. It is such a pity you didnt meet—you would have enjoyed each other. She was a thorough going democrat with a nice touch of arrogance—or so it appeared—it was really her complete security in the quality of her gift and she would have appreciated your sincerity in knowing what you know—that was the wisdom she would have liked to have shared with more and more people.

No Basket does not like cats—he is too jealous to even tolerate one in an adjoining room. Gabrielle must keep hers in the kitchen. When we had one and Gertrude fondled it Basket broke out with a violent case of eczema which took weeks to cure—poor little Grazo was given to friends in the country where he has grown into the largest cat in France. And Basket doesnt have eczema—though in the late spring and again in early autumn he was deathly sick but to the vet's surprise he is well and gayer than he's been in years. He is enjoying his old age—unconscious of any of its disadvantages and as you know a gentle companion. It is an idle hope that we will jog on together—the catastrophic proof of the futility of such dreams has been offered and gradually accepted.

A peaceful productive New Year to you and warm affectionate remembrances.

Alice Toklas

1950

To W. G. Rogers, New York/MS Rogers

6 January 1950 5 rue Christine, Paris VI

Dearest Kiddies—

I have *sold* a cooking thing I scrambled together—it has been accepted but not paid for yet. I hope they wont forget. Once when I was terribly hard up—after my mother died—I sold a joke for five dollars to *Life* (not Mr. Luce's *Life* but Tom Masson's—quite another thing indeed) and as our family was witty and amusing I made my plans when I cashed the check to provide *Life* with six per month far above the average of the one they had accepted. But they never cared for any others. Will cooking be no more enduring than witticisms. Beside one hasnt at over 70 the same aplomb one has at 17.

Fondest love to you both always and heaps of good wishes for the New Year from

Alice

cooking thing: "Food, Artists and The Baroness," in *Vogue,* March 1, 1950.

Tom Masson's: Massón had been editor from 1893 to 1922 of *Life,* a satiric weekly founded in 1883. It was sold to Time Inc. in 1936.

To Robert B. Hale, Associate Curator of American Art, Metropolitan Museum of Art, New York
MS Metropolitan

7 January 1950 5 rue Christine, Paris VI

My dear Mr. Hale—

A letter from Mrs. Harvey the day before Christmas brought me the best news I'll ever hear—that you had just told her that the Picasso *Portrait of Gertrude Stein* was definitely being returned to the Metropolitan. Before there was time to get your address which unfortunately had been mislaid a letter has reached me that it is hanging there amongst the French pictures and that it looks magnificent in a room freshly painted and recently rehung. What you have accomplished—and please believe I am not insensible of the serious difficulties you had to overcome—gives me a peace of mind that I have not known for three years. I am deeply grateful to you and thank you with all my heart.

It would be a pleasure for me to think that sometime—now or later—that there is some service I could render you and that you would not hesitate to let me know—and that sometime when you come to Paris you would permit me to thank you *à vive voix.*

Always appreciatively—gratefully
Alice Toklas

To Carl Van Vechten, New York/MS Yale

13 February 1950 5 rue Christine, Paris VI

Dearest Papa Woojums—

Our letters cross—you have my letter acknowedging all the photographs and your beautiful broadcast. Which photo of me did you show at the N.Y. Public Library. The one with you at Chartes I hope—I love it. Did you label it author of recipes? Did you say more recipes in progress? It's quite a concidence but I had a letter from a woman who crossed on the Champlain with us and she read our hands and said Baby's was a surgeon's and that mine was a writer's—you can imagine the hilarity this produced.

You may well say one has the material—everyone who has had experiences and is not dull has—but what do you expect them to do with it. *C'est le don qui conte*—so Matisse said to Leo when Leo showed him his first pictures and it's as true and trite as most of Matisse's reflections.

I have just received a magazine called *Bagou 40* published in French at the University of Houston (Texas) with an article by Paul Desfeuilles "Gertrude Stein et le Vrai Présent." He published a booklet on the continuous present of G.S. about three years ago. He is writing them as part of a book on the method of G.S. Desfeuilles is a very amusing person. It was he when he was archivist of the Chambre des Députés who permitted Baby to hold the parchment sheets of the trial of Sainte-Jeanne d'Arc—just as they did with the Gutenberg Bible at William and Mary. Didnt you take a photograph of that. When they take them out of their airtight glass cases I'm always afraid they will fall to pieces.

Fleur Cowles didnt turn up—she [*a*] *décommandée*. I had a big bold and probably bad plan to ask her to do an article on Pablo Casals' Bach festival at Prades. I knew him forty five years ago —of course he wouldnt remember that but he would not possibly have forgotten Otto Bendix and Baby who was intimately mixed up with him and a love affair of his. Happily Fleur—without an *e*—didn't permit me to make a fool of myself. It—the memory—would have burned holes in my pillowcase—and there's enough patching to do without adding any more.

Now I must go to prepare for tomorrow's fruit cake—a Russian recipe—a *black* fruit cake from *white* Russians—with no *red* cherries—but *your* pecans! It's going to be a honey (I love your using the word) because it has black honey in it. When you come over there will be one—another—ready for you.

I think I'll make yours next week—and wrap it in a brandy soaked cloth—wrapped in wax paper and kept in a tin box.

Well to the kitchen quickly.

All love to you both

from M.W.

N.Y. Public Library: The Library held an exhibition of photographs, books, and manuscripts related to Stein in January 1950.

Desfeuilles: His article "Une fervente de la répétition: Gertrude Stein" appeared as a pamphlet in 1946.

Casals: Through Raymond Duncan, who was then Casals' concert manager, Leo and Gertrude Stein had met Casals in San Francisco in the 1890's. When Leo came to Paris in December 1902 one of the first people he met was Casals. As Leo reports in *Journey Into the Self:* "I had been talking to Casals on occasion about my aesthetics and one day I said to him that I believed that if I had been born thirty years later I would have been born an artist. That night on returning to the hotel I made up a rousing fire and began to draw from the nude in the wardrobe mirror." Toklas, through her music teacher Otto Bendix, also met Casals in San Francisco.

To Paul Bowles, Tangier, Morocco/MS Texas

22 February 1950 — 5 rue Christine, Paris VI

Dear Freddie—

It has taken a long time to tell you how greatly I enjoyed appreciated and admired your book. I have just reread it—there is even more in it that I suspected to justify my earlier enthusiasm. It is a considerable achievement—no novel since *The Great Gatsby* has impressed me as having the force—precision—delicacy that the best of Fitzgerald has until yours. Limiting yourself as you have in the number of your characters has not prevented you from completely portraying an epoch.

I haven't seen as much of Jane as I would have liked. She is very delightful—she says she is working regularly—but is she. Has she any intimate acquaintance with either work or regularity —can and should one introduce them to each other.

Please write another novel. Good luck to you.

Affectionately
Alice Toklas

It is a pleasure and a satisfaction to know that *The Sheltering Sky* was written and—for me—to know that it was you who wrote it.

Bowles: Paul Frederic Bowles, the American composer and author, met Stein and Toklas in 1935. That same year he set to music a letter written to him by Stein, "A Letter to Freddy." His wife, Jane Bowles, was a writer.

To Isabel Wilder, Hamden, Connecticut/MS Wilder

16 March 1950 5 rue Christine, Paris VI

Isabel dear—

First and foremost my love and gratitude to you for improving so quickly—your handwriting was proof and then Thornton's report. Soon I'll be hearing better and more. If you are already at your sister's at Amherst I'll consider that a further step in your convalescence. May I be hatefully interferesome—when you get back to Deepwood Drive accept a lower standard of housekeeping than your old one of superperfection. Let a *few* slide for a *bit*—that will just make overexertion unnecessary—try it maybe you'll like it! My dear—this perfectly simple advice is unfortunately given by a too exaggerated example of its worth to appeal to you—but still give it a try—and let me know that you are seduced by the luxury of less work.

Now for Thornton's final arrival—in marvellous form—blossoming health—lightsome happiness. First there was the telephone message from Thorny—he really was here—and he would come to see me—and when I came back from marketing the little salon was filled with the fragrance of lilacs—and such lilacs as you cant possibly imagine—white yes white—favorite white and on five feet of wood—can you see five feet of wood—everything but a very few leaves sacrified for the one bloom. Then Thorny came and his news of you was what I hoped—encouraging—and the news of all the honors—Worcester and Harvard and the Romance Language Association—which he takes so much as a gay happy commonplace but which is so satisfying to me—to be allowed to know the recipient and to see for once acknowledgement of achievement. (How does he manage to keep—but no we will meet again and that will be one of the first things you will explain to me.) And then there was the big package to open—you know what was in it—but that will not explain—describe or half suggest my surprise and delight at the sight of two beautiful opalier bowls for the mixmaster—one anxious moment before we tried them but they worked to perfection. Oh could you remember that the original ones had been broken in '40—how came I to tell you—how was Thorny made a victim by having the care of the huge and heavy box. You are both too too good to me. The mixmaster has saved me hours of exhaustion already—beating is the most fatiguing kitchen activity *for me*. And now it's a pleasure to watch it being done. And the glass bowls are a thousand times more to my taste than the metal ones—wash dry and put away—no worry about Gabrielle's use of them—metal she says scornfully doesnt break—but what metal will resist her weight—she broke a cast iron pot by putting it bottom side up covering it with a board and using it as a stool jumped up and down on it often to break it! No I wash the dishes for pastry and desserts and have a separate closet for them—so the bowls fit in perfectly. And what a blessing they are all day long—for I'm conscious of their presence every minute.

And then next time Thornton came he brought me luxurious no mend nylons—you overwhelm me—I swim in your bounty.

Now T. is in London—possibly Ireland and back here at the end of the week or the beginning of the next one and then away away. He has taken me to a fabulous lunch of game and such a soufflé as never was. And I have made him a dish that completely *ratéd* (we are having gas and electricity strikes) and you will do better with it than I did in a properly regulated oven. It is called *Gougère*—a very old Burgundian dish and this is the way it is made (allow the proportions for one egg a person or perhaps 4 eggs for 3 persons).

1 cup of milk brought to the boil with salt pepper & a pinch of nutmeg and a liberal ⅓ of a cup of butter. Take from the stove and add quickly 1 cup of sifted flour—beat quickly with a wire whip—return to low flame and beat and stir until it separates (!)—about 20 minutes. Place in bowl—add ¾ cup grated Swiss (?) (not nippy) cheese. Beating hard add 4 eggs one at a time mixing thoroughly after each addition and beating high in the air (you'll recognise this as a cream puff recipe without sugar and cheese added). As soon as you stop beating place large spoonfuls in a wreath on unbuttered plaque in 450° oven. Do not open the oven door until it has risen(!). Once it has risen it doesnt fall.

Here is a recipe for *Potato quenelles*

Boil 6 large potatoes in their jackets for 10 minutes. Finish cooking them in the oven. Put them through a sieve while still hot into a bowl—add pepper—salt—3 tablespoons flour—½ cup grated Parmesan cheese and 2 eggs. Beat well until smooth. Roll into small sausages—poach in salted water ¼ hour. Drain well—dry on dishcloth. Place on top of *Poulet Célestine* or other prepared meat course with an ample sauce. Cover liberally with grated cheese and brown in oven.

Poulet Célestine

1 marvellous whole steamed chicken and its jelly sent by Isabel and T. Put the jelly aside.

In a large saucepan melt and over low flame allow to come to the *noisette* stage ⅓ cup butter—add 3 tbsps. flour. Stir with wire whip —slowly add 2 cups white wine—continuing to stir. This should take 20 min. Add the jelly of the chicken—2 tbsp. concentrated tomato paste and a little bag of ½ bay leaf—sprig of thyme—some parsley—whole pepper corns—the thin yellow rind of ½ lemon. Salt the same lightly—cover and reduce over lowest flame for 1 hour—stirring with whip occasionally. Add ½ lb. thinly sliced mushrooms—cook 10 minutes. Add chicken—take out spice bag—bring to a boil and serve. Excellent.

Je vous embrasse tendrement
Alice

Wilder: Isabel Wilder, the sister of Thornton.

To Fernanda Pivano, Milan/MS Pivano

27 April 1950 — 5 rue Christine, Paris VI

Nanda dear—

Thanks for sending me your letter to Carl but you know you really musnt—firstly because he is your friend now—secondly because he wouldnt at all like it. He is like that—he keeps his friendships in fairly water-tight compartments—you and I are not like that at all—but he is so he must never know that I have seen a letter from you to him—he would not understand that you were giving me an extra pleasure. I would like to read a whole volume of your letters—from one scolding your laundress to those advising a book for publication!—they would be equally interesting and entertaining. Some time all kinds of letters will be published to the ineffable delight of endless readers. From the point of view of Gertrude's democracy an important person was a person who held your attention and there were mighty few who didnt hold hers and so all letters passionately interested her—as nearly every one did—she didnt like pretentious people—no not *pomposos* and even less *pomposas*.

How pleasing and exciting it was to hear about the quarter of an hour radio [program] on Gertrude's work. It would have meant a lot to me to have been there with you to hear it though most of the commentary would have been incomprehensible for I never did know your adorable language—just enough to count the wash and order a pair of boots and read a bit of the newspaper. It was so exciting to hear you and Ettorino talking Italian together though I didnt understand a word except when I knew what you were about to say—it fired my imagination and made me long to possess it. You know Thornton's mother taught herself Italian when she was old so that she might read Dante in the original. I am sending Carl your paragraph about the reading—it will please him immensely and then he will pass it on to Donald Gallup for the Yale collection. There is just time and room to answer you about Dos Passos and Gertrude—they only met once or twice and she liked him—he had the Spanish charm—she tried to read his novel (*Three Soldiers*?) written after the other war but it didnt interest her. She told an American lady—who was in love with him at the time but we didnt know it then of course—that his brains were addled!—and she never tried to read any more of his books. (I tried *Manhattan Transfer* and it didnt hold my attention. His writing is what they call a natural now and which was called a "rough diamond" in my youth). Sartre knows nothing about American books—Simone de Beauvoir knows more but has a jaundiced eye. I think she is perfectly conscious of closing her eyes and ears to any thing that is contrary to existentialist propaganda.

Alice

Gertrude's work: Radio Italiana had presented a quarter of an hour reading from Stein's work. The program included excerpts from *Three Lives, Four Saints, The Autobiography of Alice B. Toklas,* and *Dr. Faustus Lights the Lights.*

To Fernanda Pivano, Milan/MS Pivano

[4 July 1950] 5 rue Christine, Paris VI
Independence Day

Nanda dear–

Paris has been full of Americans–two million–at least–have come to see me–they bore and exhaust me–though I only see those who were friends of Gertrude whom she would have wanted to see–so they should not bore me–but then in spite of wanting to see them all–some of them used to bore her. Did I ever tell you she once said she was going to put an advertisement in the *New York Herald Tribune* saying Miss Gertrude Stein does not desire to see any friend she has not seen for fifteen years.

Have you seen the interview with Hemingway in the March (?) *New Yorker*. It has strange revelations and exposures by himself and his wife–which were partially explained by Janet Flanner's telling me that he was mortally ill. This news has upset me strangely. With little sympathy for him it is painful to know the present situation and the horror it must hold for him. There is too much just retribution on earth–how much more comforting if one didnt pay for anything.

Gertrude liked *Sanctuary* but didnt like the next two and wouldnt try any more. She didnt think there was any influence of her work in *Sanctuary*. But I see a considerable influence (conscious or unconscious?) in *Intruder* [*in the Dust*].

Thornton is going to do an American novel (this is a *secret*) on the unfilled destiny of the American woman.

Love to both of you always.

Alice

interview with Hemingway: "How Do You Like It Now, Gentlemen?" in *The New Yorker* (May 13, 1950). The interviewer was Lillian Ross.

To Carl Van Vechten, New York/MS Yale

[4 July 1950]
Independence Day 1950

5 rue Christine, Paris VI

Dearest Papa Woojums—

I long to see the book of Leo's letters—journals—etcetera. Of course he would mention Baby on every page just as she sincerely denied in '36 that she had another brother beside Mike in California when a man who was calling on her said he had just seen a brother of hers in Italy. She really had put him and the deep unhappiness he had caused her so completely out of her mind that finally he and it no longer existed. I hadnt realised this until the incident occurred. When we saw him in '19 or '20 in the Place Saint-Germain-des-Près and I asked whom she was bowing to she answered with one word (and quite pleasantly) Leo and then she said no word more about him. That evening she wrote the so beautiful "She Bowed To Her Brother." In it she had purged him and the whole miserable time he had given her. So now I must see the book to get him out of my mind too—for goodness he made me suffer. Could you send it to me. I would read it and at once return it by registered mail. Heaps of love to Fania and to you.

M.W.

Leo's letters: Journey Into the Self: Being the Letters, Papers & Journals of Leo Stein, edited by Edmund Fuller (1950).

"She Bowed to Her Brother": Toklas is mistaken about the date, the event took place in 1931. The piece was printed in *transition* (March 1932), and later reprinted in *Portraits and Prayers* (1934).

To Carl Van Vechten, New York/MS Yale

10 July 1950 — 5 rue Christine, Paris VI

Dearest Papa Woojums—

About Leo's book dont send it—Rogers is sending me a copy. Joe Barry has just sent me a review from the *Times*. It is too easy to dispose of him by "so sad and so very mistaken"—he was as timely as a street vendor—was able to market his wares—found his salvation in a popular remedy—was able to corner the so-called intellectuals with the cure-all that they found palatable and so justified his beliefs without exposing himself. He was really generous. He believed everything that was said. I will read the book with a red not a blue pencil.

Heaps of love to you both.

M.W.

To Claude Fredericks, Salzburg, Austria/MS Fredericks

24 July 1950 — 5 rue Christine, Paris VI

Dear Claude—

The quiet life has become so hectic within a minute—it has a way of doing that in France—the French stand up against their self created excitements so much better than the casual stranger within the gates. It bores me—perhaps it is only the heat and Korea—neither of them comforting subjects—but Basket and I are going to the country at the end of the week—to a place near Bourges—where we hope to be calm and comfortable. They have poodles—it is to be hoped not too young and frolicsome for sweet old Basket. With material to sew six pillow slips—three Balzacs and Kazantzakis' last book to read and thirty letters to answer time will pass pleasantly in the large walled garden.

Finally Max White has told me what he feels about *Things As They Are*—and why he hadnt earlier. He had been at work finishing the first draught of his novel. He thinks none of his readings of G.S. gave him so completely the vocal quality she always has for him—the meaning of words never more exciting—*enfin* he is happy with it and does not consider for a moment that it has any interest merely because of its being her first writing. Now that he has commenced to speak of it the others will probably follow. The concierge does not undertake anything out of routine—so your letters will be forwarded with mine and then to you. Salzburg was an enchantment to us in late June '45—so innocent after four years of occupation—even the presence of Hitler around the corner was reduced to fairy tale proportions—we stayed at a hotel —officers—just two steps from Mozart's home and couldnt believe it. It was not a Mozartian landscape—Vienna is better—are you going there for the opera. The friends [Knapiks] who are driving me to Bourges go on to Salzburg and Vienna and then to Spain and pick me up on their return which is more than I had hoped for or deserve. Never will a railroad be a temptation again.

This is my new address

Aux bons soins de Madame Debar
La Régie
Soye-en-Septaine
par Bourges
Cher

Affectionately
Alice

To Donald Gallup, New Haven/MS Gallup

31 July 1950 La Régie, Soye-en-Septaine, Cher

Dear Donald—

I had a letter from J. M. Brinnin saying that he was doing a book on G.S.—that he proposed coming to Paris for the month of September to see me—if I would be ready to receive him. Mindful of his elegy to G.S. I hastily answered him that it was not possible for me to allow him to come if he counted upon my being able to help him—that that was beyond my capacity but that if he came I would see him—and sent the letter. The next morning with *l'esprit d'oreiller* it was clear that I had not made myself so to him so I hastily wrote again to him. It was not likely that a publisher was giving a little—if not unknown—critic advance royalty on a critical book of G.S.'s work—that he would if it was that they wanted have found all he needed at Y.U.L. So I wrote him and added that if it was an anecdotal history he proposed I would be obliged to refuse—that I had done this once and would not repeat the experiment. It was necessary for me to know what his project was—that such a book did not require my approval but Carl's permission. Of course it would have been better to have written all this in the first letter but the second was posted 24 hours later.

I have read Leo Stein's book—some of it troubled me but it did get him finally completely out of my system. There are several glaring inaccuracies—beside unconsciously wrong interpretations —but what can one expect of a person whose original valuation differed so completely from later ones of persons whose flattery won him. And of course Mabel Weeks' foreword was steeped in venom. She wanted to see Gertrude in N.Y.—indeed asked me to promise her that I would see that she did—to which I answered it was scarcely likely she would. When I told Gertrude she said simply *jamais de la vie*. The photograph marked Matisse paintings at 27 rue de Fleurus is a mistake—they were never at 27 but belonged to the Mike Steins at 58 rue Madame. It is a pity that there was no photograph in the book of him in the earlier days when he wore a golden reddish beard which hid his mouth and chin and brought into prominence the fine top part of his head. He was amongst the majority—the commonplace majority as Gertrude called him—of the sad and mistaken.

All my gratitude—appreciation and love.

Alice

elegy to G.S.: Just after Stein's death John Malcolm Brinnin wrote "Little Elegy for Gertrude Stein," which he sent to Toklas. The poem, printed in *Harper's,* is included as an "Epilogue" to his *The Third Rose: Gertrude Stein and Her World* (1959).

To Annette Rosenshine, Berkeley, California
MS Bancroft

5 August 1950 La Régie, Soye-en-Septaine, Cher

Dear Annette—

Ten days ago friends on their way to hear music in Salzburg brought me down here in their car and will pick me up in four weeks on their way back to Paris. This avoids the railway journey standing in crowded corridors. I was far too exhausted to undertake it—indeed I never will again. Two years ago the poodle on my lap—he weighs as much as a six year child—and I trying to balance on my bags in the corridor came back to Paris on a five hours journey. So the trip in the car was delightful and the place here a miracle. I had engaged to become a paying guest of a Madame Debar—having only the recommendation of a friend of hers! But the house and vast property are an enchantment. I have an immense bed sitting room with six windows and a door into the garden. The whole property is surrounded by walls so both Basket and I can roam about unleashed! Very good food cooked by my highly capable intelligent tactful hostess completes the comfort charm and agreeableness of the Régie. So much for what is happening to me.

In Paris before leaving Roubina on the telephone told me that her proceedings against Allan were coming to a satisfactory conclusion—but to my shocked surprise she said that she was no longer asking for a divorce merely a legal separation—which gives Allan the co-guardianship of the children. She offered no reason for the change.

There has been an amusing incident about the Matisses. The weeklies have kept you informed of the decorations Matisse is designing in paper for a chapel of a convent near Vence in the south of France. The Père Couturier—a very able Dominican monk —was responsible for persuading *le cher maître* to undertake in his old age this work for the Church. For years Matisse has not been a practicing Catholic. Just when everyone had become accustomed to his reentering the Church the rumor began to spread that he had become a communist. As the two things are not compatible there was a great deal of shocked surprise—was it his way to say that he would give what is likely to be his last work to the Church without believing in it. Well every one buzzed until Olga Picasso came back from the south where she had seen *Madame* Matisse who told Olga that she was the communist mayor of the small village where she lives and not her husband. The Matisses have lived apart for many years now—he has had a Russian lady secretary—model—housekeeper—attendant. You remember that he started his Russian friendships with Olga Merson.

Did you know that Gertrude's favorite cousin Julian Stein of Baltimore married Rose Ellen Hecht of S. Francisco—after she was a widow with two daughters. Later she bore him a son and a number of years ago she became a widow for the second time.

The son Julian Junior is in Paris on the Marshall Plan with his young pretty intelligent (ultra modern ideas on education government etcetera) southern wife. She has such advanced ideas that she has no sectional feeling—though so far I have not met any Negroes in their charming home in Ville d'Avray. It is possible Judy would not approve of that.

Love always from
Alice

To Ellen Alix (du Poy) Taylor Daniel, Kellers Church, Pennsylvania/MS Yale

6 August 1950 La Régie, Soye-en-Septaine, Cher

Dear Ellen—

We will have a perfect vacation in this lovely rambling old house —François Premier—with a twelfth century chapel and quite a large property entirely enclosed in high walls so that Basket can roam about unleashed. I am a paying guest and it is working out ever so much better than I had even hoped for. The place belongs to a Frenchwoman who has an enormous tobacco plantation—she grows vegetables fruits and flowers and raises rabbits chickens and pigeons—taking care of all this—beside cooking and making her clothes—with the aid of a seventy-six year old gardener who comes four mornings a week. Of course she is intelligent and active but she is also tactful and gay which makes being here very agreeable indeed. The only other person here is a young Swedish girl who has seen eighteen aurora borealises but not remarked them —she is deadly dull but as she speaks no French and very little English she does not have to be noticed.

Yes Osbert Sitwell and Gertrude liked and enjoyed each other a lot—she liked Edith too but not the younger brother. Edith took herself very seriously. Do you think she will be the next poet laureate—or will it have to be T. S. Eliot.

We saw Perdita Macpherson several times when she was young and then Sylvia Beach brought her to see us when she came to Paris after the liberation—she was in an American uniform in spite of her exaggerated British accent. I had the impression that Bryher had adopted her to relieve H.D. of all the responsibilities of motherhood. Bryher was devoted to H.D. Perdita was very Victorian middle class.

How is your book getting on—is it nearly done now. Good luck to it and to you.

Always affectionately
Alice

Daniel: An American friend who had lived periodically in Paris during the twenties and thirties. Toklas wrote that Mrs. Daniel "had been such a help in the birth struggles and early youth of Plain Editions."

Perdita Macpherson: The daughter of Hilda Doolittle and Richard Aldington, she was adopted by Kenneth Macpherson and his wife Winifred Bryher.

To Mina Curtiss, New York/MS Yale

14 August 1950 La Régie, Soye-en-Septaine, Cher

My very dear Mrs. Curtiss—

Liliane Yacoël was greatly distressed about the failure of Odile Albaret to respond to your so generous intention of seriously preparing her for an agreeable manner of earning her livelihood. When she asked me whether any other approach could help the girl understand the situation it was necessary to brutally explain that she had received more than she could digest—that the *petite bourgeoise* was doomed to at least partial failure—her aspirations knowing no limits. It is absurd to be as really democratic as we are—as passionately so—and to be obliged to acknowledge the limitations that being born a *petite bourgeoise* creates—the impossibility of freeing oneself—of escaping them during one lifetime's consciousness. It is a commonplace one likes to avoid recognising and so I really believe your hope for the girl cannot be fully realised. You have given her so much that if she only profits from half of it you will have rendered a great service—she will benefit largely—and so every one should be happy.

How strange that your friendship with Virgil and mine started at opposite ends and from there I hope the course will join and we end at the same spot. Virgil in the early days offered a familiar comradeship but inspired little devotion—there were always too many obstacles to jump. It was only after the reconciliation that followed none too quickly a break in the acquaintanceship caused by Virgil's mistaken judgement that we came to a very real devotion—which doesnt prevent both of us from an easy recital of the other's capital faults. So patience and you'll come through—will you let me say that it isnt really possible to lose any relation with Virgil *sur le plan mondain.* It is not a safe plank—nor indeed a plank at all—just a mirage. Virgil not being solidly of the world. Forgive me explaining anything to you—but Virgil is a strange plant one has to give not too assiduous but special care. I am still hoping that some day he will be prompted to do the music for a Faust libretto Gertrude did before the war.

Always your affectionate
Alice Toklas

Liliane Yacoël: Yacoël, now Mme Olivier Ziegel, was Mina Curtiss' research assistant for the *Letters of Marcel Proust* (1949) and *Bizet and His World* (1959). Curtiss' article on Céleste Albaret, Proust's *gouvernante,* appeared in *The Cornhill,* Spring 1950, and in *Flair,* April 1950. Odile was the daughter of Céleste Albaret.

To Carl Van Vechten, New York/MS Yale

27 September 1950 5 rue Christine, Paris VI

Dearest Papa Woojums—

You remember John's [Breon] friend Xaxier [Fourcade]—wonderful—marvellous—of the Gare Montparnasse the day we returned from Chartres. About two weeks ago he rang me up and said he hoped I could see him to hear something he would like to talk to me about—a few evenings later he came. He was founding a literary review with an experienced man—and they wanted something—preferably unpublished—in English. I explained that would mean the choice would be amongst the so called difficult—that it would be that possibly not only for their readers but for a possible translator. He said could he bring his editor and we could talk it over—which he did. I was impressed with their plan and their means of realising it. The money is probably being supplied by Xavier's family—that is his father—whom John described as very rich. I have made inquiries and it would seem that he is indeed very rich. All this was merely to be assured that the magazine—really a serious literary review—had the funds for sufficient life to accomplish what they propose—to publish with your consent *Mrs. Reynolds* as a serial. They both know Baby's work—Xavier's opinion not being the important one to me—and want something long—characteristic and of a form the French do not yet know. I said I would write you. Would you want them to make a formal request definitely to you. Let me know this at once. If you accept I will see if I can persuade Madame Seillière—you didnt meet her when you were here because she was out of town at that time—to do the translation. Baby thought her translation of *The Makings* wonderful.

Brinnin and his book—he telephoned me that he had arrived a week ago last Monday and came to see me that afternoon. I did not hold it in his favor that he was visibly moved to be in Baby's home—his romanticism about her puts one off. It was the first impression and remains after the last interview last evening. After he'd had his tea without coming to anything definite about his book—it seemed necessary to repeat what I'd written to him and to say what did he want of me—where were his questions—he said he would bring them—which he did two days later—futile—superficial and not helpful to any understanding of Baby's work or even of her character. What had she thought of Apollinaire's poetry and why had she not mentioned it in *The Autobiography* for example. Then we suddenly got to Leo and his book and the fat was on the fire. At once I must tell you that last evening he repeated his solemn promise not to mention it or Leo's opinions —not to defend Baby in any way against Leo's attack. It was a long argument for he felt that possible readers would be put off. But I'm really proud of having convinced him that to go into the subject of Leo would weaken and diminish the effectiveness of his book for more readers than he could convince Leo was wrong —that those who believe Leo's assertions are few but furiously loyal to their wronged hero—that those he can interest in Baby's work are many—that it was to them that he should appeal—etc. etc. ad infinitum. Well he finally came around by himself (which is of course the only way to convince). And that pleased me for the Leo subject was certainly something to be avoided. Then I got him to exclude me from his book because the atmosphere of Baby's home was a private matter—that if my existence had ever made the slightest difference to her work it was of nothing to equal the effect—for example—of landscape and was he in a position to put his finger from what he knew or from internal evidence when and how that was. It was agreed that my name could not be ignored in connection with the Plain Edition but not elsewhere. Lunch at Le Bosse with a man we knew and then to Christian Dior's collection! Heaps of thanks and love from

M.W.

literary review: The review, which was called *Elements,* did not publish *Mrs. Reynolds.* The novel was published in the Yale Edition of the Unpublished Writings of Gertrude Stein.

To Fania Marinoff Van Vechten, New York/MS Yale

28 September 1950 5 rue Christine, Paris VI

Fania dearest—

Yesterday I was taken to see the Dior collection so that I would know just what I wanted to have the furrier do with the handsome furs you sent me. Well—the muff will be flattish as it is—a bit larger (and worn on the left arm!)—the tocque will be smallish and warmish and the collar flattish—not attached to a coat—for then I can wear it with or without my coat—beside the coat isnt worthy of such permanent beauty. The tailor suits didnt please me particularly—and throughout the collection a far too generous use of commonplace buttons and pockets—large outside pockets on full evening dresses—but half a dozen superb dresses under Spanish influences that were distinct creations and marvellously beautiful—with impeccable technique. This is news for you which P.W. will probably be cold about. But we do love clothes dont we. What will Pierre Balmain think of my having gone to Dior's and not to his collection yet. I must get over to Pierre's and make my peace with him soon. It is a superstition of his that Baby and I brought him good luck and that now I mustnt fail him. And I havent seen him in months and months.

All my warmest thanks and love.

Your devoted
Alice

ALICE B. TOKLAS AND GERTRUDE STEIN, LONDON, 1936

Photograph by Sir Cecil Beaton

But we do love clothes dont we.

To Mildred Weston Rogers, New York/MS Rogers

30 September 1950 5 rue Christine, Paris VI

Dear Mrs. Kiddie–

Your wondrous gifts are my delight–the little cups served to make a new kind of pastry–an old old French pastry called Massillon. This is the recipe–

The whites of six eggs beaten with a wooden spoon. These should be beaten until they foam.
1 cup and 2 tablespoons of powdered sugar.
Then add half a cup melted but cold butter.

Gently stir in 1 cup potato flour. Bake in buttered floured little cups about 1/4 hour in oven more than medium. They are very good. Try them. They should be frosted all over with a white rum frosting with chopped pistachio [nuts] sprinkled on the top but I dont bother to do so.

Yes we knew Margaret Anderson–she was rarely beautiful–but nothing else–she was so emotional and inarticulate she gasped for breath–rather painfully–certainly for oneself–probably not for her–she doubtless enjoyed it. It was Jane Heap we liked–she went Gurdjieff and has remained over these many years faithful to his teachings.

The New York Ballet (Balanchine) is coming here later. They have not been the success at Covent Garden that the Sadlers Wells is at the Met.

Dont forget the verses.

Always affectionately
Alice

To W. G. Rogers, New York/MS Rogers

2 October 1950 5 rue Christine, Paris VI

Dearest Kiddie—

Did you see *The New Yorker*'s profile of Hemingway???!!! Nothing he has said since—not even his novel—will be as complete an exposure of all he has spent his life hiding. It's strange that he should be taking so much pleasure in destroying the legend he worked so patiently to construct. Someone—was it you—sent an A.P. man to see me and I got into a frightful row with him about Picasso's painting and Hemingway's new book (as if they could be mentioned in one sentence)—he the A.P. man said he thought Picasso was painting carelessly and Hem was writing carelessly! It wasnt quite fair because the man didnt know a Picasso from a Gris and thought a Picasso was a Braque. I liked defending Hemingway—it was the first opportunity I've ever been offered—it will no doubt remain a unique experience. It's rarely that I see *The New Yorker* which is on the whole pleasant—as evidently the office writes or rewrites so much of it. I saw the O'Hara article—it wasnt sensible. Do you know O'Hara—how old would he be—what does he look like. I ask to know as the Japanese of my youth used to say because I've a suspicion he may be the man we met in New York in '34—he was about twenty five years old then—possibly a little younger. Dont forget to let me know. The man or rather boy we met was named O'Hara and I've wondered if it wasnt the author of *The Appointment in Samarra* or Sumatra. They say he and Hem drink together.

Love to you both from

Alice

O'Hara article: John O'Hara's review of Hemingway's *Across the River and Into the Trees* in *The New York Times,* September 10, 1950.

To Fernanda Pivano, Milan/MS Pivano

10 October 1950 5 rue Christine, Paris VI

Dear sweet Nanda—

Yesterday the best possible news came—there will be nothing like it again for me. A letter from Donald Gallup to say that Yale University Press will publish with enthusiasm *(vous m'entendez)* all Gertrude's *inédits*. It was more than I had dreamed of. I had hoped faintly that they would accept *one* but no all all all. I was so overwhelmed that nothing seemed real next to this. So they want the first volume ready for March to publish in October '51. They have named Gallup—Thornton Wilder—and Sutherland as an advisory committee with Carl Van V.

Here are the only two Hemingway clippings that seem to be here —there were quantities—people seemed to think they would please me. Far from it—the whole Hemingway legend—which we saw him create and *soigner*—going to pieces as it is under one's eyes is the most pitiable embarrassing thing imaginable. The present Hemingway crack up—one must borrow from the vocabulary of the greatest of his victims—has far too much old fashioned biblical punishments and rewards for comfort to those living in the present. But of course that is just what he doesn't do—he is hopelessly 1890—and one can damn him no further. He wears like the new look but he is in the tradition of Kipling. But enough of this.

It was so like you to want flowers for Gertrude on the 27th. I went early and said these are from me and each of your friends and so your flowers were there. I stayed for the day and the next day friends drove me to the country where for five weeks I rested and even now am still feeling so much less tired than before and not too much afraid of the winter. My deep warm thanks for your thought of Gertrude but you did give them to her—then and always.

I send you *mille tendresses* and my devotion.

Alice

To Carl Van Vechten, New York/MS Yale

6 November 1950 — 5 rue Christine, Paris VI

Dearest Papa Woojums—

Cecil Beaton turned up and I went to dine with him and we had one of those devastating meetings in which everything and everyone was disposed of.

Francis Rose is in his flat all redecorated and renovated—he has the air of having settled down for good—too true to be good as someone lately said. In any case he is having a big show here and will then start painting again. Natalie [Barney] and I went to Raymond Duncan's birthday party—I made him a frosted cake with candles which I took to his home in the morning. The nicest of his harem told me that he had commenced to dress for his party—at five. And when he was all dressed in a brand new peplum and *gilet* he looked like a Christmas doll—tree—and Baby Santa Claus—and kissed all the ladies and was as old fashionedly coquettish as Mabel—quite chubby and cherubic.

All love to both of you.

M.W.

To Mildred Weston Rogers, New York/MS Rogers

10 November 1950 5 rue Christine, Paris VI

Dear Mrs. Kiddie—

The piecrust paste is wonderful! The little cupcakes I am afraid to use and the silver paper is a lifesaver with covered casseroles in oven cooking—no French covers ever cover—to say nothing of covering hermetically and the silver paper certainly does. You were an angel to send it to me and I thank you again and again.

Do you know this recipe.

False Quenelles

Roll an ordinary cream puff dough without sugar into fingers rather fat—more like a thumb than a finger—poach very gently in a great quantity of water in a wide kettle—when they have all risen to the surface and turned over on themselves cover and keep very hot without boiling. After ten minutes drain thoroughly and serve with a mushroom sauce—or a plain cream sauce sprinkled with grated cheese and browned in the oven—the mushroom sauce is better.

Love from
Alice

To Libby Holman, Paris/MS Boston

14 November 1950 5 rue Christine, Paris VI

Dear Miss Holman—

It is to your kindest of attentions that I owe an evening of sheer delight. I am deeply grateful to you for the intense pleasure the perfection of your interpretations gave me and for your thought of me. You brought to Paris what I was longing to go to New York for.

Mr. [Bud] Williams when he was here in the spring said you would be interested in seeing the pictures—mostly Picassos. It would give me the opportunity of telling you *à vive voix* all the interest and appreciation of your work that I have. I am free until I hear from you.

Thank you again.

Cordially
A. B. Toklas

To Carl Van Vechten, New York/MS Yale

16 November 1950 — 5 rue Christine, Paris VI

Dearest Papa Woojums—

I went to see Libby Holman—that is also to *hear* at her recital. She or somebody sent me two complimentary tickets in a loge. She produced what I very much wanted to experience—what I call the modern N.Y. technique. The thing that produces a two dimensional flat surface that is expressed in the novels—women's clothes—and the stage—miracle of skill precision condensation and conciseness—but only two dimensional—I ate it with a spoon—as it was an answer I longed for. Well I got it and it was more satisfactory than enjoyable. I asked Katherine Dudley to go with me and to my surprise and delight she told me she had known you when you were at the U. of C.—that you were a member of the same skating club—she made such a lovely picture of you that for a moment I was frightfully jealous—but there was no way of her having you *more* than I have—and arent there a million proofs of that.

Heaps of love and a bear hug from

M.W.

Katherine Dudley: Dudley (Mrs. Joseph Deltiel) had helped her sister Caroline Regan bring the Harlem group to Paris as the *Revue Nègre.* It was Katherine Dudley who arranged for 5 rue Christine to be cleaned and put in order for Stein and Toklas' return to Paris in 1944.

To Claude Fredericks, [Paris?]/MS Fredericks

19 November 1950 5 rue Christine, Paris VI

Dear Claude—

It was certain you would like Palma [de Mallorca]—no matter how much it may have changed since '16—such island life cant easily be influenced from the outside. The market alone is worth the voyage. Are there white melons with green or apricot interiors with a flavor that came from the sound of Cathay—and cakes called angels' tresses—and *ensimadas*—with tomatoes—citron and sardines as big as cartwheels. But none of this compares to the almond trees in blossom.

We lived on the Calle Dos de Mayo—no number that I can remember—and had a Mallorcan hound whom I taught to not eat —as he wished—but to smell tuberoses—and who was supposed to chase sheep when he escaped and went berserk. He ran away at night and once we saw him dancing with a dozen more of them in the moonlight up at Genova—and he didnt recognise us—indeed none of them paid the least attention to us—which made their dance even stranger than it looked.

Always affectionately
Alice

To Thornton Wilder, Cambridge, Massachusetts
MS Wilder

20 November 1950 5 rue Christine, Paris VI

Dearest Thornton—

There is something that has pained me and is a great trouble to me and that you should be spared but you have probably means to get me out of a hateful position. Carl Van Vechten and Donald Gallup met two of the Y.U.P. to discuss the conditions of publication. Then Carl wrote me they wanted to publish a book a year—the first one next autumn—and that a foreword to it must be written by me—that this was one of the conditions. It left me aghast—Gertrude would never have admitted such a possibility that responsible publishers could propose it. She would have despised and hated the idea. Carl said that we risked the publication of the mss.—and blinded with fear rage and tears—I accepted. Now I throw myself upon you—can you get me out of this hateful thing. Are you not one of an advisory committee. I pray that you see your way to doing this—for Gertrude. If doing this is not acceptable to you—dont think I'll ever be one iota less grateful than you have already given me so many many reasons to be.

It is incredible how many misunderstanding people one runs up against—deaf and blind to the most casual—commonplace—obvious facts.

Now let us talk about you. Are your four lectures after Christmas to follow as quickly as the four before X. In which case you will be free very shortly to wander first to Atlantic City—then to Saratoga—to a new place—(Honduras or Honolulu?) and then to Paris—perhaps you will be here by March. But when does your play go on. Everyone asks me. There are still stray Americans passing through. And Gertrude wouldnt have been amused with the present glorification of Melville—not even of *Moby Dick*—she thought that he was being grossly overrated. He was not one of the writers whom she chose as examples of expressing our sense of abstraction. Are you including Poe in your January lectures.

There is a new rage amongst the young here for Palestrina—so when you have written about your discovery you *must* allow it to be translated and published here. You are Mercury and more than Leonardo. And what a good time you have and share. Gil[bert] Harrison was here the other day and he told me how greatly you fired the imagination of the students—he seems to have known the results.

All my gratitude and love to you always—Thornton dear—

Alice

lectures: Wilder was delivering the Charles Eliot Norton lectures at Harvard.

Palestrina: Wilder had made no "discoveries" in an academic sense; he was simply enthusiastic about Palestrina and wanted to share it with Toklas.

To Mark Lutz, Philadelphia/MS Yale

[? November 1950] 5 rue Christine, Paris VI

Dear Mark—

It was ever so kind of you to write to me and to send me the clippings of the Cone collection. They interested me enormously—so much of the history of the two sisters and of Doctor Claribel's purchase of the pictures was known to me from the early days. As a matter of fact they rather than their collection were interesting—the relation between the two sisters—their markedly different characters—reactions—taste—is a passionately absorbing subject—fit for a Henry James—no less. And even in a newspaper clipping about Miss Etta's (for so she was in good Baltimore manner always called) collection something of her astounding—

her colossal personality creeps in. I imagine that most of the important pictures were bought by Doctor Claribel—that is before '28 or '29 when she died. By the way if you ever do get to see them would you look for a very early Marie Laurencin (1912?) of herself—Guillaume Apollinaire—Picasso—a Fernande Bellevallée [Olivier] and a white dog. Please do *not* send me a catalogue. I am at the age now where I am destroying papers rather than gathering them. But I was very grateful indeed for the clippings.

Always affectionately
Alice

To Isabel Wilder, Hamden, Connecticut/MS Wilder

20 December 1950 — 5 rue Christine, Paris VI

Isabel dear—

Thornton and you are such perfectionists—everything you do in affection and friendship must have the care—the detail of a finished work of art. And if that is the way you conceive it the spontaneity of the élan may see you half through—but for the other half? I know this so well because very lately I called upon Thornton for an enormous service when I had gotten myelf into serious trouble and there was nobody else who could help me out. And all the time I realised that it must be a loathsome task and at a moment when he was concentrating on his lectures and any outside activities would be the most distracting annoyance. My days will always be filled with the gratitude I owe him not only for getting me out of my trouble but for so completely understanding the situation. If a time comes when you can say a word to him of my appreciation and debt to him please do. Dear Thornie doesnt like one to say intimate things to him—his feeling of friendship is so rare that one hesitates—it's just like surprising a child in private prayer. Now we will talk about everyday things—not that the storm that swept the country was an everyday event—but it was my hope that Hamden was on higher ground than New Haven and that you would escape with such cuts of heat and light as the last years have accustomed you to. What cheerful élan to go on with your dinner party not knowing how it was to be carried through. Of course the success is some reward for the two days effort and the third days exhaustion as you say. Gradually however I'm avoiding the smallest of lunch parties even. For one thing the dining room is *consignée*. I have my meals on a tray in the salon to avoid the expense of heating two rooms. Then winter queues are beyond my endurance and winter marketing is difficult and costly—to walk to the central markets and return with my baskets out of the question—so it is easy to accept the role of least resistance—keep one's strength for where it is most needed and accept the inevitable. Basket and I have accepted our ages and limitations—he more sweetly than I—to be sure he has me to lean on and that is a comfort to both of us.

Natalie [Barney] and Romaine Brooks and the Duchesse [de Clermont-Tonnerre] had tea with me yesterday. Natalie never changes or is different or has good or bad moments—Romaine either—but poor Madame Clermont-Tonnerre is aging visibly—the death of her last daughter was the beginning of the end—she will never recover from it. She is now only a memory of what she was—but a very tender poignant one—a unique experience for me—a portrait beyond all painting.

Very trivial. For spinach soup do not chop spinach—cook in practically no water until *very* tender and with a wooden potato masher put juice and spinach through a sieve—in *ten* minutes. Dont be traditional like Gabrielle who likes to delay my lunch by chopping. I never do—knives shouldnt touch spinach any more than they should salad.

Get well—keep well—and '51 will be as happy as happy can be. Love to you dear Isabel aways.

Alice

To Donald Gallup, New Haven/MS Gallup

28 December 1950 5 rue Christine, Paris VI

Dear Donald—

The show of Picasso's sculpture is overwhelmingly impressive. It is of all his periods—that is '28–'46. Most of them I knew in his studio but the ensemble in one huge room was a great surprise. It had always seemed to me that his sculpture was an outlet before commencing something new in painting but the show is proof of how very mistaken I was. He is indeed a very great painter but an equally important sculptor.

About keeping the Gris here perhaps it is as well though I dont think there is going to be war on this or our half of the world. Quite bad enough if Asia gets it. I didnt let the pictures go to London—not because of the possibility of war but because the exhibition was postponed from October to January and February. The pictures then when I am indoors are more a part of my life than in summer so I refused. It is quite unbearably cold—though of course nothing compared to what you are having. Basket and I are clinging to the radiator—the last electric bill left me aghast and only the salon warm and the kitchen and bedroom tepid—the other rooms are glacial.

Devotedly
Alice

Picasso's sculpture: Picasso: Sculptures, Dessins at the Maison de la Pensée Française (1950/51). The catalogue contained a preface by Louis Aragon and listed sculptures from 1931 to 1944.

1951

To Paul Bowles, Tangier, Morocco/MS Texas

9 January 1951 — 5 rue Christine, Paris VI

Dear Freddie—

It was kind of you to write to me. You told me what I wanted to hear—that *The Delicate Prey* was written before *The Sheltering Sky*. (What a perfect sense for titles you have.) All reservations are withdrawn. I am rereading it as if your second book wasn't yet read and I am astonished at what you have done (it should have been said on the jacket that it was your first book instead of their foolish Gothic violence—which isn't violent to us today). And you are so right in calling them detective stories. The modern detective story which is the lineal descendant of the Elizabethan novels. The so-called detective and mystery stories of the last thirty years are hopelessly more eerie.

Affectionately
Alice Toklas

To Louise Taylor, England/MS Taylor

23 January 1951 5 rue Christine, Paris VI

Dearest Louise—

Last week Allan Stein suddenly but not unexpectedly died—so many of my past anxieties were useless—so many futile efforts to be provident and forethoughtful. As you may remember it is a long time since I saw him. We were *au plus mal.* I had told my lawyer after asking him to take a last precaution that it wasnt really perhaps necessary as I intended to outlive him. To which he answered me like a stage lawyer—I hope so Miss Toklas—I sincerely hope so!!! Did I write you that I had a few very pleasant lines from Peter Hayden. When I looked just now to find his address there was none but it was probably on the envelope which Gabrielle appropriated for the stamp—so you will be troubled to forward to him my acknowledgement. Dont you listen to Francis' arabesques. I havent known an ambassador since old Bullitt left—and *that* was no honor. Now I must go to bed or it wont be worthwhile.

Fondly
Alice

old Bullitt: William C. Bullitt, American ambassador to France (1936–1941).

To Louise Taylor, England/MS Taylor

11 February 1951 5 rue Christine, Paris VI

Dearest Louise—

Two hasty lines—first to thank you so many many times for letting me see your mother's cook books and to ask you to forgive me for sending them back to you without a word of thanks. I enjoyed them immensely—the one I liked the best naturally had the most extravagant recipes—nothing one could possibly afford but that made reading it more romantic and more of an adventure. It has given me an idea for my own humble effort. A cook book to be read. What about it.

Roubina Stein—Allan's widow—is in a mesh of lawyers—he seems to have left a successful business and a colossal amount of debts. She has a task to straighten things out—especially with two minor children which surprisingly is a complication in the eyes of the French law. So I accompany her in the early morning to the justice of the peace at Sèvres and hear her sad story late at night and avoid giving advice. She is quite alright—honest and honorable but I dont happen to care for her and wont be seeing her any morc than strictly necessary.

You are angelic to want me to come to Revere—it will be more and more tempting but it is an easy habit to resist—always I've found resisting temptation easier than yielding—it's more practical and requires no initiative! To be completely free from all anxiety—a jellyfish life for me. But always much love to you both.

Alice

To Annette Rosenshine, Berkeley, California
MS Bancroft

8 March 1951 — 5 rue Christine, Paris VI

Dear Annette—

Quite unexpectedly friends who were driving down to the midi in their car asked me to go with them. Bitter cold here when we left—we were in full moonshine after Lyon—and the next day amidst almond blossoms and mimosa. Three days at Antibes with windows open—the sea visible from the bed—a visit to the museum to see Picasso's pictures—the real reason for my going—of an unequalled splendor—a visit to Vence to see the Corbusier chapel for which Matisse has designed and painted the tiles which are to cover its walls—a long happy day with Picasso—his new pictures—new wife(?) and new children. Two days in the Provençe Gertrude and I knew and loved so well. And then back through the snow to Paris—it was a delightful break in the dull dismal winter and though it has been cold there is an air of spring being just around the corner.

Did you know that there is an exhibition at the Yale Museum of pictures that are now in America that were once in Gertrude's collection. The most important of course the Picasso portrait that the Metropolitan has loaned. The illustrated catalogue is a history of 27 rue de Fleurus from when you first knew it. And an excellent introduction and notes—it is quite a textbook. (By the way Harriet and I came over in September '07 not the following spring.)

Now I must tell you about the ladies you ask about. Mabel Weeks first because it is the shortest. She was one of Gertrude's three or four intimate friends in N. York when Gertrude used to go down there from Radcliffe and later from Johns Hopkins. Then she met Leo and the three of them with Gertrude's sculptor uncle from Baltimore came abroad together. When Leo disagreed with Gertrude about her writing and Picasso's painting and he went to Italy Mabel was suddenly sympathetic to Leo's point of view and the old intimacy with Gertrude waned.

Now about the Sitwells—Edith was a great admirer of Gertrude—wrote an article in an English review about *Geography and Plays* and came to Paris to talk to her. A warm friendship was formed which flourished for some ten years. It was she who insisted that Gertrude should lecture at Oxford and Cambridge. In the course of time we met the two brothers. Sacheverell—the younger—is less interesting and less gifted—Osbert is delightful. Then one day we asked Edith to lunch and Pavlik Tchelitchew came in and shortly after lunch they left together and we never saw either of them again for years. They had a very violent affair—Edith is perhaps still in love with him. They have written to each other every day for years and years and they each promised to give the other's letters sealed of course to Yale University Library not to be opened until 2000. I say Edith will go over for the breaking of the seals. (The sequel in my next letter!) What gossips we are. Keep well.

Always affectionately
Alice

exhibition at Yale: Pictures for a Picture of Gertrude Stein, Yale University Art Gallery, February–March 1951, and The Baltimore Museum of Art, March–April 1951.

Edith Sitwell: Sitwell had given *Geography and Plays* (1922) faint praise in her review in *The Nation and Athenaeum.* In 1925, writing about the book for *Vogue,* she hailed Stein as an important pioneer. Sitwell's "Jodelling Song" in *Façade* is founded on Stein's "Accents in Alsace" (The Watch on the Rhine section) which was published in *Geography and Plays.* Stein's portrait "Sitwell Edith Sitwell" (1925) was published in *Composition as Explanation* (London: The Hogarth Press, 1926). Her collective portrait "Edith Sitwell and Her Brothers the Sitwells" (1926) was published in *Painted Lace* (New Haven: Yale University Press, 1955).

To Mina Curtiss, Washington, D.C./MS Yale

20 March 1951 5 rue Christine, Paris VI

Dear Mina dear—

It is passionately interesting that you've gotten to the *bas fond* of Bizet's character. Could you tell me if his acceptance of his wife's and her mother's madness was from the balance in his character or just from an experience or familiarity with insanity—

so unlike the French. I long to have your book finished. You present such complete portraits—with no excrescences—as an Irish friend of Gertrude's used to say. It's the *bas fond*—the bottom nature Gertrude used to call it—that counts—everything else is futile piffle. And you few and fortunate ones seem to achieve it by a combination of all the good things the fairy gave you on the day you were born—with of course the gift to use and combine them. And that as Picasso would say is a proof that miracles exist.

Yes Janet Flanner is doing the introduction of the first volume Yale is to publish of Gertrude's *inédits.* She was kind enough to say she would let me see it when it was written. It is due at Yale before the first of the month.

Oh but you must say Gertrude—it wouldnt be friendly to do otherwise. You know it was the very young who explained that when they started the habit twenty five years ago. It was quite shocking at first but they finally convinced me and in no time it was accepted—historical and no further trouble. It was contagious so that the G.I.'s spoke not of but to her not as Gertrude but Gertie—those at the station when they came—the Seventh Army replacements—through our village. Here in the flat she was very ceremoniously Miss Stein. Afterwards on the stairway? So you are in the good tradition.

Here is an SOS I am sending out. You will please pay no attention to it if it doesnt strike you sympathetically and there are any number of reasons why it may not. Yesterday it was possible to write Virgil that our friend Bernard [Faÿ] had not been freed as we had hoped would be the case but had been placed in a hospital under the care of a good specialist and that it was possibly the first step to his being pardoned. Last evening came the news that the president had definitely refused it—though he had been recommended to do so by the *Cour de cassation.* He is afraid of his minister of justice—who advises putting it off until after the elections. Bernard is too gravely ill to envisage this calmly. So it is now proposed to have someone of sufficient importance to meet the president when he is in U.S. (within two weeks now) and present Bernard's cause as sympathetic to the American point of view. It appears that that will do the trick. Do you know of anyone who could and would do this. Do you know Mrs. Charles Dewey—whose husband negotiated some of the early U.S. loans to France. The French ambassador is strongly anti. If you feel that I've been hopelessly indiscreet and indelicate try to forget it and eventually to forgive me. It's an unhealthy habit (brooding and bursting) that comes with uncontrolled age.

Appreciatively and affectionately
Alice

Bizet's character: Curtiss had sent Toklas her article "Unpublished Letters by George Bizet," *Music Quarterly,* Vol. 36 (1947), and had discussed with her material that was later incorporated into *Bizet and His World* (1959).

Janet Flanner: Two: Gertrude Stein and Her Brother (New Haven: Yale University Press, 1951), Foreword by Janet Flanner. The title piece in the volume is not about Leo and Gertrude Stein, rather it is a portrait of Leo Stein and Gertrude's sister-in-law Sarah (Sally) Stein.

To Carl Van Vechten, New York/MS Yale

28 March 1951 — 5 rue Christine, Paris VI

Dearest Papa Woojums—

To my great relief a letter has just come from you—though I dont much like those colds you are indulging in. Cant you avoid them by strict application of precautionary measures before going into all infected areas—trams trains buses—theatres—cinemas etcetera—or better still avoiding going into them. Baby taught me how. She so protected herself in '17 when she evacuated the Spanish grip cases. Do do *some*thing—*any*thing—to cure or rather prevent having colds. They are so frightfully weakening. Do you think I want to put up with another month's silence? No siree—I dont.

Now about the Yale Fund—let us so call it. I have a plan to sell the pictures but it is too soon to get to work at that. I am waiting for Allan's wife to take the chestnuts from the fire with Danny Stein—Allan's oldest son—he is of age and perpetually hard up. As soon as I hear that she has come to terms with him I will open the subject with my lawyer—then with her as guardian of the two minor children—then with Poe who can tackle Danny—*et vous voilá*—it will then only remain for me to put through my long cherished little dream of selling them *en bloc* to a museum so that Baby's collection will not be dispersed over the landscape. This is the only thing that Allan's death will have facilitated.

Mama Woojums

To William Whitehead, New York/MS Yale

28 March 1951 — 5 rue Christine, Paris VI

Dear Bill—

Our letters with their memory of Easter '45 must have crossed and these two lines are to tell you how it pleased me that you had remembered the day. It's a different world today—not only for us—but for everyone. Alas and alas. Did I ever tell you when I was a little girl and had done something I hadnt wanted to do with as much good grace as I could muster I said gayly to my mother—And now what is to be my reward. To which she answered—The privilege of fulfilling another obligation. It impressed me a lot and gradually I accepted it even when I didnt practice it. My mother wasnt a bit austere just simply stoic. And very lovely in every way and in every relation. She died when I was nineteen. How fortunate you are to have your mother. I

GERTRUDE STEIN AND ALICE B. TOKLAS,
5 RUE CHRISTINE, 1938

Photograph by Sir Cecil Beaton

It's a different world today—not only for us but for everyone.

would like to know that she was better. This is really to tell you I am thinking of you and to send you my affectionate wishes.

Alice

To Donald Gallup, New Haven/MS Gallup

29 April 1951 5 rue Christine, Paris VI

Dear Donald—

Finally "The Making of the Makings" has arrived. You have made a wonderful story of it—a passionately interesting one to me. The [Robert] McAlmon episode was [there] in all its exasperating detail—he was irresponsibly drunk all the time (Hemingway said of him it's hard to see your editor throw up your royalties)—and then Jane Heap's efforts were quite fresh in my memory but Hem's letters were a pleasant surprise—though his devotion at that time was unquestionable. Then there is something that surprises me and only you can clear it up. What was added in '11. My memory is that Gertrude wrote continuously at it until it was finished. The typewriting that Gertrude had done on the Yetta von Blickensdorf or Henriette de Dactyle I did over on the big typewriter and caught up so that day by day the new work was typed. Then David was dead and we went to see Mildred Aldrich that afternoon and Gertrude told her she had killed her hero the night before and Mildred who was quite ante bellum in her emotions [said]—"Oh Gertrude how could you"—but perhaps I have told you this already—in which case you must forgive me. Then Gertrude wrote the "dead is dead" and it was finished—as I remember it—so you must tell me about what was added in '11.

Now I must tell you of Claire Goll and her Rilke letters and manuscripts. Do you know of her—she is the poet (?) widow of the poet (?) Ivan Goll. They went to U.S. during the occupation and became American citizens. Why they returned I dont know but he died a year ago and she lives here now. Vaguely I remember her at Natalie Barney's—she and her husband knew Rilke well and have a great quantity of his letters and a number of unpublished poems. She wants them to go to America—asked me about Harvard—whereupon I spoke up for Yale. She is emotional—wants to give them one moment—sell them another—will give them at her death. But she can be nailed to any of the three and if it interests Yale it might be advisable to conclude something before someone else gets at her. She expects to hear from you. She is addressed as Madame Claire Goll at the Hôtel du Palais d'Orsay—Quai d'Orsay. She is susceptible to flattery on any subject.

We have had four or five lovely spring days but now it is again bleak dark and chill. Thank you again—dear Donald—and for so much.

Fondly
Alice

The Making of the Makings: Gallup's article "The Making of *The Making of Americans,*" *New Colophon,* Vol. 3 (1950), and reprinted in *Fernhurst, Q.E.D. and other early writings* (New York: Liveright, 1971).

von Blickensdorf or Henriette de Dactyle: Names given to the typewriters Toklas used for typing Stein's manuscripts.

David was dead: The death dirge of David Hersland in *The Making of Americans,* beginning on page 880 (Paris: Contact Editions, Three Mountains Press, 1925).

To Claude Fredericks, Rome/MS Fredericks

24 May 1951 5 rue Christine, Paris VI

Dear Claude—

Could I tell you how lovely the lilacs were or what riches the pecans add to my shelf of provisions. You see lilacs were one of my childhood flowers—I was allowed to climb into the trees and even break the branches—by a strict grandfather who didnt permit me to cut roses or heliotrope until much later—so lilacs were a familiar flower and their fragrance still works a charm. Thanks—dear Claude for sending me such beautiful ones and for reviving a happy memory. Jamie's [James Merrill] pecans are quite the contrary—nonexistent for so long they are a miraculous reincarnation and fill me with awe and wonder. Wont they keep until September when they could become pies—and cakes! There is a California recipe for pecan pie with rum and the pecans glazed on top that I've read for years that we might enjoy and a honey ice cream with pecan sauce I invented in '38. First come back.

Once many many years ago I stayed at the Hotel Eden—the dowager queen—Margherita of Savoia—had her palace nearby and we used to see her so often that later that summer at an open air performance at Fiesole of the younger Salvini she must have thought I'd been presented and bowed to me—which made a great impression on the villagers.

Are the roses a mad riot. They used to grow all over the walls on the road to a friend's house on the Vicolo de San Nicola da Tolentina. But perhaps it is just modern flats now. It is nice to think of you in Rome—such a nice friendly place. Arent the Romans incredibly beautiful—particularly the men.

From Chicago I hear that Carl is serving dehydrated rosebuds. Violet mustard undehydrated is more distinguished—is the answer to Chicago. It has suddenly ceased raining but it is still sun-less—though murky. Someone has sent me the last I. Compton-Burnett novel—it is fantastically conceived and achieved. The drawing room table is completely cleaned and is back to its old glory as Gertrude knew it. Basket is wellish—Gabrielle is villainous and to you both I am

Always affectionately
Alice

I. Compton-Burnett: Darkness and Day (1951). Ivy Compton-Burnett was one of the few writers in whom Alice took a genuine interest. As each new novel appeared she would read it, then forward it to a friend.

To Cecil Beaton, London/MS Beaton

30 June 1951 5 rue Christine, Paris VI

Cecil dear—

Your enchanting *Photobiography* has come and is delighting me. A thousand thanks for sending it to me—it was good of you and to add your message.

The book has surprised me a bit and fascinated me—by the variety and beauty of the reproductions—by the story of how you created and developed your work and by the quality of your writing. And if all this is surprising to me it isn't because your talents hadn't impressed me earlier. What a pleasure it must be to be such a highly gifted creature. And it doesn't the least bit prevent the book from being gay and lively—at moments hilariously so. What you said of Gertrude of course touched me deeply.

As a prelude to asking a great favor of you you must know that the only photograph that I have here is the one you took that first morning in London—in profile with the little silk Louis XIth cap—all the many many others went to Yale University but

CECIL BEATON AND ALICE B. TOKLAS, BILIGNIN, 1938

Photograph by Sir Cecil Beaton

Affectionate memories—dear Cecil.

this one remains. What you will do for me next time you come to Paris—and have time—you will let me see the one you mention taken shortly before the end looking out of the window—and which I've never seen. You will understand what passionate interest it holds for me.

Your portrait of Picasso—the only one since his youth that gives him—with his force and beauty as he is. You've even been able to give the burning white light in his black black eyes. You are too indulgent to have spoken of me so kindly.

Thanks and thanks again for so much pleasure. Do let me know when you come to Paris and lunch with me. Basket and I go to Mougins about the twentieth.

Affectionate memories to you always—dear Cecil—

Alice

To Claude Fredericks, Italy/MS Fredericks

30 June 1951 5 rue Christine, Paris VI

Dear Claude—

Did you see the Russian ballerina in Florence. They say she is as great as Karsavina was. Last night I heard the San Carlos opera give *Giovanna d'Arco*—a thrilling performance with the finest soprano in exactly forty years definitely—and an old memory being what it is possibly ever. Have you heard her—Renata Tebaldi. I am going this evening again—but without knowing if she sings tonight. [Gino] Penno the tenor is a heroic tenor—the whole thing—chorus and orchestra—is in the great tradition which I'd not hoped to see again—a vibrant exciting experience. And the gorgeous Italian audience—what a seduction. Nothing else I've done of course has been nice by comparison.

Finally it is decided that Basket and I spend August at the very top of Mougins with friends who have taken a house there. If by any chance you are around there at that time let me [know]. The address after July 25th is Maison de Général de Larminat—Place Pérou—Mougins—Alpes-Maritimes. I'll have plenty of time before then to attend to your and to Jamie's [Merrill] stamps.

Cockscombs are excellent. They arent red because the thin outer skin is removed (like on feet). They are as old as the first extant recipes. Roman. And delicious. When they werent so expensive we ate them. Now occasionally I have the head minus tongue and eyes. Excellent. No the pecans dont keep over August—but a Circassian chicken requires walnuts not pecans and that's what I'll be making you. Dont they have wonderful bird dishes in Italy made without birds. Fondest good wishes always to you both.

Alice

To William Alfred, Cambridge, Massachusetts
MS Harvard

3 July 1951 5 rue Christine, Paris VI

Dear Mr. Alfred—

It is not too late I hope to meet young Charles Flood. Dentistry has kept me tied up—boresomely—occasionally painfully—pray accept this as the reason for not answering you sooner and try to pardon me. If you havent his address I will try to get in touch with him at the American Express where all our compatriots receive their mail—in fact it would be best to send him a line there at once—which I will do. It is kind of you to suppose meeting me will be of any advantage to the nice young man. What they really appreciate is sitting comfortably in a home and that is my pleasure to be able to offer them in Gertrude's home. They are a more lost generation than those who followed '14–'18. They at least refused to be attached to anything. They still had a choice. Gertrude thought that the men after '45 would have to pioneer—clear new ground and risk martyrdom—to save the country and themselves.

It is indeed excellent news that you are at work on a tragedy in blank verse—Gertrude thought that the separation between the spoken and written language was already so great that there would presently be two languages. Your work doubtless is helping to accomplish this. I hope you are satisfied with your work. And thanks for proposing to send me the recording of your poems—hearing them will be a great pleasure. Alas that Gertrude will not.

Cordially
Alice Toklas

William Alfred: Alfred, the American poet and playwright, met Stein and Toklas while a G.I. His poem "Epitaph (Lyric in Memory of Gertrude Stein)" was the prize poem in The Atlantic Contests for College Students (1946/47) sponsored by *The Atlantic Monthly.* In 1951 Alfred was working on his play *Agamemnon.*

To Annette Rosenshine, Berkeley, California
MS Bancroft

15 July 1951 — 5 rue Christine, Paris VI

Dear Annette—

You please and amuse me with your recklessness—for year by year I become more cautious careful and economical. The old woman who serves me said the other day there are moments when you are nearly avaricious secretly. I was delighted and said this is a story for Annette. Two wars help to make me hate waste but avarice is a little strong.

Madame Boiffard came to see me about six weeks ago to say goodby before going to Epernon for the summer. She says she hates it but that Amélie loves it—and she must acknowledge that it is healthy and economical. Amélie raises a great deal of their winter food as well as nearly all of their summer food. Vegetables and fruit—eggs chickens and rabbits—some of which she sells. Sometimes she brings me eggs and fruit and I give her tea coffee flour and bacon—you see how at the same age and under similar circumstances one has no false pride but sympathy. As I have the privilege of buying cigarettes very cheaply it is my pleasure to be able to give them from time to time to French friends to whom they are the greatest luxury.

How right you are about amateur players. It wasnt possible for me to escape seeing some of them do Gertrude's play *Yes Is For A Very Young Man* which is probably the one you write of. It was really wretchedly played because for one reason there was no understanding. It was a sad experience for me for it was the first time I saw it. We did have a wonderful reading of it here one evening in '45 when a number of well know actors happened by sheer accident to be in Paris—some were in combat troops others in intelligence and a lovely actress and Gertrude doubled in the womens parts. I only heard part of it because I was trying to make supper out of the tinned things the men had brought. Now it is being played in Philadelphia professionally. Amateur art isnt satisfactory—is it. It bores me frightfully. When I used to bake a cake for Gertrude I never asked is it good I always said does it look like one that came from the bakers—it should have tasted better because the material it was made of was of a superior quality to what the baker used but wasnt mixed and baked in a professional way which was what would make it look like the baker's. Well it was often that Gertrude thought it did. Finally some one said one looked as if it had come from a Women's Exchange and Gertrude said that should satisfy me.

I do hope you have found something comfortable sunny and

congenial and that you too will be drying out. Fondest wishes always.

Alice

Madame Boiffard: Jeanne Boiffard was the daughter of Madame Vernot who ran the pension at 58 rue Madame (which was located in the same building in which the Michael Steins lived, and where Rosenshine had lived while in Paris in 1906–8).

To Philip W. Claflin, New York/MS Claflin

9 August 1951

Place Pérou, Mougins,
Alpes-Maritimes, France

Dear Mr. Claflin—

Unfortunately of our brief meeting with the students at Vassar my only memory of them is of their quite exceptional loveliness. It would be a pleasure to see you again. In the meantime I am looking forward to seeing your brother and his wife. Please do not ask me to chide your wife about the Metropolitan's giving the portrait to that frightful Museum of Modern Art for ten years—since it got back to where it belongs much more quickly than one had reason to hope for. In any case your wife will tell me many things that will please and interest me.

Always cordially
Alice Toklas

Is your wife possibly connected with the Museum of Modern Art. If she is she is saving it from damnation—indeed it is to be hoped that she is doing so.

Claflin: Claflin, a New York banker with an interest in the arts, first met Stein and Toklas in the 1930's through his godfather, Bernard Faÿ. Claflin's wife, Agnes Range, was head of the Art History Department at Vassar College.

To Fernanda Pivano, Milan/MS Pivano

9 August 1951 Place Pérou, Mougins, Alpes-Maritimes

Dear Nanda dear—

About books on Fitzgerald—you should read for the preface you will write to *This Side of Paradise* Edmund Wilson's *The Crack Up* published very shortly after his death ('41?) which has letters and articles (one by Gertrude) in appreciation and many many of his letters which are wonderful. You know of course that there has been an enormous revival of interest in F.S.F. this last year in U.S. A very vulgar novel which I have not seen nor would not by a man named Schulberg (?) and an appreciative one called *The Far Side of Paradise*—by a man named Mizener which you should by all means read but which I have not seen or I would have sent it to you naturally. Of course I will tell you all I remember but it is little enough for we didnt see him half a dozen times. And surely you know the story of Fitzgerald and Hemingway. In Paris there is an American woman named Esther Arthur (the [wife of the] grandson of one of our presidents) who before marrying him was the wife of John Strachey the English minister of ? and who (she) is very politically minded but knew Fitzgerald very intimately and though I know her little she would agree to talk about Fitzgerald to you gladly. *Tender Is The Night* was largely about the Fitzgeralds when they were staying with Esther Arthur's brother!! And Thornton knew Fitzgerald after he came back from France and stayed with them for a strange weekend in Delaware. *(Entre nous* the short stories of Fitzgerald are very very poor that is why I could not write any thing about them only about him.)

All my warm loving wishes that everything may be well with you both always.

Alice

vulgar novel: Budd Schulberg's novel about Fitzgerald, *The Disenchanted* (1950).

Short Stories of Fitzgerald: Toklas' review was in *The New York Times,* March 4, 1951.

To Carl Van Vechten, New York/MS Yale

9 August 1951 Place Pérou, Mougins, Alpes-Maritimes

Dearest Papa Woojums—

The pleasant days follow each other—the Knapiks and the weather are unvaryingly agreeable—and it's pleasant basking in so much amiability—so different to life in the capitol. Basket and I take short strolls—we'd go farther but as Mougins is on the top of a hill to return one is forced to climb and neither of us seem up to too much of that. But tomorrow I am taking him in the auto car to Cannes to see Olga Picasso. When Baby and I were in Nice in the twenties we went to sit on a small isolated beach we found where Baby worked wonderfully well but I wont be seeing that tomorrow. I'd like to go over to see Picasso but it is an all day excursion with three buses each way which dont connect so I've renounced. What I am really looking for is a covered motor tricycle with a trailer. It would be so convenient and even economical—much cheaper than taxis and trains which I do not take!

We are being driven back in the same car by the same driver. We start very early the first morning and it is lovely. Baby and I once in a while used to do this—when it was still starlight—and drive until one—sleep after lunch and start off again from four to nine. Marie Laurencin wants me to join a society for the protection *de la femme seule*. Can that be equalled. Good bye—Papa Woojums dearest—have a wonderful Haitian adventure—if you are going on it. Good bye. Good bye. Good bye.

Love Love Love

M.W.

To Mark Lutz, Philadelphia/MS Yale

16 August 1951 Place Pérou, Mougins, Alpes-Maritimes

Dear Mark—

I think of you often and am hoping that your short vacation was calm and restful and that you have returned to your flat refreshed and with great courage. Having experienced going back alone to an empty house you will let me tell you how deeply I feel with you. How good you are to think of me and send me the clippings—which of course I could not otherwise have seen. Poor Fitzgerald has suffered so much for his obvious weaknesses —the fact remains however that he was the most gifted of his generation and was sensitive and articulate enough to express what he saw about it—which was more than the clerks and grocers were able to do. The young men of today seem mostly to be interested in the manner rather than the matter. But novels dont hold my attention—that is those of the young men—as they did. The vacation is half over and I havent yet gone down to Cannes. When you have time send me a line.

Affectionately
Alice

To Carl Van Vechten, New York/MS Yale

17 September 1951 5 rue Christine, Paris VI

Dearest Papa Woojums—

An answer within a week is what Mildred Aldrich predicted when Blériot flew the Channel. Poor dear she loved to see her prophesies fulfilled but she was fortunate to escape this last war. Three wars are enough in one lifetime and she remembered the Civil War!

What can I say about your suggestion that Freddie Bowles do the third foreword—preface—introduction—except that I like him a lot and liked his novel (not the short stories). Is that a recommendation—scarcely. As you say "a suitable preface by someone familiar with her work." Is he—I am sure I do not know. But then Janet though suitable was not familiar with her work and her foreword is considered highly satisfactory—so perhaps your stated condition (with which I wholeheartedly agree) may be too exacting. However my one objection to Freddie is that his gift is not in the direction of scholarship as yours Donald's and Thornton's would be and that it seems wiser to lean in that direction rather than friendliness (Janet's and as far as I know Freddie's). It is sweet of you to ask me at all at all—as we said when we were *fin de siècle*—so that if you and your advisory committee feel he is suitable he certainly is. If he is chosen because he is a popular young writer today is that any guarantee he will be two years hence.

And Edmund (ex. Bunny) Wilson—isnt he Queen Victoria living on to point the moral that high minded clear thinking can land one in the ditch with one's private tastes exposed to the eyes of the casual passerby. His cross-examination of Baby at the Algonquin that morning was a scream—he just wouldnt separate civic virtues from aesthetic purposes.

M.W.

I am sending you by boat mail the *Lucy Church* [*Amiably*] and Max's [Jacob] letters.

Wilson: Edmund Wilson had just reviewed Stein's *Things As They Are* (1951) for *The New Yorker.* The review is collected in his *The Shores of Light* (1952).

To Carl Van Vechten, New York/MS Yale

10 October 1951 5 rue Christine, Paris VI

Dearest Papa Woojums—

It is now ten days since Gabrielle has gone and the second liberation is gradually becoming a convincing fact. The end was so quiet it made one nervous. Gradually the flat is being put into order. Gab. was clean but disorderly with a passion for collecting—empty bottles tins and bags—string corks—all worn—as well as clippings samples stubs of pencils and labels. For two days I've had a nice *femme de ménage* mornings and peace and quiet cheerfulness reign. There will be extra work for me but I can manage that easily and it will be an economy. When Mildred Aldrich moved out to the country she said to me—Someday you will appreciate closing and locking the shutters of your home. To which there was nothing to say—no you dear old New Englander you were born so—not I. And it's a horror to me now.

Well—to change to something gay and lively. [For *aïoli*] pound to a paste as many cloves of garlic as you can stand—in the *midi* they count two per person or 4 per yolk of egg—add salt to taste (no pepper or mustard). Then the yolk or yolks of eggs—pound and stir until it becomes an emulsion—then add olive oil drop by drop. (It curdles more easily than simple mayonnaise.) When it begins to become firm add lemon juice. When it is once more firm add a tablespoon of boiling water if two yolks of eggs have been used. This will keep several days.

Edward [Waterman] sweetly asked me to lunch with him at a bistro in the quarter. It wasnt what one could properly call a bistro—it was a serious students' little restaurant with the best *gigot* I've eaten in years. Then he took me to the show of the impressionists from the German museums (we were both furious that they hadnt been taken for reparations)—he converted me to and I him to Courbet (there was a wonder—how Baby would have loved it—she did love his pictures in a particular way). And then Edward went to get his mail and I went to the commissary to get him some crackers he likes and we didnt ever meet again. I stood for forty minutes and caught a dreadful cold (a box and a half of Kleenex!). But I forgive Edward and will ask him to lunch with me when I've settled down a bit (23 letters and heaps of sewing).

I'm so touched that Judith Anderson remembers me. She moves me like no one has for a long time—she has a power of concentration—her mere presence in a room changes everything—that ought to be rationed in small vials.

Basket has been sick and needs a deal of watching. But he will be peaceful soon—he hates disturbances—he shrivelled under Gab's temper—not that she showed it toward him—but he couldnt understand violence.

Love and love and love from

M.W.

To Donald Gallup, New Haven/MS Gallup

18 November 1951 — 5 rue Christine, Paris VI

Dear Donald—

Two days ago I got over to Lascaux's show—you have had the catalogue and even photographs so you are prepared for the unexpected extraordinary development in his work. What you will not know and it is not the easiest thing to make clear is the change in his palette. The color is warmer more closely related to the composition and without losing any of the light which was so characteristically his special gift. It is very closely knitted—the color and composition—and strangely enough his pictures are more spacious. At first the landscapes seduced me but when I said this to Kahnweiler who appeared shortly after I got there he said—For me I prefer the still lifes. And he as always was right. There is a greater freedom in them and at the same time a greater concentration. He (K.) thinks that Lascaux's joy at being back in Paris has worked the miracle—and naturally his more frequent contact with other painters. As you know they spent their holidays not far from Vallauris and he frequently saw Picasso but whatever he may have felt there is no direct Picasso influence in the pictures. The integrity of Lascaux's character is beyond mere praise. But you know him better than I so it [is] useless to speak of it to you except for the pleasure it gives one. The whole development is quite miraculous. Next summer will suddenly have become a long time hence to you. Kahnweiler says that the pictures sell well especially to Sweden—that he is satisfied but that it annoys Lascaux.

By the way there were no ceramics shown at [the] Lascaux exposition and I didn't like to ask for them—though it was foolish not to have done so.

Thanks and thanks and thanks to you—dear Donald.

Always appreciatively and affectionately.

Alice

To Samuel Steward, Chicago/MS Bancroft

19 November 1951 5 rue Christine, Paris VI

Dear Sam—

I've an idea about getting a passage back on the French Line. Why dont I make the reservations here. That seems sensible doesnt it. Give me the date or boat or both and over I fly to the rue Auber—where I've not been since we bought our tickets *aller et retour* in '34 for the dear old Champlain. What a lovely boat it was and how uncertain we were—about the venture of Gertrude's lecturing. Every hour I repeated—But if for any reason we dont like it we will go right back on the Champlain again. And how we loved it all. Here I am reminiscing like my two grandaunts—my grandmother never did—not she—she considered her sisters as agreeable but weak and didnt take time to disapprove. They played concertos on two square pianos with the pedals raised as they were so short. They looked like Renoir's portrait of Malibran. That is Fanny did. Mathilde looked like nobody but herself. She weighed ninety pounds and had Manchester terriers that weighed three—and had her [hair] cut short seventy years ago all in ringlets black around her white face. Towards the end she was blind but could find a lost needle—she said it was magnetism. Grandma was politically minded and read the London *Times*—they'd gone to school in England—and crossed her legs and was altogether advanced and *outrée*.

There's a long and curious story about Gabrielle that must keep until you come over. She put me through two months of mental anguish and in a great flare up she consented to leave which was what I most wanted. And go she did. And it's calm and peaceful now and she's forgotten and after everything is in order again life will be possible. After all havent I found time to reminisce—more's the pity if that is the way time is to be wasted.

Good night and my love to you always—

Alice

To Carl Van Vechten, New York/MS Yale

27 November 1951 5 rue Christine, Paris VI

Dear Papa Woojums—

If you didnt hear from me after Gabrielle left it was because the work kept me so busy that there wasnt at first time to even hunt a *femme de ménage*—and guests for lunch twice and Basket not well and the doorbell ringing when it wasnt the telephone. But now a nice woman comes to do the heavier work and everything is more or less in order. Gabrielle was clean but incredibly disorderly. So there was a lot to do but I'm seeing ahead with satisfaction to a day when there will be time to tackle a number of things.

The other day in the bus—there was someone wearing the purest most beautiful canary yellow gloves—she looked familiar—she came over to sit next to me and say—You dont remember I am Mercedes de Acosta. She has become so very bourgeois looking and comfortably middle aged. She said she would come to see me. A few nights ago she rang up and said she and Cecil and Greta Garbo had rung the doorbell several times the night before but no one had answered (Basket and I really need a stronger bell) and could they come that evening which they did—Cecil very tousled exhausted and worshipful—she [Garbo] a bit shy—quite Vassarish—unpretentious but very criminal. She asked me with simplicity and frankness—Did you know Monsieur Vollard was he a fascinating person—a great *charmeur*—was he seductive. She was disappointed like a young girl who dreams of an assignation. Do explain her to me. She was not mysterious but I hadnt the answer. The French papers say they [Beaton and Garbo] are to marry—but she doesnt look as if she would do anything as crassly innocent as that. *Expliquez moi* as Pablo used to say to Baby.

Are you coming over if they give *4 Saints*. Love and love and love from

M.W.

Mercedes de Acosta: An American writer of Spanish descent, she wrote screenplays, poems, and plays. Her memoir *Here Lies the Heart* (1960) recounts the same version of her meeting with Toklas. She was for many years an intimate friend of Greta Garbo and Marlene Dietrich.

Monsieur Vollard: Ambroise Vollard had opened a small gallery in Paris in 1893. Among the artists he exhibited were Rodin, Pissarro, Renoir, Dégas, Bonnard, Cézanne, and Picasso. The Steins bought a number of pictures from him. (See *AABT,* pp. 35–40, for a description of the Stein's purchase of Cézanne's *Portrait of Madame Cézanne.*)

To Claude Fredericks, Pawlet, Vermont/MS Fredericks

30 December 1951 | 5 rue Christine Paris VI

Dear Claude—

At last the luxury of a free hour to talk to you quietly. Jamie [Merrill] came with his mother his stepfather and your gorgeously enveloped token. But what my dear boy do you take it token means—your memory doesnt go back far enough to take for granted—as mine permitted me to do—that anything so long so thin so dazzingly gay must be a candy cane striped and pepperminted as they were for my first remembered Christmas over seventy years ago. So that evening unhesitatingly it was opened. (This a little scandalised Jamie the next day when he came to see me again and we had a very happy and for me enlightening talk.) A cane can become an umbrella but it's extraordinary that such an elegant exterior penetrates to the heart. But the umbrella is indescribably distinguished—mysterious—evocative—it should belong to some great heroine of the past—a tragic one whose umbrella couldnt console or save her from her inevitable doom—Anna Karenina or Christina Light—someone in the grand manner. But though you have chosen to give such an umbrella to the plainest of old women it is not wasted upon her. From it comes a sense of other days other times and in them the umbrella

PORTRAIT OF ALICE B. TOKLAS
AT 27 RUE DE FLEURUS, 1922

Photograph by Man Ray

Other days other times.

beckons me to share the feeling of such a world. How can one say in return for this thank you many many times for your beautiful gift. Immediately I commenced to take it out with me in the afternoons—against the fog—but on Christmas Day which I spent with the Barrys at Montmorency it rained and it was baptised—Claude naturally after the donor. And it is raining again but I've only been on errands and marketing and Claude would be unhappy and displaced in the rue Dauphine—as it is today—and the rue de Buci—but tomorrow Natalie Barney has asked me to lunch and she will see all the great passionate drama the umbrella is. For the New Year all my fondest good wishes for the realization of *all* yours.

Always affectionately
Alice

1952

To Samuel Steward, Chicago/MS Bancroft

30 January 1952 — 5 rue Christine, Paris VI

Dear Sam—

There isnt much news. Max White who is a great admirer of yours by the way went to Spain in early summer and was happy—it held him as it had some twenty years earlier and he would have stayed on indefinitely if he hadnt been called home by the serious illness of an aged mother. He was here briefly. He is quite irreplaceable. The Knapiks are angelic to me. Virginia more beautiful than ever and in a nice way—you will be surprised—is doing bookbinding—she takes her lessons right around the corner from here and will come to see me this evening. Francis [Rose] is doing some important work—around Venice in late summer and at Cassis now—he rents his flat furnished and lives on it and the small sale of his pictures. It is of course a good sign that people dont like them easily—but a discouraging one. His private life is quite a bit more fantastic than it was. If Glenway Wescott could have been useful—*bien*—but as a judge of literature—hell. He writes pretentious unreal and stilted letters to any and everybody. I've seen a couple and it's my idea that he hopes that they are being kept and published—in his lifetime. He has by untiring effort over some thirty years become what he believes to be a cultivated man of the world.

And still he wrote a very good old fashioned novel (tradition of W. D. Howells!).

Do you remember the Dora Maar landscape—she painted three very beautiful ones last summer and more exciting still lifes. And I've seen twice Fernande Olivier—after more than forty years. She's unchanged—except physically—she's a monumental wreck. And they brought Greta Garbo to see me. And with many questions answered by me of her friends the *mystère c'est dévoilée.* And not so interesting—she looks without makeup not more than 36.

Love from
Alice

Max White: An American writer whom Stein and Toklas had met in 1935.

To Brion Gysin, Tangier, Morocco/MS Gysin

26 February 1952 5 rue Christine, Paris VI

Dear Brion—

Security—what a fearfully limiting experience it would be. As for capital I've not had any—when I was young I ran up debts—which was pleasant. Then I came over here and never knew where money was to come from—mostly it didnt. G.S. bought pictures and spent no money on anything else to be able to do so. Except during the two wars when we didn't know or care what we spent we lived like church mice and it amused us to go about like gypsies. Now *mes petites économies* are not so diverting and put one in the banal majority. So you see our situations have points of resemblance. Your particular gifts and my lack of any certainly flourish best in a not too great luxuriance. Surely you would have been submerged if not drowned as a professor—your book would then only have been for other faculty members. It would be too heavenly if you'd get the first volume published in my time. Are you in Central Africa—have you been and returned.

There is nothing about Santa Teresa except in *Four Saints.* It is probably going to be given here for the May musical festival. Virgil is supposed to bring over a new Negro cast and to conduct it. No one confirms this though it was in the *N. York Times.* Jane [Bowles] is strange as an American but not as an Oriental—especially an Oriental D.P. It was to this conclusion that seeing her with Libby Holman brought me. If accepting this makes her more foreign it at least relieves the strain—that morbidity—she originally seemed at first to be consumed by. Morbidity is really Scandinavian—not Latin or Oriental—in spite of the Italians' weakness for feeling they suffer from it. Racial characteristics—so abjectly true as William James once said.

I'll be writing again soon—nagging to hear from you.

Affectionate good wishes to you—dear Brion always.

A.B.T.

Gysin: A painter and writer who had met Stein and Toklas briefly in the 1930's while he was in Paris. For many years he lived in Morocco and was a close friend of Paul and Jane Bowles.

To Carl Van Vechten, New York/MS Yale

29 March 1952 5 rue Christine, Paris VI

Dearest Papa Woojums—

Mina Curtiss is here—she is staying in a flat on the Quai de Bourbon with eleven full length windows looking down on the Seine—furnished in the mode of *The Second Mrs. Tanqueray* with Chinese gold and silver walls and furniture that is elegant but equivocal—objects of value that are both useful and fragile and flowers that stagger belief. It all suits her reincarnated Byzantine empress beauty. It is a puzzle to me how she adapts herself to Williamsburg Mass.

Dora Maar is putting Basket into the portrait which pleases me a lot—she is coming to make some more drawings of him—it is to be hoped she will give me one of them. It is the habit here when a painter asks someone to sit for him—to give the portrait to the sitter but Dora Maar evidently doesnt for the smashing portrait she did of Marie Laure de Noailles is in her studio still—so she should give me a drawing of Basket—which of course I'd promptly send to Yale. If not promptly at least as prompt as I ever am. All my love to you both always from

Your grateful
M.W.

Dora Maar: During the late 1930's and through the war years Dora Maar, a painter and photographer, had been the mistress of Picasso. After the war Stein bought one of her landscapes (now in YCAL). Toklas gave the portrait of herself and Basket by Dora Maar to the YCAL.

To Donald Sutherland, Boulder, Colorado
MS Sutherland

7 April 1952 — 5 rue Christine, Paris VI

Dear Donald—

Finally after many false alarms *Four Saints* is to be given by ANTA for two weeks and then come here for two performances of the musical and artistic festival at the end of next month. Virgil is training the singers (Negroes) and orchestra which he will direct there and here. They tell me that this production will be much more elaborate than the original one. More's the pity—for Miss

Stettheimer combined cellophane and silk velvet in a luxurious sense of economy—as Freddie Ashton did a fantastic ballet and religious procession. No one knows these things any more. The French radio has been talking of Gertrude's work and the opera—and Virgil and Jean Cocteau are to do a séance about the opera just before it is given.

They are also importing from Austria *Wozzeck* which friends have asked me to hear with them. Mittel Europa's art leaves me cold—particularly since Rilke has been dropped overboard. Frankly a Boston symphony concert would have been preferred!

Bernard's [Faÿ] affairs have been worrying—his health is very bad—his finances rotten—he has papers to stay securely where he is but is not permitted to earn his living. Will his old publishers commence again. If the necessary *sous* are forthcoming it would be a temptation to go to see him for a long weekend.

Thank you a lot for taking time to explain the use of Greek words by helping me to find out more by myself—which makes you the ideal teacher. By the way the *Oedipus* [*Rex*] of Stravinsky is advertised as having been translated into Medieval Latin by a Monsieur Jean Danielou and then translated by Jean Cocteau into modern French—a truly Russian salad with a *piquante* sauce.

Yes it is a shocking fact that everybody but the author makes money from books that are going to live—this didnt surprise Gertrude as much as the number of people who could earn a little because the book had come to be written. It was true of Doctor Whitehead's work. He lived on his salary and later two pensions.

Yes Picasso's sense of volume and space and light are born together with his subject and material and he once said that it was this—which he accepted as normal—that prevented him from having a problem to resolve. He is well again. Françoise Gillot is having a show but I have avoided it. Rare as a meeting with Picasso is it would be fatal to run into him having seen her pictures.

Fond love to you both.

Alice

Faÿ: Through the intervention of friends Faÿ had managed an escape from prison and had gone first to Spain and then to Switzerland. Because of her known sympathies, Toklas was thought to be involved, and a number of her friends were called before the *préfect* of the Seine.

To Carl Van Vechten, New York/MS Yale

7 May 1952 5 rue Christine, Paris VI

Dearest Papa Woojums—

It was too sweet of you to remember an anniversary of what happened so frightfully long ago. A few weeks ago the date popped up at me on the calendar when I was looking for something else so that when the day came it was easy to confuse it with others—but the oldest friend on earth—such a lovely and singing person—Danish—rubbed it in—that we were both too old and so this was the last not to grow any older. And then Carlo and Fania's love and kisses came. Then a very nice Martha Stout and I went to two exciting picture shows and later she made me meet her and Ludwig Bemelmans (whom she had brought to see me a few days before and who is wittier than his books are funny) and some other people for lunch near here. And it was ever so nice. And now Bemelmans sent me a no. 106 of a book of his with an original gouache.

I got off my article to Mrs. Norcross for *House Beautiful* and being a pessimist about what she will think of it and an optimist about receiving a cheque for it—no sooner had I posted it than I flew over and had my photograph taken and then to the embassy for a passport—so that I can go to see Bernard a long weekend away from here leaving Basket at the vets. The vice consul—who (like they all do they say) has modelled herself upon Miss Shipley in Washington (who you will remember made so many difficulties for Richard Wright)—was an angel to me and came way out to the street to bring me my *carte d'identité* which I had left on her desk.

Tomorrow I spend the morning with her filling out blanks for an application so I'll have the passport by the time I hear from Mrs. Norcross that she doesn't want the little effort.

Then Mrs. Bradley sent word through Mina Curtiss that she had an offer for a cook book from someone for me and as I wanted to see her about Bernard's manuscripts it was easy to combine the two things in one visit before she left for N. York. It was from Harpers. It will be necessary to find out from the man at Rinehart if they are ready to give an advance. Mrs. B. thought she could get 2 or 3 thousand from one of them. That would suit—to have something to ease the present situation and something ahead.

The Knapiks took me to *Wozzeck*—it was tremendous—music—drama—orchestra and voices. The Viennese opera at its most direct and purest.

Virgil sweetly had someone from the committee come to see me about tickets for *Four Saints* and now I am to have two invitations for each performance—and I've asked one of the Knapiks to each—and Virginia and I are going to the *Socrate* together. You know Virgil played and sang it to Baby and to me in '26 up in his little red plush bedroom.

The Judy Steins are bringing some young Americans so it is time to go and find some glasses and something to drink.

Hugs and hugs and bear hugs to you both from

M.W.

House Beautiful: It's not clear which of two articles Toklas is referring to. Her first to appear in *House Beautiful* was "Secrets of French Cooking, Part I," November 1954. This was an excerpt from *The Alice B. Toklas Cook Book.* Subsequently, *House Beautiful* printed "Secrets of French Cooking, Part II" (December 1954), "Blessed Blender in the Home" (July 1955), "Cooking with Champagne" (October 1955), and "How to Cook with Cognac" (March 1956).

To Carl Van Vechten, New York/MS Yale

7 June 1952 5 rue Christine, Paris VI

Dearest Papa Woojums—

It was a *Four Saints* and Baby Week indeed. Virgil finally turned up a week before the first performance—the next evening we met by accident at a restaurant of all places—the drollest place for me to be found in. Four evenings after he and Maurice [Grosser] came to see me—they are less separable than formerly. Seats (two) for each of the two performances were forthcoming—Virginia and Harold [Knapik] already having accepted. Then Nanda [Pivano] turned up unexpectedly the day before. Fortunately she was able to go with me to the *générale*. She kept whispering to me—Is that the way it was in the original performance—what did Gertrude say to this or that. The performance struck me as musically more sound than I remembered—the singing of the soloists better—the chorus a bit too forceful—the ballet lamentable—the décor heavy. Santa Teresa sang like an angel—she had a great success. The audience was not a bit scandalised—very enthusiastic and appreciative. You will have all the clippings that Virgil is to receive.

It seemed as if two parties (the flat not being large enough to hold all at once) should be given for the cast of *4 Saints*—but Virgil said Mrs. Reiner disapproved—so he arranged to have the two Matthews and the ex Mrs. M. (the *commère*) Leontyne Price and Martha Flowers and a dancer who was born in S. Francisco—and I asked a dozen people and by the time they all came and the four very large cakes and *petits pains (au paté)* I had baked were disposed about a punch bowl and tea for those who wished it—the rooms were crowded. It went off very nicely. I loved the singers—most of all Inez Matthews—we were friends at first sight. They all have so much grace and distinction and the prettiest manners—Saint Ignatius too—everyone was pleased with everyone else—so in spite of the pall of Baby's not being here it wasn't too bad.

Jo [Barry] and his family return on the 14th and very likely I'll go to Spain with them for four weeks—that is from the last week of this month. They are going to America to live—it's an irreparable loss to me. He is going to have a large salary and not too much work with *House Beautiful.*

For August I go to Cannes with the Knapiks—Virginia has found the house and we have paid for it—a good garden and view—two bathrooms and everything else to correspond. All this tells you how unhappy I am at not being able to see Fania—it was what I most wanted and if I hadn't engaged myself for my vacation in August so much in advance—as I have done for the three previous vacations—it would have been such a joy to see Fania once again—I am writing to her.

M.W.

To Donald Sutherland, Boulder, Colorado
MS Sutherland

6 August 1952

26 bis rue Louis-Perrisol,
Cannes, Alpes-Maritimes

Dear Donald—

Two months have passed since your first letter arrived—another was waiting upon the return from Spain and the aesthetic of the *Iliad* which kept me in snatched moments immensely illuminated. The heat here exhausted me for several days. Yesterday I read the introduction over again and found a mine of understanding and explanation not only of the *Iliad* but of painting & of literature. The geometric abstraction you made so clear that the detached units in Picasso's still lifes flow and scan like lyric poetry—yet remain realist and geometric. Then what you say about the insignificance of the verb and the importance of the noun in English literature explains Gertrude's writing. And then your explanation of the dance and the art of movement was what Gertrude discovered in the walking marathon she saw in Chicago. And Santa Teresa's double quality was what attracted Gertrude and which in a vague way—from the confusion that is natural to me—came to me in the marvellous day spent in Ávila where G. and her saint were alive and near. On nearly every page there is something that illustrates Gertrude. Homer's interest in the violence and splendor of life and of death (and Picasso too)—and his morality—being based on handsome conduct. And the repetitions composed in time. It is a thousand pities that you didn't talk to G. about this because of the enormous pleasure it would have given her. If this is the introduction what immense importance your finished work will have.

Quite unexpectedly the Jo Barrys asked me to go with them for the greater part of last month on a motor trip to Spain—down the Mediterranean coast to Murcia—by way of Granada to Málaga and Cádiz inland to Cordoba Seville Toledo Madrid the Escorial Segovia—Ávila Burgos Valladolid. It was the landscape—pictures and a few churches that I wanted and had. Endless Grecos from private collections we'd not seen in the old days and Zurburáns (do you know his Virgin at the Metropolitan—do see it when you get to N. York again)—the Goyas no longer hold my attention. On the way down we stopped an afternoon to see the cathedral at Albi (did you get a p.c. from there—it has the weight of Spain) and on our [return] we stopped at Bayonne to see two late Goyas and found incredible Ingres—particularly a sculpted hand—and the cave paintings at Lascaux surprisingly post Cézanne—having missed those at Almería. If I'm alive next year I go back by hook or by crook to Castile.

And now I am here in the Mediterranean at its most banal in the most unpleasing spot on its French shore but staying not too uncomfortably with agreeable friends. Harold Knapik a composer is at the piano most of the day—he would be there constantly if he didn't cook and so very well. The house is at the edge of the communist working quarter and yet only a short walk to the excellent

26 bis rue Louis-Perrissol. Cannes. Alpes-Maritimes.

6 · VIII · 52.

Dear Donald: Two months have passed since your first letter arrived—all other was waiting upon the return from Spain and the aesthetic of the Iliad which kept me in snatched moments immensely illuminated. Then the heat here exhausted me for several days. Yesterday I read the introduction over again and found a mine of understanding and explanation not only of the Iliad but of painting and literature. The geometric abstraction ~~of Picasso~~ you make so clear that ~~his~~ Picasso's detached units in ~~his~~ Picasso's still lives flow and scan ~~like~~ like lyric poetry—yet remain realist and geometric. Then what you say about the insignificance of the verb and the importance of the noun in English literature explains Gertrude's writing. And then your explanation of the dance and the act of movement was what Gertrude discovered in the walking marathon she saw in Chicago. And Santa Teresa's double quality was what attracted Gertrude and which in a vague way from the confusion that is natural to me came to me in the marvellous day spent in Avila where G. and her saint were alive and near. On nearly every page there is something that illustrates Gertrude—Homer's interest in the violence and splendour of life and of death (and of Picasso too). (You illuminate Homer through my understanding of them—an abject admission of not only limited understanding but woeful ignorance.) And the morality being based on handsome conduct. And the repetitions composed in time. It is a thousand pities that you did not talk to G. about this because of the enormous pleasure it would have given her. If this is the introduction what immense importance your finished work will have.

Quite unexpectedly the Jo Barrys asked me to go with them for the greater part of last month on a motor trip to Spain—down the Mediterranean coast to Murcia—by way of Granada to Malaga and Cadiz inland to Cordoba Seville Toledo Madrid the Escorial Segovia Avila Burgos Valladolid. It was the landscape—pictures and a few churches that I wanted and had. Endless Grecos from private collections not seen in the old days and Zurbarans (do you know his Virgin at the Met—do see it when you get to N. York again) the Goyas no longer hold my attention. On the way down we stopped an afternoon to see the cathedral at Albi (did you get a p.c. from there—it has the weight of Spain?) and on our return we stopped at Bayonne to see the late Goyas and found incredible Ingres fish—fruit—vegetable and flower markets—so far as I penetrate. Though before leaving at the end of the month when we go back to Paris I will go to see Picasso at Vallauris.

To Louise Taylor, England/MS Taylor

14 August 1952

26 bis rue Louis-Perrisol,
Cannes, Alpes-Maritimes

Dearest Louise—

Do you happen to have a good recipe for gaspacho—either the one they make in Málaga or Cádiz or Seville or Cordoba or Sevilla or Toledo or Segovia or any other heavenly spot. When I tried to find it in a Spanish cook book on the Siesper—the man who owned the bookshop said laughing lustily—Oh *señora* only peasants and foreigners eat it—we never do. Do you think this is true. At any rate no cook book mentioned it. So I just bought one that specialised on cakes! And it's an excellent one for pastries. If you ever go to Ávila there is the greatest baker ever was around the corner from the cathedral and you must taste *one* of *all* his specialties—including small *mille feuilles* meat patties. And think of me and I'll pray for your tummy! No we didn't get to Ronda. But have you eaten an artichoke omelette?

Claude Fredericks was briefly in Paris on his way home. He is going to spend three months a year at his mother's restaurant at Houston and nine months in Rome living on what she will pay him! We should go over to U.S. and make a fortune! Or do we prefer not to?

Fondest love
Alice

To Isabel Wilder, Hamden, Connecticut/MS Wilder

25 September 1952 5 rue Christine, Paris VI

Isabel dear—

It is a week today that I had the delight of seeing Thornton on his so brief visit to Paris and if no word has come to you from me before it's because the very naughty *femme de ménage* has not turned up since then. (She has said it is because she had a *crise cardiaque*—because a dear cousin died—because her daughter returned from the country and had been unprepared to enter a technical school—she—Madeleine—will give me a further choice when she finally comes back in three days!) So that I have had poor Basket to care for—he really shouldn't be left alone as his blindness not only makes him lonesome but embarrasses him when he stumbles against things. Then there has been a sad disquieting unexpected turn in the life of a friend which involved me—all to no purpose alas. And here finally a long contented breath—exhausted but free finally to tell you what a wicked person you are. Thornton called for me to take me to supper with such gaiety such Wilder cheer (you two of course but your brother Amos doesn't look so like you not to have the characteristic too) and then breathless but not speechless (that's Wilder too—isn't it) proceeded like a magician to produce from a valise more than a valise ever held before—real Kentucky whiskey—tins of lobster—nylon stockings (not that they took up any space—never have I seen such spiderweb fineness)—cigarettes. It was angelic of you to want me to have them but surely you know you are making the simple daily routine impossible when these wondrous unbearable life luxuries are on my shelves or in my drawers. They arent suitable to my age or station! And how to thank you and not scold you. And you not here to taste—to see—to smoke all these goodies. Well you will be for all—well except the cigarettes—will be found when you come. And the whiskey—well when Thornton comes back we'll open it and I'm going to taste it too and then it will be corked and put away in the furthest dark corner of a little hideaway shelf and when you are merry *we'll* have a nip. It will be a wild moment—wont it. And then Thornton took me to Casenares for supper and he said to me—Where is the lady. And I said you hadnt arrived yet but would soon—because it was what we both hoped. And I had delicious oysters—the best string beans of this year and a yellow peach which Thornton shared with me. And then we went to pick up his air ticket for the next morning and then he brought me back here and now he's in Venice and will be back here in a couple of weeks to meet Ruth Gordon (the stage is so casual with prefixes—they just arent used any more—in my youth there was Mrs. Fiske and Miss Rehan and Mrs. James Brown Pattes) and do you think he [Thornton] will really play in it. If he's not a great actor who is—I ask you. He'll have a tremendous success. (Little hope for Miss or Mrs. Gordon being noticed at all.) Of course in the back of my head there's "The Emporium" that isnt ready for rehearsal yet and the revised and extended Harvard lectures not published yet and of course neither of these two works should be postponed and what an abundance he has to draw upon and disperse in any direction he pleases.

Winter is on the way—only a couple of days into autumn and woolens are being worn and the heater is going. It isnt amusing—but though I may be less than agreeable I dont have colds ever—as everyone else does. The microbes arent heated enough to breed! And there are quantities of wool with which I cover myself—so many layers that *les blouses* are already not buttoning too easily.

The cook book is started and very soon bending over an imaginary stove will keep the temperature a-mounting and a-mounting.

Oh yes—there is Marian forgotten! She rang up two days before Thornton was to arrive telling me she was here with the Mr. Hauser of ready molasses and power through repose (as if we could believe in that) and she had read in that morning's paper that Thornton had disembarked at Southampton. What was to be done about that—what could be said. To hastily deny it was safe but what was to follow. Before there was time to decide on what course to choose Marian said she would ring up all the possible hotels and would let me know when she would come to see me. Which she didnt do. And I would so like to know if the largest diamond was still being worn though on what grounds would never be known. From Venice Thornton sent me two lines that he had talked with her upon his return to the hotel far until after midnight—which was over an hour and a half. What an inexhaustible restless disturbing and pouring of unemployable energy. Someone has just told me of a friend's having invented a lovely new word—underwhelmed. Poor Marian is indeed underwhelming. And with this I must close. You have dear Isabel my warmest thanks and appreciation for the beautiful gifts and my fondest love always.

Alice

Madeleine: Madeleine Charrière, Toklas' *femme de ménage.*

The Emporium: An unfinished play by Wilder. He had read parts of it for a benefit.

Marian: Marian Preminger, a friend of the Wilders.

To Samuel Steward, Chicago/MS Bancroft

24 October 1952 5 rue Christine, Paris VI

Sam dear—

The poor sweet old Basket who is blind and deaf fell off the roof to a roof some twelve feet below and in the dark I couldn't find him but the concierge rescued him and beside the shaking up Basket got off fortunately with a slight cut which is healing nicely. But with the misadventure he lost the little confidence he had been slowly achieving—so that he needs someone to stroke him frequently. Isn't it too sad that this is the way he is to end his days.

It is useless to say that this doesn't make the beginning of winter—autumn is winter here—more to be dreaded than usual. So that writing to you will cure me of all dismalness—you are not only sweet and good—when you are good—but gay and understanding and angelic. And the gadgets are exactly like you—all these things—and some of them with sharp edges too! And I refuse to do any kitchen work that doesn't include the use of at least one.

The weenie eggbeater with the long handle created a version of mayonnaise that is rapid and economical. Dry mustard—salt—pepper or paprika in quantity in a bowl with one entire egg. Beat with the Sam gadget eggbeater for three minutes—while you do something else with the left hand—then gradually add oil in the usual way—and when it is stiff lemon juice in small quantities. When a third of a cup of oil has been added stir in a dessert spoon of boiling water. Add a few tablespoons more oil. *Eh voilà.* As it will be more than you need for one time it can be put in the ice chest for the next day but no longer because of the white of egg. Cannot be made without the use of a Sammie gadget eggbeater. The knife sharpener is so good that it is put away every other day far from the kitchen—Madeleine would wear it out cutting Baskets meat and I would lose too many fingers.

Now you must hear about Francis. He is in Portugal and Spain with Mrs. Pacevitch but before leaving was in a good deal of trouble with Luis his *valet de chambre* boy friend whom he now says is his illegitimate son. Francis is saying he is going to recognise him so that he will inherit the title!! As yet this tale has not been confided to any English friends—who would put him straight about bastards inheriting titles. Just we Americans—who are indifferent about English honor—we rather like it. Of course Francis can be much less amusing than this. The tale before this had Francis involved with the Spanish ambassador—the Spanish minister of justice and a stray Spanish duke—in which a Frenchman said to Francis—Trust Miss Toklas—she has good judgement. And you may say here is where we wake up. And you would be right. We do but Francis doesn't—not he.

Jo Barry is going to lose his youth in U.S. He wont be disillusioned—only saddened. I give him a year. He says it is so wonderful he wants me to come over to share it!!! Not that I dont think the U.S. beautiful—next after Spain—and I do love my combies—but renaissance—*ah ne pas cela*—not in any country. Isnt the election exciting. I wade through all the speeches—pretty third rate as they are. Shouldnt there have been a woman candidate for the vice-presidency or did Mr. Truman's administration discourage them. The doorbell is ringing. Much fond love from

Alice

To Norman Holmes Pearson, New Haven/MS Virginia

1 November 1952 — 5 rue Christine, Paris VI

Dear Mr. Pearson—

The card has just come—it has excited me and gives me so much pleasure that it is impossible to realise that I am not going to be there to hear you. You have all my fond thoughts and hopes and wishes. If your address is printed would it be possible for me to have a copy—it would be sent on to Yale where everything concerning Gertrude's work goes—indeed belongs. Your interest over the years is a great comfort to me. Gertrude enjoyed the U. of Virginia enormously—its beauty and the few people she met. After her lecture a student—the president of the Poe Society?—gave her a key to his room. I found it in her coin purse—she always carried it—she was very proud of it—she said it made no difference that it was a Yale key and that there had been dozens of them.

Always cordially
Alice Toklas

Pearson: A professor of English at Yale, Pearson had become friendly with Toklas during Stein's American lecture tour. He had sent an announcement of a lecture he was to give on Stein's work.

To Carl Van Vechten, New York/MS Yale

24 November 1952 5 rue Christine, Paris VI

Dearest Papa Woojums—

Basket is no more—he died quite suddenly at the vets today—he had had a bad attack Friday evening. Early the next morning I took him over to the vets who found his condition serious but yesterday he was better and ate his three meals—the same today until he collapsed—he was in no pain after Friday evening. His going has stunned me—for some time I have realised how much I depended upon him and so it is the beginning of living for the rest of my days without anyone who is dependent upon me for anything.

The work with [Leon] Katz is interesting and diverting and the notes are so much fuller than I had suspected—I only had seen those made in connection with the diagrams—which are perhaps a twentieth part of the whole. After the questions are all answered —of which in four séances a tenth are finished—he will give me all his material to read. Katz has seen Francis Rose and gotten all Baby's letters to him to copy.

As soon as I discovered that there was no question of immediate publication or rather one of vague date my answers and asides (!) became of an indiscretion that will please you. It is to be hoped that Katz's work will not be open to even students for a considerable period. At first I kept saying—Not for the book just for you—until Katz said that it wasn't for immediate publication. Katz is ever so nice—gentle and sensitive and amiable. I asked him to go to the concert at which Fizdale and Gold were to play. They play like angels and were altogether adorable. They played Satie like no one ever had—Stravinsky as if they were a full orchestra—Bizet deliciously. I sent them a few lines to ask them if they have time to come to see me again. As I was about to take it to the post your *perfect* photographs of them came so I scribbled a line on the back of the envelope to them. You have caught the vibrating sensitiveness marvellously. Unquestionably you are the only person who has portrayed the beauty and pain of youth. You should have a show of the portraits of couples of young men. Let me know pronto that you are *en train* of arranging it. Love love love.

M.W.

Katz: Among the unpublished manuscripts that Stein had sent for safekeeping to the Yale Library in 1936 were the copybooks and numbers of loose pages for *The Making of Americans.* Included in the manuscript were a mound of small notebooks whose pencilled scrawls contained the writing notes and comments Stein made to herself, without any self-conscious concern for their bluntness. They were the notes from which Stein worked directly for most of her writings from 1902 to 1911. These notebooks were transcribed by Leon Katz, who subsequently spent several months (1952/53) in Paris drawing on Toklas' memories and recollections. An edition of "The Notebooks" together with Toklas' commentaries and Katz' annotations is to be published by Liveright.

To Samuel Steward, Chicago/MS Bancroft

19 December 1952 5 rue Christine, Paris VI

Sam dear—

About Francis—the story has become as involved as only his can. Frederica has been dragged into it for material and practical reasons—not at all certain that Francis is the father. With her permission Francis has recognised him—giving him French nationality for the moment—but when the boy L. comes of age he wishes him to take Spanish nationality so that he may have the Spanish titles Francis has the right to through his grandmother! Can you but so equal it. Bernard [Faÿ] says—Is one sure of the paternity—is his now legal father his father—his mother his mother! May we ask a leading question—the only one that interests me. When in the course of the story did Francis hear that the boy was his son—from the beginning—soon after—or just when—do you know. Frederica has had an operation in London and wishes Francis to be kept on this side of the channel so that she may have a quiet convalescence and a quiet recovery. It is my difficult task to accomplish this—but without knowing just where in the south Francis is wandering. It will be necessary to locate him and tactfully keep him where he is. If only he were here I'd menace him but you can't write that sort of thing! Fancy getting into one of Francis' stories at my age.

You knew didnt you that Dora Maar was doing a portrait of me—well she finished it and brought it to me a few weeks ago—there is some very fine painting in it and now the question is where to hang it. Of course I wont disturb any of Gertrude's hangings which means that Francis goes off the mirror back to the door on the left of the fireplace where it had been originally and the portrait takes its place on the mirror. What will Francis say. But there doesnt seem to be any other solution.

It isn't too cold but it's as moist as usual—the days are lengthening but imperceptibly—my *femme de ménage* says they lengthen in from the afternoon end! The French are so original. When once I remarked to Jeanne Roupelet that there were 13 moons a year she replied—Not in France!

Sam dear—a good happy year—good happy work—all my thanks and love.

Devotedly
Alice

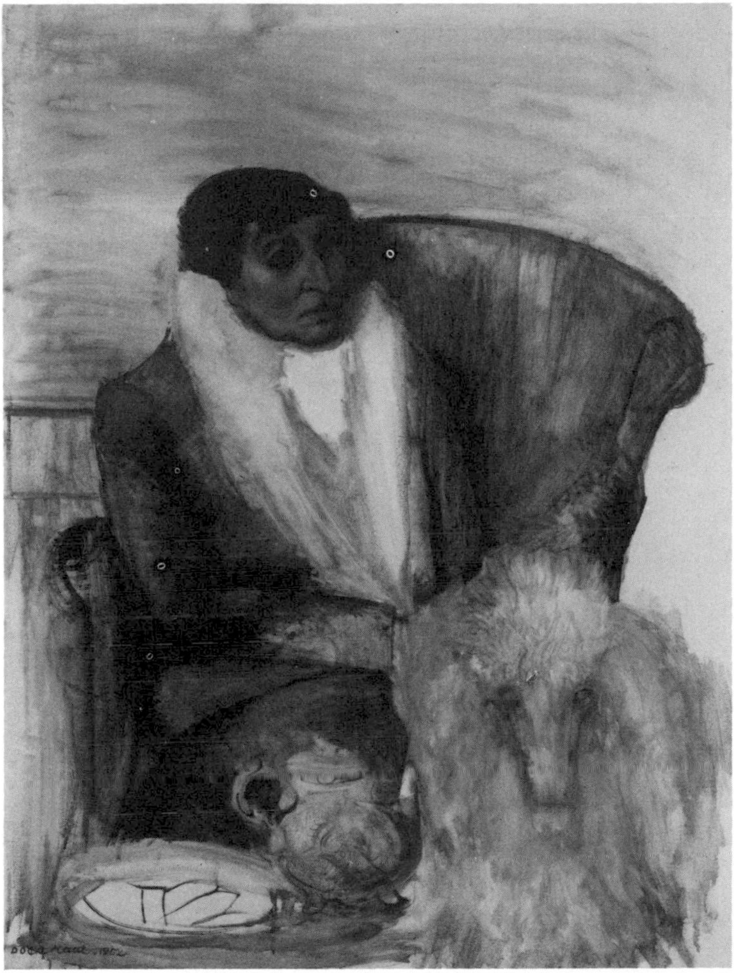

"PORTRAIT OF ALICE B. TOKLAS," BY DORA MAAR
OIL, PARIS, 1952

Courtesy The Yale Collection of American Literature, The Gertrude Stein Collection

1953

To Donald Sutherland, Boulder, Colorado
MS Sutherland

8 January 1953 — 5 rue Christine, Paris VI

Dear Donald—

It is two months since your first letter came. Always I think of you—and with much affection and deep gratitude. There have been too many difficulties to cope with the spineless state that extreme cold—deranged plumbing—and electricity—put one into and very humiliating it is to have to acknowledge one's complete inadequacy. It is no use saying that with warmer weather it will be different—just will it. In any case it is a good break to be writing to you and you'll pardon this complaining when you see how quickly you'll have disposed of it.

It commenced with my getting myself into deep water with a nice person named Leon Katz appearing with Gertrude's notes of 1906–1918—some 400 typewritten pages—mostly for *The Making of Americans* but including *Many Many Women—A Long Gay Book—G.M.P.* and the early portraits. He had C. Van V.'s and the Yale U. Library's permission to work upon them. Some of these notes are colossal—Gertrude at her clearest—fluent and with a brilliancy she usually avoided. Katz is sensitive with a sleuth-like gift of running down the answers to the many questions he has asked himself—is going over the notes line by line—word by word. Well and good. But in the notes are the preparations for the portraits of people who are to become the characters and her whole study of the two basic groups of characters. Still well and good enough for Katz. But Gertrude—alone with herself and the originals of her characters and portraits—could be of a frankness that makes indiscretion appear pale. Carl and Gallup hastily looked through the notes one afternoon after Katz had copied them with their permission and like Mr. Wilson in the winter of '16–'17 were surprised to learn how greatly Gertrude had exposed not only people she knew—friends—Leo and Sarah Stein—but herself. They—C. Van V. and Gallup—then said that Katz could go ahead —he had received a Ford Foundation grant by this time—on the condition that his book finished the sealed manuscript would be deposited at Yale Library—its publication date at its discretion. So Katz came over for me to supply names dates and places—not all of which was uncovering skeletons. There were however questions that bothered me—one answered by refusing to answer very much like an F.B.I. investigation. You now see that eagerness to see the notes of which Gertrude showed me only a small part—led me on. Nothing but really nothing could have stopped me. Now all this story does not come to an end with my dilemma. That will settle itself on its own. But the real question is—what did Gertrude intend for the future of the notes. She had them go to Y.U.L. with the manuscripts. They had been tied up and put away for thirty years and fairly certainly she never reread them. She had forgotten them as she had the *Q.E.D. (Things As They Are)* as she had Leo. (She told a man who said he had lately seen her brother in Florence—But no my brother lives in California. I only have one brother and he lives in California. After the man left I asked her why she had denied Leo's existence. Oh Leo—she answered—I have forgotten him—for years.) About the *Q.E.D.*—Haas who was here lately told me that when he wrote to her to ask if it should not be included in the bibliography Gertrude answered—No. And still Carl had it printed. But should one therefore suppose the notes would be printed too. And this question of the notes is what Pablo calls a bouquet by comparison with the bomb C. Van V. dropped in his last letter. Wouldnt it—he asks —be nice to have Katz do the introduction to the volume of poetry due in '54. Completely undone I answered at once that I had understood that it had been definitely decided that you were to do the preface to the volume of poetry—that Katz was in no way prepared to do it—that his period was up to '20—that this was his opinion. It is too absurd to keep me in ignorance—pop a question and then retire into another long silence. You'll understand I hope this having unburdened myself does not imply that you are being appealed to for either sympathy advice consolation. If it's been a bore to wade through the story please forgive me. Indeed a sharp word might buck me up.

About your lovely plans for this summer—nothing could be more cheerful for me than to dwell upon them. Surely they cant refuse T. Wilder's recommendation if they could [refuse] you without it. Those funds and grants and foundations have a higher law by which they act. The Guggenheim refused Gertrude's recommendation three times and Pablo's twice. T.W. is of a *genre plus sérieux*. So you and Gilberte should be coming over soon—that is in early summer.

Love to you both always
Alice

volume of poetry: Sutherland did the Preface to *Stanzas in Meditation and Other Poems* (New Haven: Yale University Press, 1956).

To Louise Taylor, England/MS Taylor

14 March 1953 — 5 rue Christine, Paris VI

Dearest Louise—

About the cook book. You wont think too badly if I throw myself upon you with a thud will you. This is the situation—Harper is willing to give me an advance and a contract when 30,000 words are in their hands (12,000 more to go) and they want the rest—40,000 more—for the first of May. You will see the grind this is. So one chapter (how pretentious for me to write that) will be devoted to recipes of friends—undoubtedly the only thing of merit in the deadly dull offering. The two Van Vechtens—Virgil—Pierre Balmain—Marie Laurencin—Francis—Dora Maar—Isabel Wilder—Virginia and Harold Knapik have consented and the Low-Beers and Brion Gysin will undoubtedly. Now may I add Red's Circassian Chicken and one from your inexhaustible supply with permission to use your names. And if like angels you do accept will you please be kind enough to tell me Red's name!!!! (ad infinitum). It is evidently not Redfern nor Redfield—but was he baptised Redvers or still something [else]. Let this conspiracy of silence herewith end. And does one use the "Colonel"—unless he is a general. *Grand Dieu* and I never knew it.

I havent been well—exhausted—and then that is now pernicious jaundice—a most beautiful but entirely misplaced Chinese yellow! neither grave nor painful—at first sleeping and dozing—now just sleeping—a nice highly unalarmist doctor says that all is well it only requires patience—quiet—a rigid but agreeable diet—all and every kind of food except no fats. Madeleine has come up to scratch wonderfully—competent and devoted—which makes me very ashamed of my past impatience. You have these details so that you are not to imagine anything. The only thing is when had you planned to come over because the doctor wants me to continue the rest cure for some time yet. I see no one—do not telephone—and am feeling better. Now dont think of me as miserable—neglected lonesome *et Dieu soit loué*—on the contrary the enforced rest is a luxury.

Are you having spring too. It is wonderful to get dried out. Even the flat has.

Endless love to you both always.

Alice

cook book: The Alice B. Toklas Cook Book (New York: Harper & Brothers, 1954) contained a section "Recipes from Friends."

Redvers: Although Toklas had known Redvers Taylor since the late 1930's she had always simply called him Red. The problem was not unique with Alice, as Colonel Taylor wrote: "My name Redvers is a West Country name and has caused confusion as long as I can remember. Redwing–Redfern–Redwin–Redmond–Redford–being just a few variations on envelopes received. The trouble is that at the beginning one doesn't bother to correct the mistake and then later you feel too embarrassed to do so." (Letter March 19, 1973, Taylor to Burns.)

To Carl Van Vechten, New York/MS Yale

24 April 1953 — 5 rue Christine, Paris VI

Sweetest and only Papa Woojums–

You are more darling than ever to understand my not writing more often but the difficulty in getting the miserable cook book finished has been a tormenting and a very unsatisfactory effort. My head is empty. It shouldnt have been so long. So I plod on despairfully. And this is not jaundice. The doctor thinks my recovery unusual for my age. New tests–blood etc.–will show–the result of the analysis will be ready today–if there are any new symptoms or after effects. And I'm getting stronger.

I did meet Georgia O'Keeffe. She came to see me–at very short notice–and I found her wholely delightful–rarely pure and beautiful in an unexpected way. I liked her a lot and am delighted you sent her.

About Baby's last words. She said upon waking from a sleep–What is the question. And I didnt answer thinking she was not completely awakened. Then she said again–What is the question and before I could speak she went on–If there is no question then there is no answer. And she turned and went to sleep again. Were they not a summing up of her life and perhaps a vision of the future—often they mean that to me and then they are a comfort.

All love to you both always.

M.W.

To Harold Knapik, Paris/MS Knapik

6 May 1953 5 rue Christine, Paris VI
Monday Evening

Dear Harold—

Your recipes are perfect—precise and seducing—and I thank you more than I can say for so generously giving them to me and for having taken time to work them out. Recipes are just as symptomatic as anything else of the person from whom they come and Gertrude liked to say that any and everything was symptomatic. In which case we would like to live and be judged by yours.

The sweets are my joy. With considerable discipline they are doing the diet no harm and me a world of good—and they are one more debt I owe to you. But not any more than the electricity bill Virginia says you paid long ago. There is a small cheque (Mougins) or two I am depositing in the "cellar" which will perhaps cover my share of the bill—half of which would be less than fair for me.

You don't half know what your note meant to me—it makes a great difference to my days.

Dearest love to you both always.

Alice

cellar: In 1948 Virginia Knapik, who was employed at the American Embassy, had declared Toklas to be her aunt. In that way it was arranged that Toklas could have commissary ("cellar") privileges.

To Nancy Harrison, Washington, D.C./MS Harrison

28 June 1953 5 rue Christine, Paris VI

Nancy dear—

The first thing to tell you is that you are a wonder to take your son's arrival so calmly—as if you were going to have your first son every other morning—you are of course not less excited than I am! are you? or are you not? Well—any whicher way you are a wonder and fill me with admiration—you set a new standard! Bless you. And all good things are three—a new home—a new son—and Gil holding down a big new job—and you have all three of you—that you do know surely—all my thoughts and loving good wishes. It is my greatest pleasure to think of your happiness and the lovely future you are sure to realise. Bless you all three!

And now you must tell me how you and Gil come to combine two such Republican names as Blaine and Harrison. It's a joke this—for of course they are easily explained—the one easily understood—the other inevitable—but when I saw them together on Baby David's first appearance it amused me—he will have to work hard in the other *political* camp to explain the combination. My family was all Republican (left over Civil War connection) and they voted for the one part of Baby's name and were all prepared to vote the other if they'd only been given the chance. Take as good care of yourself as you do of Baby—for a little while it's important that you should—later it wont make any difference if you are once more your own sweet reckless self.

All love to you all three always.

Alice

The coverlet will come along in time to put it in mothballs for next winter.

Nancy Harrison: Mrs. Harrison, the wife of Gilbert A. Harrison, was the great-granddaughter of Republican Presidential candidate James G. Blaine.

To Janet Flanner, Paris/MS Library of Congress

1 July 1953 5 rue Christine, Paris VI

Dear Janet—

A bad dream is no reason for taking your time—so at once may I ask for Madame L. Tisan's address which carelessly was thrown away after the very pleasant evening she spent with me. Not only is she charming but she knows the country Gertrude loved so well and when her husband called for her he turned out to be a comrade in the Resistance of one of our friends who had brought him to see us at Culoz—so it was a lovely evening you gave me and thanks for it—and so much else—Janet dear.

The dream was only bad and sad because it was vivid and unexaggerated. You and Noël [Murphy] refused to recognise me and I asked—Is it irremediable. And Noël answered—Irremediable—and you both walked out through a doorway. When I was awake "Did you know why" kept going through my head—but there was no answer. As Gertrude so rightly said there is none—in which case there should be no question. So it isnt possible now to ask if such a thing could happen. It couldnt—*could it.*

Forgive my taking your time.

Devotedly
Alice

To Janet Flanner, Paris/MS Library of Congress

8 July 1953 — 5 rue Christine, Paris VI

Janet dear—

You are too sweet to have sent me the wire. The dream of course couldnt be true but your message brought your precious friendship nearer. But you really are a wreckless and reckless soul to have wired.

As Gertrude always used to say as soon as you have disturbed someone you can find the missing object yourself. With the wire still in my hand there in the drawer with other addresses where it belonged was Madame Tenan's [*sic*]! Can you forgive me twice in one breath and not remember the disorder in which my life proceeds.

Thanks—thanks and more thanks. Love—love and more love.

Alice

To Annette Rosenshine, Berkeley, California
MS Bancroft

10 July 1953 — 5 rue Christine, Paris VI

Dear Annette—

Have I written you that there is a man working on the voluminous notes. Four hundred and fifty typewritten pages that Gertrude made from 1906 to 1914 when she was working at her study of characters—what she called the bottom nature of each kind. They are brilliant beyond words and are passionately interesting. It has been a marvellous experience to go over them with Katz. Then this month a book of some of the letters written to Gertrude is to be published. They have just sent me an advance copy—which I read last night. They revive old days and like all memories they make one sad at the same time that one is clearly conscious that one is fortunate to have them. Do you remember Max Jacob—later he spoke of those days as *L'Age Héroïque* and there was something heroic in their devotion to their work. Poor Max died at the hands of the Germans—a good deal of a martyr—saint and hero. I see Pablo once in a while—he is my near neighbor but is rarely in Paris. He came up for a show of his latest work last year and some of this year's. His painting is more beautiful than ever—the color has a new sensuous beauty and the composition is simpler and more complex—simpler in its fluidity and more complex in the relation of the forms. There were several landscapes of a freshness and vigor that only he can produce but a seated woman is perhaps his greatest picture. If the portrait of Gertrude was his first great picture I hope this new one isnt going to be his last. He is in vigorous health and has finally regained some of his early beauty that he had lost in his middle years. He is very sweet to me but I dont bother him. He knows I've had a real affection for him over all these years and he has *au fond* a loyalty of his kind for a very few old friends.

Roubina wishes the children to be American. It was she says Allan's intention. They certainly will not adapt themselves to American ways to say nothing of not appreciating American ideas. Michael is inflexible—Mimi more pliant and open minded. Roubina came to ask me a favor which it was impossible for me to grant and I have not seen her since—nor am I likely to again as she has already allowed some time to elapse. She is a good mother—according to her lights.

Yes Leo and Gertrude knew Gladys Deacon through Berenson years before she married. Gertrude thought her quality genuine enough but not interesting. Leo told me she once announced at a dinner party—Stein and I are the only two people who have had enough courage to [put] the manners they were born and

ALICE B. TOKLAS, SAN FRANCISCO, *ca.* 1905

Photograph by Arnold Genthe

ALICE B. TOKLAS, NEW YORK, 1935

Photograph by Carl Van Vechten

bred with completely aside and have therefore been able to live an unencumbered life.

All my best wishes to you—dear Annette.

Always affectionately
Alice

Gladys Deacon: An American who was studying painting in Paris in the early 1900's.

To Lawrence Strauss, Carmel, California/MS Bancroft

11 July 1953 — 5 rue Christine, Paris VI

Dear Laurie—

The cook book is finished and sent off and I'm coming to terms with my age—so that's that.

What you would most like to hear is news of Paris but of that unfortunately I have little to offer for I've not been about much—but of the Luxembourg Gardens it is of the very best—they are getting back to some of its old beauty and elegance—a great part of the balustrade and urns have been repaired—some replaced—the herbaceous borders are replanted but with commoner flowers. On a sunny day—and they are rare this year—all this with the children and their boats and the water make as lovely a picture as they did when you first knew them. And the Seine—just two blocks from here—is more beautiful than ever—particularly in the early morning—when the traffic is light and doesn't interfere with the river noises.

No a dog to succeed Basket offered too many difficulties—Paris is no place for a big dog unless one has a car to take him several times a week for runs in the woods and a small dog would have had to be the same kind as the wholly adorable devilish little Pépé —a Chihuahua—and naturally they are not found here.

Alice

Strauss: Laurie Strauss, a Californian, was in Europe from 1906 to 1911 studying voice. He was part of the Stein circle and lived at 58 rue Madame, the pension in which Annette Rosenshine also lived.

dog to succeed Basket: Stein and Toklas had had a succession of dogs: Basket (I), so named because Toklas thought he should carry a basket of flowers in his mouth, something he never did; Pépé, a chihuahua, the gift of Picabia; Byron, a gift from Sir Francis Rose; and Basket (II). Both Baskets were white poodles; Stein and Toklas had bought them because ever since Toklas had read *The Princess Casamassima* she had wanted one.

To Janet Flanner, Paris/MS Library of Congress

17 July 1953 — 5 rue Christine, Paris VI

Janet dearest—

You are so right in your vigorous attack upon dreams—as of course you are about everything else. (And it doesn't tire her—Gertrude used to say.) To the superficial mind they are real and so they impress me. In seventy years there havent been a half dozen remembered dreams—so you understand why the last one worried me. You are angelic—archangelic—seraphic—that is the correct consecutive order—isnt it—to console me as you have.

A très bientôt
Alice

To Louise Taylor, England/MS Taylor

24 August 1953 5 rue Christine, Paris VI

Dearest Louise—

Did you ever spend an August in Paris—no one but literally no one is in town—all the little shopkeepers have gone off travelling to foreign parts—Italy or Spain—Papa and Mamma and the children and one mother-in-law and aunt or cousin all piled into the car with the dog or cat. This with the strike made a quiet Paris—happily it has been cool. A woolen blanket and a ditto coat have never gotten put away in naphthaline! We are getting ready to leave within the week. Two of us fly but one must go by train to take the bags. We are at 27 paseo de Generalissimo—San Feliu de Guixols—Catalunia for the month of September. None of us have any money to travel or to stay longer—flying is the same price as railroad fortunately—for the railroad is anathema to me—as the métro is.

Yes Francis has a son. Dilkusha de Rohan wrote me—I hear Francis has presented you with a grandson. Isn't he wonderful—he thinks of everything.

Off to the locksmith for keys for my bags—for the million things for a summer vacation of a month! paper string ink needles cotton—a new thimble—I wear holes in the tip every few years!—What do seamstresses do!

Love always to you both.

Alice

1953

To James Merrill, United States/MS Merrill

5 September 1953 — San Feliu de Guixols, Spain

Dont tell me—my dear Jamie—that it was only a coincidence that I was rereading "The Wintering Weeds" when your postal came. It was sweet of you to think of me after what must have been my inexplicable silence. Its reason—a hideously long and tedious illness—is only now no longer valid and so post haste you are to hear how greatly I enjoyed and appreciated your poem—and still do. It has a disciplined flow a cool fine exterior music and a deep full movement and meaning. It is years of mellowed experience—older than the early poems without having lost their freshness—the only illustration is surprising but appropriate. *Enfin* it is a big step forward but a very natural development. It is not certain that I should add a wee criticism for it is a prejudice of mine—several unnecessary adjectives for what has already been described or implied. I like the poem a lot and I'm glad it is you who have written it.

I think of you often.

Alice

Merrill: Merrill, a poet, met Toklas through his friend Claude Fredericks.

To William Alfred, Cambridge, Massachusetts
MS Harvard

12 September 1953 — San Feliu de Guixols, Spain

Dear William Alfred—

San Feliu is a fishing village—it was once a smart bathing resort—but when sunbaths and living all day on the beach were discovered the beach was too small in which to deploy so the *beau monde* went away. The friends with whom I am visiting found a typical Spanish house with fourteen beds—one inadequate bathroom—three dining rooms and a hundred chairs. The garden has camellia trees and a fountain. It is all very amusing.

Orwell describes the Catalunians very well—that is he sees them as I do! *The Homage to Catalonia* gave me a lot of pleasure. *Prisoner of Grace* none at all. Joyce Cary has become a pet aversion—his real affection for sordid detail and commonness inspires a similar style which is thoroughly distasteful to me. Please do not mind this violence it gets it out of my system. It is as an American woman whom G.S. and I used to call Pomposa once said—It is important to know what you think. *The Power and the Glory* is my dish of tea. I enjoyed it immensely and am going to read more of the right Greene.

Basta—basta. No more—except my deep thanks and warm affection.

Alice Toklas

To Nancy Harrison, Washington, DC/MS Harrison

18 September 1953 San Feliu de Guixols, Spain

Dear Nancy—

If you havent heard from me in all this time—not even a thank you letter for sending me David's adorable photograph—it was because I was too ashamed to do so until your son's coverlet was finished. Last night it was—some five months too late but it goes to the post this morning. I can just hear David saying to you—Mummie what kind of a friend is she. Is she waiting for me to go to college. I love the photograph and see a resemblance in it to each of you—he already shows a mighty strong character and is probably already keeping you busy and guessing. His names suit him—he has their dignity and promise. *Enfin* he is a very sturdy and handsome boy and thank you—dear Nancy—for sending it to me.

Now here finally is Gil's favorite potato recipe.

Peel as many small potatoes of the same size. Wash drain and dry thoroughly. Into an iron pot half their weight in butter (it does use a considerable amount but what remains can be put aside and used again) and place over high flame. When the butter bubbles put the potatoes into it. The pot should be large enough to only have one layer of potatoes. ˣ As soon as the butter reboils and covers the potatoes remove from heat and allow the butter to completely cease bubbling—until it is still. ˣ Then replace over high heat and follow completely the first operation ˣ⁻ˣ. Repeat ˣ⁻ˣ once more—in other words it is cooled three times. Then replace over high flame to heat but this time the potatoes *simmer* in the butter for about ¾ hour. They should be golden brown—melting not crusty. A great chef at Chablis taught me—so you are his grandchild! Good luck. And not only for cooking potatoes but *for everything* for all three of you.

Fondly devotedly
Alice

To Mercedes de Acosta, United States/MS Rosenbach

26 September 1953 — San Feliu de Guixols, Spain

Dear Mercedes—

You are good to want to send me books—but there wont be time upon my return and later someone will bring me the Lindbergh and Tolstoi—the two which would interest me. The Kinsey reports are too hopelessly dull. As you say so rightly American sex is the most banal point from which to study our compatriots—it is so small a part of their character—and completely lacking in their subtlety and complexity. Sex is perhaps like culture—a luxury that only becomes an art after generations of leisurely acquaintance.

Why we scarcely approach either as individuals—it's mass propulsion still!

You are too flattering about my handwriting—your simile is too poetic for anything connected with anything I can produce. It was the necessity for economy of paper and time that forced the reduction in size—during the other war. It was very nearly as large as yours but lacking your magnificence and generosity. You see we share still one more taste. From the enormous correspondence Gertrude received it was easy to eventually gather knowledge of it as an exact science. So that when you have time and would be so good do tell me what you find in mine—dont fear to offend me by anything it may reveal—for after a long life and these years alone it isnt possible to ignore futility and failure. Heaven only knows why so much happiness came to me.

Always affectionately
Alice

books: Mercedes de Acosta had sent Toklas Charles Lindbergh's *The Spirit of St. Louis* (1953) and Alexandra Tolstoy's *Tolstoy: A Life of My Father* (1953).

To Carl Van Vechten, New York/MS Yale

25 November 1953 San Feliu de Guixols, Spain

Dearest Papa Woojums—

About Natalie's [Barney] doing an introduction. If my memory doesnt fail me—and alas it does all too frequently these days—the question has already been asked and the answer was—Admirable—except that she probably has never read any book of Baby's through. Perhaps if she accepted to do an introduction she might make the effort to do so. If it werent for this reason I think she would like to do it and would then do it very well. You know that Janet Flanner was never able to say that she had read a copy of the manuscript for which she did the introduction—so why not Natalie. Perhaps that is the way ladies do it best. Natalie on the whole would do a better piece than Janet. 1st she would stick to all the facts she possessed—second she knew Baby better—3rd she is genuinely witty—what Lady Cunard called "memorable sayings."

The stay here doing nothing in this air and sun has made me feel so well. I hope Paris wont destroy it. We have been indulging in all kinds of luxuries in the way of food—beside the usual good Spanish cooking which I prefer to any other—such paella and Mediterranean seafood as you cant half fancy. Grapes melons peaches and pastry out of this world—as you have taught me to say. Today our landlady took us to one of the largest cork manufacturies in the world which she owns. It manufactures practically all the champagne corks for the world—they go directly from this little port to every corner. She is immensely wealthy—inherited and made by her. She comes from Barcelona—where she lives—once a week to give it the onceover. She is going to take us to her country home to spend the day. "We" have been reduced to two—Harold [Knapik] and me—poor Virginia having been called by her chief to a conference at Rome and so losing almost two weeks of her vacation. Before she left we went in an autocar to Gerona to see the two magnificent churches there. It's a fascinating picturesque old town with seductive modern luxury shops—where Virginia picked up some bargains in leather. Last night the Habasques picked me up in their car and I dined with them at a hotel on a bluff overlooking the sea—a real Pinero setting—Mrs. Patrick Campbell coming on any moment—a few kilometers from here where they were spending the night. Good bye from San Feliu and your devoted—loving

M.W.

an introduction: Natalie Barney's Foreword to *As Fine as Melanctha* (New Haven: Yale University Press, 1954).

Habasques: Guy Habasque and his brother Robert had been neighbors in the Bugey.

1954

To Thornton Wilder, Hamden, Connecticut/MS Wilder

8 January 1954 | 5 rue Christine, Paris VI

Dearest Thornton—

There is no use pouring out to you an old woman's lot of woe—you'd disapprove of it and of me if I did—so *schwamm darüber* and try to understand and to forgive me. Everything got straightened out finally and in spite of the extreme cold it is quite comfortable. The pennies that finally were sent as royalties (!) are now royally paying for as near adequate heat as the radiator can produce—*assez.* But nothing was so warming so comforting as your dear Christmas wire—which came early as I was making coffee. You were seraphic or archangelic—which ever is the more important—to send it to me. I loved it and you more—more than the wire and more than ever. No matter how much my bad conscience hurt for not having answered two lovely letters the constant thought of you was almost as warming a presence as when you come into the room here.

Did Florida fix you up. Is the cold over—done with—disposed of so that it wont return. Is the ear better—if not cured. Do see a good specialist—a great one who can and will cure it—and send me as good as a Christmas wire to say that it is cured. That would be joyous news indeed.

Could you not let me have a copy of your homage to John Marin—when we were over we saw a lot of his work. He seemed to me to be a legitimate successor of Winslow Homer whom I adore—the great American painter isnt he. By the way, do you know the pictures—but recent—of Loren MacIver. They have been over here since last summer and are gay charming things. But she really paints extremely well and knows what painting is *(chose rare* amongst our compatriots) and what she is doing. Her earlier pictures—from photographs—were uncertain—too fanciful and decorative. They are returning to New York soon. If she gives a show of her last work do look at them.

Picasso is very sad. Françoise when she left him took their two young children and permits him to see them once a month. He loves children and adores his and it's a very feminine revenge Françoise is taking. She has all the pettiness of the *petite bourgeoise*—it is that that it means. Kahnweiler is doing the authoritative book on Picasso—as he did for Juan. This seems to be the little news for today.

Take good care of yourself—you are a worry—driving and thinking of something else--relaxing in moist climates—going on for days with insufficient sleep. So many horrors pop into my head—which is one way of saying I love you—Thornton dear.

Devotedly
Alice

John Marin: Wilder was preparing a commemorative tribute to John Marin, the American painter (1870–1953), to be delivered at a special meeting of the American Academy of Arts and Letters.

Loren MacIver: MacIver, an American painter, and her husband Lloyd Frankenberg (who had written the introduction to Stein's *Mrs. Reynolds* (New Haven: Yale University Press, 1952) were friends with a number of Toklas' friends, including Mercedes de Acosta. Although she knew their last name, Toklas repeatedly referred to MacIver and Frankenberg as the "Falkenbergs."

To Samuel Steward, Chicago/MS Bancroft

28 January 1954 5 rue Christine, Paris VI

Sam dear—

News! There really isnt any. Winter is winter and there is no use going into that—most particularly not the kind we've been indulging in these last few days—minus fifteen centigrade outdoors—plus twelve in the salon—but it is supposed to break today and the first airplane has flown over the house this very minute—which is more encouraging than any meteorological (too many syllables?) report. We indulge in so much foolishness—P.T.T. strikes and a proposed plan of having lanes around the Arc de Triomphe to relieve the traffic congestion and a mauve and green and red curly decorative cabbage—non-edible of course—which is the latest and still rare novelty. News of this is front page news like Hemingway's accident has been in *Le Figaro.* But when we were in Chicago and they shot a young gangster (Baby something) he was first page news because he was bad—the good boys were definitely not—they were second page news. Appalling this exaltation of crime in U.S.

Yes Katherine Anne Porter had a story back of her venom. She was quite an admirer of Gertrude's work previously to a visit of a well mannered good looking young G.I. whom I found talking to Gertrude on the sofa here. Do I read Katherine Anne Porter said Gertrude to me. Oh God no—said I—and left the room—whereupon the youth said—But you know my aunt. To which Gertrude answered—So very many people came to the rue de Fleurus. When the [Porter] article appeared in *Harper's* (you probably saw it amongst a book of criticism of K.A.P.) Joe Barry answered it and very well indeed but *Harper's* didnt print it but gave it to K.A.P. who wrote him an enormously long incredible letter in which "as an artist I" occurred several times ending with—In case on re-reading my article you find other things to object to please let me know before it is reprinted in a book of essays. Of course Jo didnt answer her but sent her letter to Yale Library. Dont repeat this please only you and Jo and Sutherland know the *bas fond* of K.A.P.'s point of departure.

Endless thanks and love from an appreciative and loving

Alice

Porter: Porter's articles on Stein and her exchange of letters with Donald Sutherland pertaining to this incident are published in *The Collected Essays and Occasional Writings of Katherine Anne Porter* (1970).

To Lawrence Strauss, Carmel, California/MS Bancroft

1 February 1954 5 rue Christine, Paris VI

Dear Laurie—

Do you remember taking me to hear Felia Litvinne at the Opéra Comique. You loved her you said because she wore a red red rose right there—and you pointed to a spot arms length from your waistline to indicate her. And Bertha Bardy (?) who danced so divinely. The memory is very vivid to me though the names may be wrong. Since those days there has been time for the Seine to overflow its banks several times.

One more reminiscence and then good night. Do you remember Picasso's Fernande. Well a young professor was translating Guillaume Apollinaire and writing a preface to the volume and as Marie Laurencin refuses to talk of that part of her past I looked up Fernande and she came here to meet the translator. It was the first time in twenty-five years that I saw her. She had grown enormous—like several bags of potatoes piled one on top of another—but still retaining vestiges of her old beauty and grand manner. From time to time I find pupils for her—but she bores them with her egotism.

Affectionately
Alice

young professor: Roger Shattuck, who had translated *Selected Writings of Guillaume Apollinaire* (1950), was in Paris working on *The Banquet Years* (1955).

To Princess Dilkusha de Rohan, London/MS Texas

1 February 1954 — 5 rue Christine, Paris VI

Dear Dilkusha—

It is a complete misunderstanding of my financial situation under which you are laboring. Perhaps it's belated symptoms of jaundice on my part that made me sound [so] to your vivid imagination—if it has ears—that could allow you to suppose me in want as Mildred Aldrich was. Not at all—at all—at all. I have the right to sell a picture or pictures for my maintenance. That does not happen to be a thing I would care to do. So please put [away] your idea of coming to my rescue by having a subscription taken for my benefit or turning the flat into a tourist center or any other equally absurd project. Frankly—my dear Dilkusha I would be very angry indeed with you if it wasnt certain that you have allowed your too lively imagination and sympathy to run away with you. You'll be forgiven only—but freely—if you will tell me you have completely misunderstood the situation—that [if] you have spoken to anyone about it you will at once correct it—and that you forget the whole episode—even if you believe it to have been entirely my fault—

which it wasnt. After you have let me know that this is understood we'll not refer to it again.

In spite of all!

Devotedly
Alice

Dilkusha de Rohan: Dilkusha de Rohan's father was a British Army officer, her mother was an American. She was born in India and given the name of Dilkusha after a village near which her father was stationed. She married a Prince de Rohan, an Austrian, who was killed by smashing his car up against a tree.

Mildred Aldrich: An American writer who lived in France and was a close friend of Stein and Toklas'. In the 1920's Stein had organized a fund to provide an annuity for Aldrich.

To James Merrill, United States/MS Merrill

22 February 1954 5 rue Christine, Paris VI

Dear Jamie—

Bravo for the three act play—it pleases me that you have tackled it—a long breath is a test and you will have achieved something from the attempt—but naturally I'm not hoping for less than something that satisfies you. I expect a great deal from you and your gift. Tithonus—was it not he who was changed into a cricket —and for what reason—oh dear I'm like a friend of Gertrude's who said that she was woefully ignorant—wasnt it amazing that she got on so well.

Good luck to you and to Tithonus.

Always fondly
Alice

Jane Bowles' play would appear to have affected the audience strangely—no one agreed and that may have been the producer and actors' fault more than Jane. She is a strange creature.

play: Merrill's play, *The Immortal Husband,* was given an off-Broadway production in 1955.

Jane Bowles' play: In the Summer House (1954).

To Brion Gysin, Tangier, Morocco/MS Gysin

24 February 1954 — 5 rue Christine, Paris VI

Dear Brion—

Thanks for your letter though I cant say I care for its news. It is so beastly to be harried—especially when one is young—one's senses are blunted when one is old. What difference does it make then whether one has more or less peace of mind—the only thing [that] counts is the creature comfort that comes—if it does—from not being congealed.

My only drag with Unesco is through the sister of Natalie Barney —I know her slightly—it would have to be through N.B.—who is in the *midi* but returns early next week. Let me warn you— Unesco's investigation of your credentials covers a vast area of your public and private life—early education—later education— they appreciate university degrees and honors—political opinions and affiliations and frequentations. Will your having been amongst the Arabs help. They put a friend through this—everything was smooth sailing—he was all but accepted when they sprung the private life. When he balked because he said that there was no part of his past that he would deny or change Unesco dropped his candidature and none of us ever knew whether that past held anything blameworthy or not. Let me know where one brings pressure and I'll do all I can.

Ever devotedly
Alice

To Mercedes de Acosta, United States/MS Rosenbach

24 February 1954 — 5 rue Christine, Paris VI

Dear Mercedes dear—

When I asked you to tell me about Jane Bowles' play it was not to ask you to take time to analyse it in detail as you did but what you had to say fascinated and interested me beyond words—for it was an exact portrait of Jane herself and as I suspected the play is nothing but a projection of herself—ergo neither she nor the play are adult. As you so very clearly saw. What in her seemed based on fear—her strongest realist emotion—you have put your finger on—fear of taking an adult attitude to her weakness—more particularly even fear of facing adult responsibilities. If mistakenly I mistook the reason of her fears the moment you gave the right one we were agreed. And I was relieved for it had worried me a bit—of course it diminishes one's interest in her to have the answer. Years ago we took our nice intelligent Bretonne servant to keep house for us in Spain. As she was lonesome we found a French maid who was working in the household of the French consul and saw that they saw each other as often as suitable. Jeanne was pleased with the new acquaintance but not overjoyed. After spending a long [evening] together Jeanne returned and observed—I didnt know why I didnt like her more but now I know —*Elle est sotte.* If I wasnt shrewd enough to find it out for myself—I do thanks to you know now what worried me and why there could be no real pleasure in knowing Jane.

The freeze is over—for the moment. It is rainy and warm—with moments of spring—the sap is running in the chestnuts.

Fondest good wishes for the book and love to you always.

Alice

To William Alfred, Cambridge, Massachusetts
MS Harvard

4 March 1954 5 rue Christine, Paris VI

Dear William—

Your Bill Alfred has precipitated me into my addressing you thusly—another meeting and it would have happened naturally. It is the young of this generation who can so easily name you Bill. So what we eventually would have arrived at has now happened. It does not embarrass you I hope.

Enfin it is a pleasure to tell you that I enjoyed your letter—all except the news that your play has been postponed—but if it is quite definitely being produced in October it [is] not so long to wait. It will be exciting for me to hear about the performances. What will it be for you. You will remember how actable it seemed to me. You will supervise the rehearsals—so that they do not hunt for hidden meanings but just speak your beautiful words clearly and the audience will be enthralled. That is what my wish is for the production of your play.

How you can work with interruption is beyond my understanding—Gertrude was forced and gradually enjoyed working after two in the morning—but after long years of this the doctor found that the late afternoon and early evening walks in no way replaced those of the early morning. It was then Gertrude commenced working in the late morning and early evenings. This is to warn you. Anyway next autumn you will have a room whose windows will not betray the light in which you are working to the outside world.

Gratefully and affectionately
Alice

To Carl Van Vechten, New York/MS Yale

23 March 1954 5 rue Christine, Paris VI

Well—dearest Papa Woojums—

What do you think is going to happen to me. I am going to fly to Italy on April Fool's Day—for ten days. Rome Florence and Italy —with a fat fee by the editor of the *House Beautiful*—she wishes to *consult* with me! blah blah! about American architecture and household furniture in 1900. Do you suppose there isnt anyone else alive whose memory goes so far back. At any rate I'm very pleased to go and to return with a fat check.

Do you know a Sybille Bedford—she has written a delightful book *The Sudden View*—about a year she and Esther Arthur spent in Mexico. She is a strange and charming creature—unfortunately for me she doesnt live in Paris

There have been a great many people here. Antonina Vallentin who has just done a life of Einstein. I think she would have liked to do Baby's. (She has done Greco's and Goya's and Leonardo's.)

Have you ever made smoked salmon scrambled eggs. It is very nice—the salmon must be soaked overnight in milk.

Natalie [Barney] has returned and came to see me with Marie Laurencin and Jean Denoël.

Frederica Rose brought the Baronne de La Grange whom we used to meet at Bernard's.

It is no longer cold but it rains—growing weather for those who have gardens!

So much love to Fania and to you from

M.W.

To Louise Taylor, England/MS Taylor

30 May 1954 5 rue Christine, Paris VI

Dearest Louise—

About the Italian trip. It was lovely. In Venice I loved the light the food and food shops and the Venetians—the canals and the outside of the palaces bored me. Five days there and then by automobile to Itri (do you know the palace there)—to Padua (ah the Giottos bowled me over)—and to six lovely days in Florence—so much more wonderful than I remembered—in spite of the devastation the beastly Huns perpetrated—over a much greater area than I had realised. But it was wonderful to be there again and to find the Florentines so beautiful and dignified. And oh such food!—And such spring gardens and objects and architecture and furniture. Well well you see I lost my head and my heart most completely—except alas to Fiesole of so many happy memories—changed beyond recognition. There were in the little square dozens and dozens of sight-seeing buses from Denmark and England and Sweden and France to say nothing of Italy with thousands of automobiles all belching their occupants compactly over the hillside. It was frightful. When finally the dear old Casa Ricci was located and I saw its façade all covered with stucco and balconies and gingerbread and the terrace with a pitiable pond of goldfish replacing the 15th century well—I fled. It was heartbreaking. Came home by train to Milan and thence by air. Now

HARRIET LEVY AND ALICE B. TOKLAS, FIESOLE, 1909

Fiesole of so many happy memories.

it's the usual routine and so cold. At eleven o'clock I will turn on the radiator!

Be a good girl so that you get all well nicely soon. Lots of love to you both.

Alice

Fiesole: All the Steins spent about six months of the year at Fiesole. In 1908 Michael Stein rented the large Villa Bardi; before that the Steins had all stayed at the Casa Ricci. In 1908 and 1909 Harriet Levy and Alice Toklas rented the Casa Ricci. In later years Gertrude and Alice would spend their days walking through the hills, visiting museums and libraries.

To Isabel Wilder, Hamden, Connecticut/MS Wilder

11 June 1954 5 rue Christine, Paris VI

Dearest Isabel—

How are there enough hours in a day not to get hopelessly overwhelmed—exhausted and dazed by the rush of events. Your Marian visitation is the maddening climax of the daily tangle. Lately Francis Rose has been in several unpleasant tangles about their flat. Frederica who is admirable—competent—and devoted had straightened out the difficulties following the flat being sold over their heads—only saving two small rooms on the fifth floor where Francis was looking forward to painting after some improvements were to be made. She went down to Corsica to finish a long overdue book and for which she had had a substantial advance. Whereupon Francis got himself involved with the telephone company for an instrument and number which the British embassy secured for him personally in '45 and which the man who bought his flat refuses to give up. The telephone company is the government. It threatens to take his identity card away from him. He had a plan to steal the instrument! Then he was paid for a picture with a cheque on a bank where there was no deposit. A crime in France to pass such a cheque. An order for a portrait was not approved of—all of which he brings to me to solve—so it goes—he is a sweet fantastic thing who has an abounding energy and wears me out at nearly double his age.

Which brings me to what I've wanted to say to you well over a month. First to thank you *de tout mon coeur* for your dear wire for my birthday—it was a warm comforting note on a bleak occasion and to ask you—if I am still here—next year to just pass it over in silence. You will understand how one feels about hanging on—though you wont know it happily—because you will always be so useful—so needed—so indispensable—no negative qualities these.

The really good thing to tell you—is the stupendous retrospective of Picasso's early pictures 1900–1914. The museums of Moscow and Petersburg sent half—the rest came from private collections in Paris—ten from here—leaving large bare spots in the room and for three months. The pictures are beautifully presented—hung with great intelligence and taste. I had tickets for the small press *vernissage* and Harold Knapik took me. We came away weak and limp.

Devotedly
Alice

To Donald Gallup, New Haven/MS Gallup

12 July 1954 — 5 rue Christine, Paris VI

Dear Donald—

You will have seen in your newspapers something of the excitement we have all been having with Tschoukine's daughter's claim to her father's pictures that were being shown by the Soviet government at the Pensée Française. But what you probably did not learn was that she claimed the picture no. 10 in the catalogue—which was one of the ten loaned from here. It is the long narrow one that hangs in the *petit salon* and has Russian letters in it and it is for this reason that she claims it! But there is Kahnweiler who will testify this afternoon that he sold it to Gertrude in 1914 and that it has never left her flat. And on the back of the canvas is stamped "This picture belongs to the estate of G.S."—which I stamped upon all the pictures when I was frightened Allan forcibly would take one or more to sell for his own needs. The Russians took the pictures of T. to their embassy to protect them—the ten from here are still at the Pensée Française—who asked me if I wished to remove them. Kahnweiler advised me not to. If a favorable decision is rendered at once—which it easily may be—the show will open again. The pictures are probably well protected by two French laws—so my lawyer tells me—but the decision may drag. What a foolish person Madame T. de Kellner is. It has caused almost as much excitement as *l'affaire Indo-Chine*—that is in Paris. It is useless to tell you how considerate and efficient Kahnweiler has been.

Having extravagantly indulged in a Parker 5 I am plagued to death in using it—must it be discarded or must a terrible scene take place to have it put in order. Something better than this struggle must be arrived at. Do drop in as you suggest. Oh it would be too wonderful. I am putting an extra good bottle of brandy aside. Do come and have a nip.

Love to you—dear Donald—
Alice

claimed no. 10: Picasso's *Woman With Mandolin (With Russian Letters)*, Paris 1914, now in the collection of Mr. and Mrs. David Rockefeller. Kahnweiler has explained that Picasso took the letters from posters of the Bolshoi Opera which the Russians had used to repack paintings Kahnweiler sent to Russia for exhibition. (Interview with Kahnweiler, July 17, 1973.)

To Henry Rago, Chicago/MS Indiana

10 August 1954 | 5 rue Christine, Paris VI

My dear Rago—

You are so right about the overemphasis at the U. of Chicago of rationalism—it is of course itself all wrong but to teach it with conviction is unpardonable. It is a comforting thought that you are leaving all this beyond you. You know Gertrude had a frightful row with Mr. Hutchins in '34 about the answers they expected from their students in their philosophic discussions. He and Mr. Adler asked her to preside at one of their meetings and when it was over the latter asked me—How does she get them to talk so freely. It was necessary to answer that she herself was not certain [of] the answer to some of their questions—that she had a good deal of elasticity—admitting more than was simply demonstrable. Happily your new work will be along other lines than the old was. And it is a pleasure to know that the new poetry is coming on so well. It ought to get published—there is obviously too much bad poetry—as well as bad painting in U.S.

Affectionate good wishes to you both.

Alice Toklas

To Louise Taylor, England/MS Taylor

19 September 1954 | Lou Fougou, Grasse, Alpes-Maritimes

Dearest Louise—

We've been having continuous sunshine since we came back—now Saint Matthieu's Day we're to have rain—possibly a hailstorm before night—which will spoil one day's jasmine gathering—the season lasts until the middle of next month. The snails are plentiful and excellent—small and very tender and prepared with chopped onions and tomatoes cooked so long they are quite thick and garlic of course. And *aïoli* with them too. Harold Knapik has built—with tiles and stones as a background—means of cooking on a spit. When I get back I'm going to try using more gas and keeping the oven door open and seeing if that wont improve roasting that is baking meat. Yes the milk here is unusual—nothing like it since U.S.A. Most French milk is too generously watered. Harold has just finished Faulkner's *A Fable* so I'm getting at it. Hope to finish here and send you it—but down to Grasse—too many far too many people and such strange ones—where do they come from. The only human beings were such nice young clean American sailors from a war boat in the harbor. I overheard one ask "Didnt someone say there was a cinema in this town." "Yes" was the answer "there are several but they are all in French." They sit at café restaurants drinking beer and asking oh so politely for *"frites s'il vous plait."* They are very different from those we used to see.

How smart your flat will be all cleaned. I envy you—5 rue Christine is quite disreputable—the carpets and curtains are beyond repair—what I can afford isnt enough to show or feel—it will have to see me through as it is. Do you remember how pretty it was all new and clean.

Good luck for the little red apple crop. Keep getting better and better.

Fondest love to you both always.

Alice

To Donald Gallup, New Haven/MS Gallup

12–19–21 October [1954] 5 rue Christine, Paris VI

Dear Donald–

Your letter of the twenty-seventh and the first copy of the book were here upon my return—alas that it should only be today that there has been a moment to thank you with all my heart. It is a beautiful piece of bookmaking. Natalie's [Barney] foreword is even better in print than in manuscript—but it's not necessary to tell you that the pieces selected and their arrangement move me deeply. Gertrude always used to say—Let's put them first into groups and then break them up by contrasts—which is just what you have done. You and Carl have done such marvels because of the purity of your purpose which permits inspiration to flow unimpeded. Thank you—dear Donald. Are dust covers ever interesting? I dont think so. They perhaps protect the book when it's at the bookshop. I always take them off at once and get rid of them—they never have anything to do with the book.

Upon my return I found the Wilders here. Thornton from the successful performance of his play at the Edinburgh Festival and a two weeks lecture tour of the German universities. The play has been so successful in the provinces that the theatre in London where it will go on at the beginning of the month has been engaged by the year. In the meantime Thornton has retired to Aix-en-Provence where he will be joined by *two* ladies—and where he will write another play. While he was here we saw the two big picture shows—which I had already seen several times—the Cézanne and the Picasso—which will be over Monday so that finally the pictures will be returned. For the show they put *L'Étudiant* under glass. You will remember how the collage was deteriorating. Kahnweiler thought it and the early dark Gris still life needed serious and immediate attention. Both Gertrude and Picasso several times spoke of this and always ended by saying—not in our time—let the museums do that. Now la Maison de la Pensée Française did it and is returning the picture under glass—and I am not removing the glass. I only wish it would happen to the Gris!

Before we left Grasse I took the Knapiks over to Vallauris to see Pablo. It ended with our lunching with him and spending a long and happy day—at his home—in the chapel that he has just decorated with two wonderful decorations—a third smaller one to follow his greatest achievement—of incredible beauty and power. P. is as gentle and sweet to me as ever—but he himself is calmer more content and less feverishly active than he has been for years. I suspect getting rid of Françoise—which was a shock and losing the children was certainly a blow—was on the whole a great relief. He has a new lady—official? I dont know. It looked just out of a bare box! She is a well bred—well educated bourgeoise of about 26 with fine eyes but no particular looks. She is in full possession but is it lasting? Is she sampling life with P? Paulot is living permanently with his father and admits he would prefer living in Paris—living with his father has done him a world of good. Olga is slowly dying in a clinic at Cannes. She says Pablo has been very good to her in every way.

I hope you werent as shocked as I was by the notice in *Time* of the hashish fudge. I was also furious until I discovered it was really in the cook book! Contributed by one of Carl's most enchanting friends—Brion Gysin—so that the laugh was on me. Thornton said that no one would believe in my innocence as I had pulled the best publicity stunt of the year—that Harper had telegraphed from London to the Attorney General to see if there would be any trouble in printing it! [Simon Michael] Bessie—Harper's present editor was here—and the lunch cooked was a triumph of ineptitude—*petit malheur* and an immobilised right hand!

Alice

book: As Fine as Melanctha (New Haven: Yale University Press, 1954).

his play: Wilder's *The Matchmaker.*

a new lady: Jacqueline Roque, later Madame Jacqueline Picasso.

To John Lucas, Paris/MS Lucas

1 December 1954 Tours, France

It was kind of you to send me the p.c. of Dali's jewelry. He is always what a little boy called a typical type whose tricks become stale.

A.B.T.

Lucas: A poet and professor of English, Lucas and his wife Pat had met Toklas in the early 1950's. They saw her regularly either in Paris or Rome.

typical type: A remark attributed by Toklas to Allan Stein.

1955

To William S. Byler, New Haven/MS Virginia—Barrett

9 January 1955 5 rue Christine, Paris VI

Dear Mr. Byler—

Thank you for asking me to contribute to the number of *The Yale Literary Magazine* to be devoted to Henri Matisse.

It is many years since I last saw Matisse—he had misconstrued—not understanding English—what Gertrude Stein had written in appreciation of Madame Matisse's beauty—and she was very beautiful. So that there was no further acquaintance with him. But that is not a suitable subject to enlarge upon. I shall try to find something to make evident my appreciation of the great painter he was —and send it to you within a fortnight.

Sincerely
Alice Toklas

my appreciation: For the Fall 1955 issue of *The Yale Literary Magazine* Toklas contributed an essay, "Some Memories of Henri Matisse: 1907–1922." In the *AABT* Stein had compared Madame Matisse's beauty to that of a horse.

To Ralph W. Church, Santa Barbara, California
MS Bancroft

25 January 1955 — 5 rue Christine, Paris VI

Dear Church—

About the pen and ink portrait of Gertrude by Tonny—after going through everything here and not finding it I came to the conclusion that it was amongst the things I loaned to the Allan Steins immediately after Gertrude's death. Allan as you may know died several years ago and his widow has refused to return to me what was loaned to them. She is neither an easy nor a pleasant person to deal with. I have not been in communication with her for some time. My lawyer says it would require a lawsuit to force her to return what she is keeping illegally—naturally—and for obvious reasons—I am not undertaking that. I am very sorry that I cannot send you the Tonny portrait—that I should have given you a false hope.

You are kind to be so indulgent about the cook book. It was undertaken solely to earn some pennies.

The news is that the Seine is too high. The cellars are filled with water. And that there is to be an important retrospective of the work of Picasso in May at the Louvre in honor of his seventy-fifth birthday.

And forgive my being a disappointment to you.

Warm and fond good wishes to you always.

Affectionately
Alice Toklas

Tonny: Kristians Tonny, a Dutch artist whose work had briefly interested Stein.

To Annette Rosenshine, Berkeley, California
MS Bancroft

2 February 1955 5 rue Christine, Paris VI

Dear Annette—

Matisse's death probably awoke as many memories in your mind—or even more—than it did in mine. His health was so precarious for several years that when it did come it was no shock. Mrs. Walter Haas who came to see me once several years ago has just sent me a line to tell me that she and a friend are giving the portraits of Mike and Sarah to your museum of art as a nucleus for a collection of pictures in memory of Mike and Sarah. It is a beautiful and generous *geste*. Mrs. Haas is to be in Paris soon and then I'll hear more of the detail. *The Yale Literary Magazine* is preparing a special number "Homage to Henri Matisse"—the proceeds to found a scholarship for a French student at Yale. Amongst the people asked to contribute they asked me to send some early memories of Matisse. They are indeed the only ones there are—for I hadnt seen him for over thirty years. He disapproved of Picasso's cubism—it was difficult to find suitable material—finally I got enough together and sent it off saying that they should cut anything that they found useless.

I believe Madame Matisse is still alive—they were separated for years and years. She and Margot were deeply involved in the Resistance and a few months before the liberation were caught by the gestapo. Madame Matisse was sent to prison in France but Margot was sent to Germany—whence she returned in a bad physical condition. We met her at a dinner party and Gertrude drove them home later. Margot was very sympathetic. Madame Matisse's excellent training was obvious. Later she came to see me and she showed some of that heroic quality of Madame Matisse.

From the ubiquitous Mrs. Sprigge I heard of her visit to you—she can write but can she read. When she left here she had read very little of Gertrude's work. She is a successful person if you accept her standards.

Not for another two months will Harpers give an account of the sale of the cook book—they write that it has sold well. It would be nice if it would permit a two month's vacation—everything is so frightfully expensive here—but that is true the world over. Have you read Louis Bromfield's *A Remedy for a Tired World.* His is not an inspired vision—but he is nicely practical so that he may have something to say that would make encouraging reading—he has been deeply interested to the exclusion of everything else for many years now in the problem of the exhaustion of farming land in U.S.

I hope you are well and send you many warm good wishes.

Ever affectionately
Alice

Margot: Matisse's daughter, Madame Marguerite Duthuit.

To Donald Gallup, New Haven/MS Gallup

13 February 1955 5 rue Christine, Paris VI

Dear Donald—

I havent seen the catalogue of the Cone show but I know most of the pictures they have. *The Blue Nude* was over the sofa at the rue de Fleurus—in the division of the pictures it fell to Leo who exchanged it (with other pictures) for a Renoir. Leo's portrait was a gift from Picasso to Leo. At the division he [Leo] didnt want it (he was bitter even about that) so it remained at the rue de Fleurus until Gertrude sold it to the Cones. You know Gertrude's Uncle Sol in N. York offered when she went East with

Bertha to buy the photograph she had of her grandmother (his mother)—Gertrude was outraged and said—One does not sell one's grandmother's photograph. If later she sold her brother's portrait she would have answered that that was a very different matter indeed—which indeed it was. How could she hope to forget him if he hung on the wall. Bye the way it was very resembling to him as he was when I first knew him.

Fondest love to you—dear Donald—from

Alice

Cone show: In connection with the publication of the *Handbook of the Cone Collection,* the Baltimore Museum of Art mounted an exhibition of works left to it by Dr. Claribel and Miss Etta Cone. A number of the pictures in the Cone Collection once belonged to the Steins: Matisse's *The Blue Nude* (1907) and Picasso's *Portrait of Leo Stein* (1906), among others.

To Louise Taylor, England/MS Taylor

24 February 1955 — 5 rue Christine, Paris VI

Dearest Louise—

The clipping about Picasso's behavior to Olga shocked me—it is quite false and shocking to read at this moment. May I tell you the facts. Picasso did leave her but there were good reasons. They should never have married—Russian and Spanish temperaments are too opposed—they havent the same approach. Eventually Picasso couldnt work—she poor thing couldnt believe that every one didnt feel like Russians feel. He made a very generous allowance for her and the boy to live on. She was unhappy of course but so was he. Gertrude and I continued to see Picasso and did not see Olga again—until Gertrude met her on the rue Dauphine—this was just a very short time before Gertrude died. And then Olga came to see me and though I still feel she had acted foolishly I was filled with pity and sorrow for her. It is not true that they didnt meet after the separation—they met from time to time. When she was sick Pablo would go to sit with her—send for great specialists—insist upon trained nurses and so on. The portraits he painted of her were shown at exhibitions—of course they were not for sale—he kept them as he has many of his pictures. The boy grew up self willed—wild—was in Switzerland. Picasso wouldnt let him earn his living—he had no particular gifts—except mimicry if it is one. During the war he went back to Switzerland and worked as a volunteer naturally—for the Red Cross—which when the war was over offered him a paid job but Picasso answered: "It is I who earn the living for the family." Olga and I saw each other so it was necessary to tell P. that we did. He said nothing so I repeated she was an angel to me when I was first alone. She—said P.—*c'est bien elle*—when one has need of her she is there. When the franc devaluated he increased Olga's allowance way beyond the difference of the new value—each time. She was not in hiding these last years but in the best *maison de santé* in Cannes—very luxurious—where he and Paulot went to see her. These last four years that my vacation took me to the south I would go to see her there—a nice frail thing with her lovely eyes—she would wear her lovely jewelry—heavy jewelled bracelets which Picasso of course had given her. The last time I saw her in October she was wasted but still lovely and she was content because P. was so good to her. Hers was a typical Russian tragedy. The son does drive his father's car—it is the one thing in life he enjoys—and P. encourages it—for he wont speed recklessly with his father as he would if he were alone. And poor P. has no desire to marry again. The clipping said he couldnt divorce because Olga was a Greek Catholic and her church doesnt permit divorce. The Orthodox Church not only admits divorce but its priests marry and divorce. P. is of course a R. Catholic—he never wanted a divorce. It would surprise me greatly if he married again. Why should you have to hear all this—goodness knows. I love Spain and things Spanish and Picasso!

So much love to you both from

Alice

To Princess Dilkusha de Rohan, London/MS Texas

6 March 1955 5 rue Christine, Paris VI

Dear Dilkusha dear—

You put a chill down my spine with your accident. Havent you learned yet that it isnt age but lack of experience that makes us fall off ladders or have radiators fall on us. Keep off ladders for *all the rest of your life*—dont bother what has accumulated up on high or behind radiators. Dust the objects—clean the silver if you must and forget the rest. That's what this winter taught me and it's a satisfactory course of action. Rinse the dishes in boiling water—scrub the bathtub and let the rest go—as a matter of fact it doesnt go anywhere! Is this understood and accepted.

There is new evidence of La Sprigge's unworthiness—colossal—but too long—but it puts her *hors concours*. No more to add now—and nothing new to fest. She is classified and will soon be forgotten. A p.c. has come from her from Grasse. (No she cannot sully it.) Her rather smelly friend Priaulx Rainier lost her handbag—passport purse—personal treasures—money—thinks it was stolen!! What kind of a person is this friend—is La Sprigge to allow it to be stolen. Did the French ever steal your handbag—they never stole Gertrude's (she never owned one!) nor mine nor anyone I knew or heard of until now! I dont believe it! Not I.

Love from
Alice

To Princess Dilkusha de Rohan, London/MS Texas

7 March 1955 5 rue Christine, Paris VI

Dilkusha dearest—

Thanks for the so very *original* story of Gertrude and Picasso being lovers. If that had been true one could have added incest to the scandal for she really felt herself as an older sister to him —taking him by his lapel and gently shaking him once I remember when she was displeased with him to which he responded by kissing her on either cheek. They understood each other in spite of saying dreadful things when they were irritated. This is an incident for you alone. Gertrude thought nothing of the poetry he wrote but when he first read it aloud to her (they were each of them holding one page of the notebook from which he was reading) and he had read all he had done to date—she looking down at the page said—*Que c'est beau* and repeated it—*que c'est beau*— as was her habit. I knew what she meant but didnt think P. did. It was the disposal of the written words on the sheet! Several years passed and she never said another word to him about his poetry. Then one evening Dali came to see Gertrude and after considerable palavering he asked Gertrude what she thought of P's poetry. And she told him and all the reasons in detail were included. After Dali left she said to me—Pablo sent him to find out what I did think. Well when we saw P. the next time he pounced on her and said—Why did you tell Dali what you hadnt told me. To which Gertrude replied—You know very well that it is not necessary to explain to an intelligent person—one only explains to a stupid one. Isnt it a deliciously characteristic story of each of them?

Here you have an old woman's garrulousness—but dearest Dilkusha much love and so many good wishes too from

Alice

To John Schaffner, New York/MS Columbia

18 April 1955 5 rue Christine, Paris VI

Dear Mr. Schaffner—

Thank you for your letter. It was a pleasure to have news of Perdita. It was at Burier that I first saw her as a child and the last time was during the winter of '44–'45 when she came here with Sylvia Beach and Mr. Norman Pearson. The change from a child to a competent woman in uniform left me breathless. That was the last time I saw her—but she left a vivid charming memory—so will you please say many kind things to her from me.

Mr. Beard was too indulgent about the book of recipes. He saw two pieces I did or perhaps only one on cooking with champagne which he said required amplification—more anecdote—more preparation—more comment—more introduction. It was I knew hopeless advice—there wasn't a word more in me. I was like those passionate one book ladies Mary McLean and Marie Bashkirtseff—except that the subject of my passion was food. There was nothing to do but to cut out the little comment and keep the recipes—which of course was unsuitable for *McCall's Magazine.* I was very much ashamed to appear ungrateful to Mr. Beard whose visit had been a rare treat. This is why you didn't hear from me. Nothing would please me more than a nice long piece but there is nothing but a large cardboard box of recipes. If this is a disappointment to others how much more so it is to me.

Thanking you for thinking of wanting to help me.

Cordially
Alice Toklas

Schaffner: John Schaffner, a literary agent, was married to Perdita Macpherson. Among the writers he represented was James Beard, author of cookbooks. Stein and Toklas had met Perdita when she lived with her mother Hilda Doolittle at Winifred Bryher's home in Switzerland. During World

War II Perdita worked for the O.S.S. in London, and when they opened their Paris office she was sent over. Shortly afterwards, Norman Holmes Pearson, who was with the O.S.S. in London, came to Paris and brought Perdita to meet Stein and Toklas.

To Dilkusha de Rohan, London/MS Texas

13 June 1955 — 5 rue Christine, Paris VI

Dilkusha dearest—

How are you—is your foot better. Is it less painful—can you walk with less difficulty. A cane is an enormous aid. I've taken to one and it is helps to get about quicker and with more security. Have you started to walk again. You *must*—at once and regularly. That cant be fatiguing—on the contrary it will be help to further effort. *Ce sont des bandits* but one lives by and for them—the miraculous commonplaces.

There is some very nice news. Max White (whose health has been miserable) has become a Catholic—brought to it by a wonderful Jesuit priest the abbè Teilhard de Chardin—who was to have baptised him but who died suddenly after going to mass on Easter Sunday. Max wrote—I dont know why I waited so long—I am very happy.

I was taken to Reims—happily by car—the trains are loathsome. It was a scream—we were lunched and dined royally—drank champagne from eleven o'clock on all day—saw the cellars—and much much better the incredible abbey with its newly uncovered eleventh century abbey and met endless hospitable and amusing people. No sooner had we returned we were off to Cognac and Jarnac. The thought of two times cognac was a nightmare—unswallowable firewater that it is to me. (Do you remember your Bloody Mary for your birthday—but vodka is better than cognac.) But you appreciate cognac by its odor not by its taste so all was well. Once more wined and dined and I returned a wreck—but the telephone and doorbell were pitiless.

Antonina Vallentin was there—she is so gently persistently thorough—she goes into all the little dark corners and crevices and sifts the dust for the truth. I admire her enormously.

Get well and keep well—Dilkusha dear.

Ever fondly
Alice

To Carl Van Vechten, New York/MS Yale

14 July 1955 5 rue Christine, Paris VI

Dearest Papa Woojums—

There were lots of people I knew [at the Picasso vernissage] but one was a surprise—Peter Rhodes—whom we knew in Lyon immediately after the liberation—and whom we never saw here. (He was demobilised in N. York.) We were terribly fond of him and he and I had a few excited moments and he brought his wife to see me and some photographs of Culoz and Baby which he took in September '44. And two of me at the vernissage—which he will not send to you. (Someone said one of them was in *Time*. Perhaps.) A photographer wanted to take my photograph—No—I said—go away. To which he said—You are either the wife or widow of a great painter. No—I said—I'm neither Madame Matisse nor Madame Dufy.

Janet [Flanner] brought three people from the N. York Museum of Modern Art to see the pictures and nice Mark Tobey too. It was the time for my *best* manners and they were elaborately brought forth—so that when Miss Dorothy Martin (?) [Miller] and one of the men said they had never seen such fine Braque painting to the Picassos I held my tongue—that was in the other room. Then they came in here and repeated their error. *Silence de ma part.* They appealed to me—was it not—pointing to the big picture over the fireplace. It would be if it were—I permitted myself to answer. And I plied them with sherry—*pâté brioche*—and my best little cakes—allowing myself to tell the story—*sans discrétion*—to anyone who will listen.

Then we had the three productions included in the official American *Salut à la France*—*Oklahoma* to which Janet [Flanner] and Noël [Murphy] took me—the President of the République—the national guards in their Napoleonic uniforms—our ambassador —officers in dress uniform—very brilliant audience for a tuneful (so tuneful someone said that you can sing it all and forget it) but otherwise dull evening. Then there was *Medea*—for which Guthrie McClintic sent me tickets and to which I asked Edward [Waterman] to take me. Judith [Anderson] was spendid—the first time I saw her act—she read the miserable lines as if it were the original Greek. It was a poor production but she was great. I love her.

Then there was Thornton's *The Skin of Our Teeth*—I wish Fania had been the fortune teller in this performance. Mary Martin was adorable—Helen Hayes excellent—the men inadequate. There was a reception afterwards—Isabel Wilder had taken me the previous evening to the rehearsal where I had met Mary Martin—her husband and her daughter (who is in the cast) [and] Helen Hayes and her husband. And Judith looking beautiful—she was off for two days to a festival in Greece—Euripides? I gave a tea party for Mary Martin—Helen Hayes—their families—etcetera. Mary Martin unspoiled spontaneous and deliciously feminine. A lunch for Guthrie McClintic with Natalie [Barney] and Francis [Rose]. Through Guthrie McClintic I met Francis Robinson of the Metropolitan Opera—sympathetic.

You see what a social life I've been leading.

To go back to your letter. Arnold Weissberger turned up unexpectedly and asked me to lunch—a very pleasant occasion indeed. I like Arnold W. a lot. Your letter arrived after he did so

ALICE B. TOKLAS, 5 RUE CHRISTINE, 1951

Photograph by Ettore Sottsass, Jr.

You see what a social life I've been leading.

I hadnt known about his doing all the small dirty work to secure the royalties for me. I had supposed he was doing it from kindness to you—to Virgil—even to me—beyond the insignificant (to him) percentage for his fee. Now you tell me there hasnt even been that. What is there I can do—can I send him something—a rare old book—if I can find a suitable one in English—on what subject. Please let me know soon. His mother sends me by him nylon stockings. It is all too good too kind. And I've gotten to like him a lot for himself alone. He has extraordinary gentle ways.

We had a terrific electric storm day before yesterday and we are in for one again—so I'll fly to close the shutters and windows.

Happy days always to Fania and to Papa Woojums.

Love—devotion—gratitude

M.W.

To Anne Low-Beer, San Francisco/MS Low-Beer

29 August 1955 — 5 rue Christine, Paris VI

Anne sweet—

Yesterday in going over the last piece of furniture for a very delayed spring cleaning something pushed me to open what Gertrude called her secret draw which is as obvious as the five others in the row. It hasnt been used but once opened I looked and felt—certainly there was something under the bit of silk that covered the bottom of the draw. It was an envelope and in it were two photographs of your mother—one alone and one with you in her arm on her lap. I was so certain that they had been burned with the few letters I had had from Gertrude—after I returned here alone but no—they had been carefully hidden from me and my memory. It was beautiful to find them and to have them but the old question is to the fore again—what is to become of them—they cannot—they must not fall into the hands *de n'importe qui*—and I havent the strength to destroy them. May I send them to you—will you accept them. Even if they are duplicates can you not place them amongst yours. I hope you will say yes.

The many months that have gone by since I wrote were crowded but dull—it is only now that there has been a bit of breathing space and in three hours I'm off on a late vacation to stay with friends at a village above Grasse for few weeks. There have been two long weekends and a beautiful though brief visit to see Bernard Faÿ at Fribourg—his doctor seems to have stopped the progress of his malady—but his general health is no better—a new medicine helped at first and then no longer did. He is in wonderful form and his mind is clearer and goes further than formerly. He is probably coming home soon now. But to what—French politics are more confused than usual—bad internally—worse in Africa. It is a hopeless mess—but France will survive.

Dearest love to you and to Bela always.

Alice

Anne Low-Beer: The daughter of Alice's close friend Clare Moore de Gruchy. Dr. Bela Low-Beer was Anne's husband.

To James Merrill, Amherst, Massachusetts/MS Merrill

25 September 1955 Saint-Jacques de Grasse, Alpes-Maritimes

Dear Jamie—

I came down here to stay with friends a month ago. And I've sat in the sun ever since—doing nothing though resolutely the attaché case for letters is at my feet—a book next to it and some handiwork on top of it and there they are untouched all day. At night I carry them up to my bedroom and say tomorrow. Finally tomorrow has become today. So now you will have my prettiest thanks as they say in Baltimore for your letter and such news as I have.

Yes untouched California is first rate and only second to Spain and it pleased me a lot that you saw and liked it. By now you must be at Amherst where you surely are more at home than either in N. York or in Florida. You are the fine *fleur* of that strangely rarefied and vigorous place that it was to us in thirty-four when Doctor Stanley King was its prex and was considered a possible presidential candidate.

And your work—the new novel—is it finished—is there enough new poetry for a book. Are you satisfied in the new work in the new surroundings. You are not too annoyingly the beloved of a good piece of the faculty and the students. When you have time you will tell me this and more.

In the picture world there were two splendid shows—a loan collection from U.S. of paintings from David through the Douanier —which first outraged the French—how dare Americans own French paintings which should belong to France and then they were flattered that this should be so. And a breathtaking fifty year's retrospective of Picasso's work—the finest of them the last twelve painted from an eleven year old memory after Delacroix —all twelve painted within three months. He is still the youngest of painters. The Metropolitan sent over the portrait of G.S.—you will understand how much it meant to me to see it again.

Do you know this part of Provence—below Grasse but still on a hilltop—surrounded by olive and cypress trees with very tall clipped rosemary and laurel hedges with quantities of jasmine in the fields below—all deliciously fragrant.

And thanks a lot for your recipe for shrimps with orange. It is an inspired combination but on a third preparation of it I added to a pound of shrimps—two tablespoons of burned dry curaçao and the tiniest pinch of cayenne. This just before I left so I'll try it again when I return the middle of October—indeed I should have before venturing to mention it to you. Forgive my tampering with your creation.

And forgive this hodgepodge scrawl—it is only to tell you that I think of you often and fondly.

Alice

new novel: The Seraglio (1957).

To Carl Van Vechten, New York/MS Yale

13 November 1955 5 rue Christine, Paris VI

Papa Woojums darling—

In yours of the 31st of October you wrote Knoedler wants "to borrow a selection from the paintings at 5 rue Christine." Now you say they want all the Picassos and all the Gris—a very different proposition indeed. The Gris—there are only seven—of which three are in Berne—are not all of them in a condition to travel (collage). In any case I definitely do not consent to lending all the Picassos. Nor would I accept their invitation to be their guest and "be at the gallery as often I can." *Ça n'est pas dans mes moeurs.* So I shall answer Miss Wittler. She is a very nice person and will understand that honoring Baby is one thing and advertising K. another. I know you think it would help sell next year's volume but if it takes all the pictures it's not possible which as I say I shall tell Miss W. They are as much an honor to Baby here as *chez* K.

Hurrah—*Painted Lace* has just come—the copies Donald [Gallup] sent to Virginia (to save duty and having to go to the customs).

It's a beauty physically and Baby at her most adorable perfection —of course the contents are a lovely transporting surprise to me and Kahnweiler's preface reads extremely well. The dust cover isnt as good as the binding—as you said—but that's not important. Oh dearest P.W.—*Painted Lace* makes me ecstatic too—and more than ever your loving grateful

M.W.

Knoedler: Lela Wittler, then a European representative for the Knoedler Gallery, had proposed an exhibition in New York of the pictures from the collection of Gertrude Stein. Toklas did not want to lend the pictures and had done so in the past only at the urging of Picasso or of Kahnweiler.

Painted Lace: Painted Lace and Other Pieces (New Haven: Yale University Press, 1955).

1956

To James Merrill, Amherst, Massachusetts/MS Merrill

5 January 1956 — 5 rue Christine, Paris VI

Dear Jamie—

To tell you at once about *The Bait.* It is admirably constructed and reads so fluidly that it must act well. But more than its reasonable evolvement. If one knows more at the end of the characters—of your approach to them and the subject—it is not that you havent told all from the beginning except the direction. But what fascinates me is the underlying question or rather fact or understanding of pure abstraction as only a highly gifted American knows and can tell it—as Poe and Hawthorne and your E. Dickinson (I'm a lttle fed up with hers) so simply told it. It is an enormous pleasure that amongst your generation you are the only one whom I have run across who knows what it is and who has it. Dont lose it—hold on to it. Nothing can replace it. The play has made it abundantly evident—the poetry was gifted and lovely—but *The Bait* is more.

Winter was mild until a week ago but it has commenced—there is a question of my having more adequate heat—which will be a blessing. They asked me to translate a slight but delightful book by a very young Belgian girl which has just been posted. She has a child's shrewd wisdom and comprehension of beauty—natural of course—people still are absurd and contemptible. It's an excellent antidote to that abomination *Bonjour Tristesse.* I'm sorry that the *Louis XVI* has been out of print—but they promised it for the beginning of the year and isnt that where we are.

Cooking has been put aside for a bit but some herb recipes are calling loudly for attention—soon—I hope they'll get some enthusiastic consideration—though U.S. should have its excessive interest in them soft pedalled.

I've been reading Santayana's letters with passionate interest—his dropping his Spanish inheritance in his youth was only equalled by what remained of it to distinguish him for the rest of his life. He writes like an angel—doesnt he.

I hope the novel is coming on as you want it to. So many fond wishes for it and for you for this year and for always.

Love from
Alice

book by a very young Belgian girl: Anne Bodart's *The Blue Dog and Other Fables for the French* (Boston: Houghton Mifflin Company, 1956), translated and with an introduction by Toklas.

Louis XVI: Bernard Faÿ's *Louis XVI, ou La fin d'un monde* (1955)

Santayana's letters: The Letters of George Santayana, edited by Daniel Cory (1955). Santayana had been an Assistant Professor of Philosophy at Harvard when Stein was at Radcliffe.

To Annette Rosenshine, Berkeley, California
MS Bancroft

10 January 1956 — 5 rue Christine, Paris VI

Dear Annette—

At our age—though you are younger than I by several years—one doesnt react from the unexpected blows that come at one from dark corners. Daily life continues because it is largely routine—if it is too hot in July and too cold in January—which it is now—there is little to do about it. There is always more to do than one can accomplish—which is a blessing—although I always did long for leisure. I see too many people but they keep me lively and moving about. What I have enjoyed doing is translating a short but delightful book by a very young Belgian girl—for which I have just gotten Picasso's permission to use a reproduction of one of his drawings as an illustration. Then the cultural attaché at our embassy in Brussels who is a friend of mine has asked me to go there to give a *causerie*. I accepted because I like travelling expenses paid and now I know I was brash to have done so. Someday it will be imperative to decide what is be said that will not disgrace my country—for I shall no longer be an old American lady who lives in Paris but simply an American.

The other evening I was dining (a cup of broth and a baked apple for me) with some people and one of the guests said to me—Did you know in California a painter named Stackpole. What a panorama that name unfolded. Of course I did though there werent any pictures—or were there and I didn't know—"black and white" illustrations—and all the names—Maynard Dixon and Leslie Hunter and something Armstrong—well well well. Well Stackpole lived in Paris—married a French girl—lives in Auvergne—and was asked as the only foreigner to compete in some French contest (sculpture?).

And now I would like to know how your book is coming on—have you a few chapters completed that you could send me—as I think we arranged.

It is snowing and the thermometer by my side is registering 52° which is not enough.

I send you very many fond good wishes for a happy New Year.

As ever affectionately
Alice

your book: Rosenshine's unpublished memoir "Life's Not a Paragraph," a typescript of which is deposited in YCAL.

To John Brown, Brussels/MS Brown

19 February 1956 5 rue Christine, Paris VI

My dear friend–

Thank you for your kind letter–all you suggest shows so much amiable consideration that I am quite embarrassed and deeply touched.

The end of the week I kept free hoping you would be here and it was a disappointment that you didn't come.

1. What about "Memories of the rue de Fleurus" as a title?

2. Would it be possible not to decide upon car or railroad for another week. The calendar announces rain and wind for the first quarter of next month. I do so hate train travel.

3. It is sweet of your wife and you to ask me to stay with you. I should love to if it would not be a trouble or a nuisance to either of you. It would certainly be more comfortable and happier for me. So many many thanks.

4. Having consistently refused to talk on the radio (what could any one hope to do with me on television) on G.S., Picasso and lately again on Marie Laurencin it isnt possible–is it–to do so in Bruxelles.

Enchanted at the prospect–weather permitting–to see Ghent and Bruges. Also to meet the ladies of the Women's Club–adore my compatriots.

5. *The* [*Alice B. Toklas*] *Cook Book* was published in London by Michael Joseph–26 Bloomsbury St. If any bookseller in Brussels wants any copies he should say that it is urgent for the Paris booksellers said that M.J. is slow in filling orders.

Appreciatively and gratefully
Alice T.

John Brown: An American diplomat and writer, Brown had invited Toklas to speak at a meeting of a women's club in Brussels where he was serving as cultural attaché. Later, in the 1960's, when he was attached to the U.S. Embassy in Rome, he and his wife Simone proved helpful to Toklas in arranging for her stays at a Roman convent.

To John Schaffner, New York/MS Columbia

20 February 1956   5 rue Christine, Paris VI

Dear Mr. Schaffner—

Your letter has just been delivered—delighting and exciting me. Your proposition enchanted me until alas and alas and alas I remembered a clause in the Harper contract which reads (I have just looked it up):

"17. The Author grants the Publisher an option on his next book, manuscript of which he will submit. The terms shall be subject to mutual agreement."

It sounds final and fatal—doesn't it. Surely there is nothing legal —nothing honorable—that can be done about it. The only loophole is "manuscript." Would there be a manuscript?

I am sad because it would have been so nice to have worked with you and made some money together. Of course if you see any solution to what would seem an insurmountable difficulty—you will let me know.

Affectionately and cordially
Alice Toklas

proposition: Schaffner had proposed that Toklas write her memoirs. The book was eventually published as *What is Remembered* (New York: Holt, Rinehart and Winston, 1963).

To Carl and Fania Van Vechten, New York/MS Yale

16 March 1956 5 rue Christine, Paris VI

Dearests—

Herbs and Spices has been my delight since it came on Monday. I steal minutes off from all there has been to do since my return from Brussels a week ago—it's a drug lulling me into a blue world of happy unreality. Thank you—thank you—thanks. What pleased and surprised me was to learn that paprika which is my favorite seasoning and which I used sparingly fearful that it was too heating is a prime vitamin C and that the man who discovered this got the Nobel prize for having done so. I am pathetically ignorant. So now I go to it. Paprika is everything to replace the sour oranges of our present market. *Herbs and Spices* is my Stars and Stripes. Useless for me to do an herb book—I'll do flavorings which can include wines and liqueurs—we'll see.

Now for the Belgian trip—it was lovely—driven up by the embassy chauffeur—stayed with the John Browns in their so comfortable—spacious home—dinner party that evening to meet some of their friends. Mrs. Brown a French Canadian—excellent cook—housekeeper and hostess. They took me to see fabulous private collections—the museums. Was presented to the Queen Mother—82 years old and as gay and lively as a bird—looks sixty—had me sit at her right—great bouquets of orchids a yard long—ropes of pearls—unheard of canapés and cakes—*hautes toutes*—asked me to send her a copy of the cook book—and told one of her ladies in waiting who told the Browns she wanted more Americans like me to be presented to her. Was my head turned? Perhaps. Went to Ghent to see the Van Eycks—cocktails at a country estate—lunch in a 14th century house on the quays. The *causerie* went off well—my *frousse* disappeared as soon as I got started—cocktails for a chosen few afterwards. Dinner at the Poets Club (poets dine very well indeed in Belgium). The first toast to me! Stephen Spender also guest of honor. Met Anne Bodart whose book I translated—had enough conversation with her to write the introduction to her book in haste upon my return and got the photograph of a Picasso wash drawing which is to illustrate the book. And so from prima donna back to routine here—from wearing Fania's coat everyday to kitchen attire.

Miss Wittler of Knoedler's left me breathless with a letter saying it was getting time to arrange for the autumn show of the pictures. Sly that—I answered that she had evidently forgotten my last letter to her. To which she answered—Under what conditions would I consider it. Does she think the pictures are vegetables and I am a market woman?

Heaps of love to the darlings from

M.W.

To Isabel Wilder, Hamden, Connecticut/MS Wilder

8 April 1956 5 rue Christine, Paris VI

Dearest Isabel—

When I came back a week ago Thornton's and your sweet Easter greetings were under the door—you are so good to remember me. It just added to the joy and peace that had come to me at Solesmes where most unexpectedly I found myself Holy Thursday through Easter morning. Thank you for the happy telegram. A friend was driving to the Benedictine monastery at Solesmes and asked me to go with him. *Poupon ne refuse pas*—so I threw in some linen and toilet articles—your stockings—your flowered washable bag—your little rolled face cloth—thanks and thanks again. It was still quite cold but the forsythia—willows and some grass were out—but oh the endless dead fruit trees. The chanting of the service was ineffably beautiful and elevating particularly the midnight mass for the resurrection. It washed out the annoying past—La Sprigge—her hateful manuscript and her visit to defend herself and her vulgarities and insinuations—all forgotten. Anyway Gertrude and her work need no defense against her attacks.

I have a new trick for jellied eggs—poached they take too long—so after a few hours in the refrigerator pop them into boiling water for a bare four minutes—then under the cold water faucet (fast running) until you can handle them—shell at once—the white is quite firm—the yolk not cooked. When 1 packet gelatine has been soaked in ½ cup water add ½ cup hot water (for 4 eggs) put in ramekins after adding ⅓ cup Traminer wine or any dry perfumed white wine. Before it hardens put an egg in each ramekin and spoon jelly over it to completely cover—sprinkle minced chive over egg and a garland of giant shrimps around. Dainty delicious—great success. Do not keep in freezer—*any French kitchen.* Takes ½ hour for a dozen eggs and is made hours in advance. You see my preparations are modern—no real troubles—though mixer hasnt yet seduced me—no chicken à la king—no readymade piecrusts biscuits cakes or muffins—not yet nor likely in the future.

Keep well and take care of yourself and much love from

Alice

To Mercedes de Acosta, New York/MS Rosenbach

28 June 1956 — 5 rue Christine, Paris VI

Mercedes dear—

Marie Laurencin's death was a great shock to me. She was in good health and excellent spirits when I saw her for the last time about two months ago. This afternoon I saw Jean Denoël and he told me about Marie's last days. He saw her four days before she died when she was perfectly well. He went off to visit in the country and then came back to Paris when he heard of her death. Two days before she complained to Suzanne of not feeling well and the doctor was sent for and said it was the usual intestinal trouble and that she should remain in bed. The next day Marie felt even less well and before the doctor arrived she told Suzanne she was going to die and Suzanne should send for the priest. The doctor said the heart had been affected. There was no hope. She died the following morning. Natalie thinks that the difficulty Marie had (three lawsuits) to recover her flat and putting it in order and moving in exhausted her—after the years of extreme calm. Marie was part of my happy early life in Paris—forty-eight years ago now—she was enchanting—quite legendary. At times she did not like to be reminded of it. Then again she brought me photographs of herself —of her mother. Her disappearance is another break with my past. It makes me feel more alone. If there were not still things to do for Gertrude there would be no reason for me to live on.

Natalie [Barney] is having a lovely new blossoming—she looks wonderfully flourishing—she's the one bright spot in a fairly cheerless world.

I am going to mail you a nice box Marie once gave me. It has had rough treatment at the hands of brutal *femmes de ménage*. It should have been put away but Gertrude and I never liked the idea or the practice of puttings things away but you will see how it *was* like Marie—dainty and romantic and charming. *En souvenir* of Marie and with much fond love from

Alice

Suzanne: Suzanne Moreau-Laurencin, the adopted daughter of Marie Laurencin.

To John Lucas, Rome/MS Lucas

10 August 1956 5 rue Christine, Paris VI

Dear Mr. Lucas—

Thank you a lot for sending me your impressions of the paintings of Piet Mondrian and of Gris at the Biennale. It is unfortunate to have seen more reproductions than originals of the former—it doesnt help one to appreciate his color—then there has been so much controversy concerning his painting. One used to say of certain work—It is painting—are they pictures. With Mondrian isnt it perhaps the other way round. *Au fond* it is painting—not ideas that are important. Doesnt it boil down to Matisse's *"C'est le don qui conte"*—Gris' essence is in his most abjectly realistic still life which makes him a very pure painter of abstraction. (I say it badly but it is true I think.)

Cordially
Alice Toklas

To Bernard Faÿ, Fribourg, Switzerland/MS Faÿ

19 December 1956 5 rue Christine, Paris VI

Dear good kind friend—

To my deep regret and shame many weeks have passed since your beautiful letters came to cheer and encourage me—but Madame Azam will tell you of the disturbed days of these last months—just enough to explain my silence and that now my life will be more peaceful. Try to forgive me—please.

Madame Azam—who is so human is for all that quite angelic to me

—she gives a radiance—a sweet understanding—all minor miseries vanish into thin air. And this privilege of knowing her is due to you—for which and for much else I am grateful to you.

One of the good things that happened was a performance of Gertrude's little play *In a Garden* made with some witty music into an opera. A little opera company from N. York was asked to give it and two other one act operas at the Edinburgh Festival. They were so successful there that they conceived the idea of touring with them. They piled themselves—the scenery and costumes in a station wagon and performed in London—Copenhagen—finally Vienna and here. Gertrude would have loved it. The singing was good—very musicianly—and their appreciation and animation were contagious. I met them after the performance and then they came to see Gertrude's home. By the way they sang a charming opera of young Chanler.

No one sends me novels any more—they send me cook books! a number of which—written by foreigners—are very amusing. Frankly those by Americans on American food are deplorable. But I'm mailing you an anthology of American poetry (published in England) in which you will find some old friends. It has a not uninteresting introduction by Auden.

Sylvia Beach came to see me to ask my(!) permission to include in the autobiography she is writing *(Shakespeare and Company)* a portrait Gertrude did of her in the early '20's. She told me she had two visits from the redoubtable Mrs. Sprigge who told her that her English publisher said she should make some discovery concerning G.S.'s writing and that she had. She had discovered that it was I who had written the books. Sylvia answered her—"It does not surprise me that you should think so—you have not read the work of G.S. It has been said that I wrote James Joyce's work—by people who did not read him."

Ever affectionately and devotedly.

Alice

In a Garden: The After Dinner Opera Company had presented Stein's *In a Garden* as set to music by Meyer Kupferman. The play was originally written for three children (Rose d'Aiguy, Mark Godet, and Maurice Godet) who lived near Belley. It was performed on the terrace of the Chateau Béon and Pierre Balmain came from Aix-les-Bains to help with the costumes.

Chanler: Theodore Chanler, an American composer and brother-in-law of Mercedes de Acosta. Toklas was strongly affected by Chanler's deep religious feelings; meeting him helped to pave her way to the Catholic Church.

To L. Arnold Weissberger, New York/MS Weissberger

26 December 1956 — 5 rue Christine, Paris VI

Dear Arnold—

It is exactly two months ago today that you mailed me the clipping of Leonard Lyons about Picasso—thanks a lot for having done so —though frankly I find him very inexact—he has his preconceived ideas and anything he hears must not disturb them. Gertrude said that was the way newspapermen were when they came to interview her but the photographers who came with them could listen —hear and understand. As a lawyer you know better what people say and mean.

Ever appreciatively and affectionately.

Alice

1957

To Robert Bartlett Haas, Los Angeles/MS Haas

Easter Sunday 1957 — 5 rue Christine, Paris VI

Dear Bobchen—

The better the day the better the deed—and I hope it is being a joyous day to you. Last year I spent Holy Week at the Benedictine monastary at Solesmes but there is no gasoline this year for the friend to drive me there as he did last year. I was glad to have your sweet letter and now ashamed to see how long it has remained unanswered. As one grows older the daily chores take longer to accomplish—which is a great bore. The winter was mild and now the country is almost summerlike—the chestnuts and fruit trees—with the exception of the late apples—have lost their blossoms. I miss Bilignin.

A most beautiful and exciting thing has just happened—Bernard Faÿ has been pardoned. He was required to spend nine weeks at the detention prison at Fresnes but when he came to see me a few days ago after his release he was in excellent form and fair health. Would that Gertrude could have known of his pardon and freedom.

Another beautiful and exciting event in the exhibition of fifty pictures of Picasso painted in '55 and '56 in which there is the material for painters for the next fifty years. There are some incredible interiors with black—blacker than black—good Spaniard that he is.

Love to Louise and to you always.

Alice

Bobchen: The nickname given to Robert Haas by Stein. Haas had become friends with Stein and Toklas through several years of correspondence. With Donald Gallup he prepared the 1941 *Catalogue of the Published and Unpublished Writings of Gertrude Stein.*

To Samuel Steward, Chicago/MS Bancroft

[25 April 1957] 5 rue Christine, Paris VI

Sam dear—

You are really too sweet to send me the burlesque pictures—the only thing that would or could completely and entirely take me out of distressing *tristesse* of this winter weather. And would you believe that there are two of my favorite heroines of my early youth—Lillian Russell and Fay Templeton and that my memory of them is not at all as they are pictured in the book. Lillian Russell gave no suggestion of knowing a Diamond Jim Brady and Fay Templeton was less than half the weight—who wore a pair of tights a high belt a bunch of violets and a smile—so proper that my mother took me to a matinée! And one afternoon before the other war on the rue de Rivoli on the way to Galignani Gertrude and I stopped breathless at the sight of Lillian Russell—yellow hair—turquoise eyes—pale rose complexion in a black tailored suit buttoned down the front like a riding habit from neck to waist into which she had evidently been poured. How otherwise had she gotten into it. Oh yes she had an enormous black velvet picture hat with long black feathers. Of course none if any of this was of the mode of the moment. She progressed very slowly. Dumb-

GERTRUDE STEIN AND ALICE B. TOKLAS,
THE TERRACE AT BILIGNIN, 1938

Photograph by Sir Cecil Beaton

I miss Bilignin.

founded the traffic stopped—staring at her—made room for her to pass. It was probably one of her last triumphs. There are probably dozens of more treasures for me to discover. The book came this morning and so I havent dug into it yet.

Angelic Sammie—all my grateful thanks and love.

Alice

To Doctor Jeanne Eder-Schwyzer, Switzerland
MS Ulla Eder-Dydo

5 May 1957 5 rue Christine, Paris VI

Dear Doctor Eder—

I am very grateful to you for writing to me what your daughter—at Vassar—felt about the play. You will understand how much her appreciation of it meant to me.

As a little girl I was allowed to meet Susan B. Anthony when she came to San Francisco. She was the first great woman I met and she made a lasting impression upon me. She was beautiful and frail and quite naturally dominated the group of women who had been asked to meet her.

Thank you again very much.

Cordially
Alice Toklas

Vassar: Dr. Eder-Schwyzer's daughter, Ulla Eder, was teaching at Vassar College where the Music and Drama departments had mounted a production of Stein's *The Mother of Us All.*

GERTRUDE STEIN AND ALICE B. TOKLAS,
AIX-LES-BAINS, 1928

To Brion Gysin, Tangier, Morocco/MS Gysin

11 June 1957 5 rue Christine, Paris VI

Dear Brion—

Useless to tell you now that your New York show was redeemed after the event by more than the average encouragement of critics and warm appreciation of stray but influential people. *(House Beautiful*—Museum of M. A.—*Vogue).* That is a galaxy for publicity that is Heaven sent. Do you know something called a following up letter. You must not allow them to doze even in the heat of summer upon their enthusiasm for you—your pictures—your articles. Forgive grandmotherly advice but that is how it was necessary to proceed when Gertrude's books were printed here and it was necessary to find booksellers to market them in U.S. Keep at them gently—charmingly with distinction!

Did I write you that Bernard Faÿ has been pardoned—and all his civil rights recovered. He came into France and gave himself up to be relieved *"de la peine."* Nine weeks at Fresnes during the retrial. If it had not been a favorable verdict he would have gone back to prison for eleven years—but he would have died long before that. He is wonderfully courageous—in excellent spirits—but only in fair health.

Natalie Barney has they say a new love affair—isnt it a miracle? Picasso has had an incredible show of his latest pictures—more miracles. And André Masson an impressive one.

So many good wishes to you and fond love from

Alice

To Nancy and Gilbert Harrison/MS Harrison

19 August 1957 — 5 rue Christine, Paris VI

My dears—

Loving welcome to little Joel. Three [boys] are fine to spoil a little sister. Do they look alike—David—Jamie *et* Joel. When you have a moment let me know about them and yourselves. Bless you all. Joel's blanket will be almost as late as David's was. But it will come along the end of next month!

There is a great deal to tell you. First many thanks dear Nancy for offering to send Ford's book—we knew him in 1912 when he had married(!) Violet Hunt—Holman Hunt's daughter—very pretty she was—and knew him intimately through three marriages (! ! !) over the years—with Stella (whom Gertrude called a drunken fairy) the heroine of the second of the novels and a character in Hemingway's novel *The Sun Also Rises.* He [Hemingway] made her a Canadian which infuriated her—she was an Australian. G. dedicated a book to their daughter Julia—a charming child. Someday I shall tell you some killing stories of him.

Then have you read Miss Ivy Compton-Burnett's books. There are half a dozen of them here and I'll send them on to you if you havent. They are rich reading—witty and amusing beyond words. She told a woman who told me—"I dont understand why I am not a best seller—dont I write about the scandalous subjects people love to read—adultery—incest—embezzlement." Let me know—they are cheap and light and will be no trouble to wrap and mail.

Donald Sutherland was in fine form—he lent me the new volume of Joyce's letters—incredibly woefully ignorant uneducated and blastingly uncultivated. Do you remember what Gertrude said of Joyce in *The Autobiography*?

Endless love and good wishes to all the Harrisons.

Alice

Ford's book: Ford Madox Ford's *Parade's End* (the Tietjens tetralogy, containing *Some Do Not* (1924), *No More Parades* (1925), *A Man Could Stand Up* (1926), and *Last Post* (1928). Ford was the editor of *The Transatlantic Review* when it published excerpts from Stein's *The Making of Americans.* Stein's book *A Book Concluding With As A Wife Has a Cow* (1926) is dedicated to Ford's daughter Julia.

Joyce's letters: James Joyce Letters (1957), edited by Stuart Gilbert.

To Samuel Steward, Chicago/MS Bancroft

14 September 1957 Magagnosc-par-Grasse, Alpes-Maritime

Dearest Sam—

There were many weeks of too much work with the natural exhaustion that followed—broken by the shock of the unexpected death of a friend—by Francis getting himself into a scandalous scrape and being taken to hospital.

James Purdy bores me. He asked me to write something about his latest effort—that I would be amongst friends—Carl and Edith Sitwell but I ignored his request and the book. He—his subject matter and his treatment of it lack taste.

Two weeks ago tomorrow Virginia Harold and I were driven down here by a friend of theirs. It was a lovely trip—sunny—by way of Grenoble—the *route Napolienne.* The friend went on to Mallorca and we are here in a convenient if not too comfortable house in a little garden with huge olive and willow trees with the fragrance of not too distant fields of jasmine blossoms. I sit all day in the garden and havent yet ventured to go to Grasse—to say nothing of Cannes where I want to go to see Picasso—who never comes to Paris any more. If I can manage it I shall take the treatment of the mud baths (not alluring in themselves) at Acqui in Piedmont—Anita Loos was lately miraculously cured of long standing arthritis. It would be pleasant if it did as much for me. I am

ALICE B. TOKLAS AND HAROLD KNAPIK, MAGAGNOSC, FRANCE, 1957

. . . huge olive and willow trees with
the fragrance of not too distant fields of jasmine
blossoms.

writing today for terms. The cure is short—three weeks—so that the return to Paris would be before the end of next month.

About Francis [Rose]—he suddenly appeared in Paris about a month ago—complaining of Frederica—she had sold the two wee rooms in the Quai d'Anjou—she could no longer afford to pay the taxes. He hasnt been painting but was earning a lot for textile designs—he apparently has great aptitude for them. The next thing one night quite late there was a telephone message from a strange rough voice—announcing that Francis was at the British military hospital at Levallois. Then the visit of one of the resident doctors who was very upset by the *voyou* whom Francis brought with him from London and who had beaten him up in a drunken brawl—and who had brought him to the hospital and who called it a serious heart attack. The doctors say there is nothing the matter with him except his character. It is too sad.

The equinoctial mistral is blowing and I must go indoors. When you have time write to me.

All my fondest love.

Alice

James Purdy: American writer whose book of short stories, *Color of Darkness,* had just been published. Purdy had strong Chicago ties and was a friend of Wendell Wilcox and Osborn Andreas in addition to Steward and others.

To William Alfred, Cambridge, Massachusetts
MS Harvard

10 October 1957 [Acqui, Italy]
Monday is the fête day of Santa Teresa of Ávila.

My very dear William—

Your beautiful letter followed me from a hilltop near Grasse where I spent a quiet month resting and then here—at Acqui—in

Piedmont where the baths have been so beneficial. If they have been so for me at my age what would they have for you. If you come over next year I do so hope you will come here—just for three weeks—perhaps but two. This is not an answer to all the wonderful things you wrote to me about—they will hear print for surely what you say moves me like nothing has these last solitary years and in the direction I want you to lead me. (No the book about Gertrude troubled me for but a short time. It is quite forgotten now.) Will Saint Anthony find a ray to show me the way to God. Yes I was baptised a Catholic as a small child with my mother's knowledge—then I wandered—only the saints remained. Of my few friends half are Catholics—three recent converts.

Tomorrow I go to Milan and Saturday to Paris.

Dear William—thank you from the best part of me. I shall be writing to you soon. Love and gratitude from

Alice

book about Gertrude: Elizabeth Sprigge's *Gertrude Stein: Her Life and Her Work* (1957).

baptised a Catholic: A search of church records in San Francisco and Seattle failed to turn up any baptismal certificate for Toklas, but it is possible that records were lost during the San Francisco fire.

To Nancy Harrison, Washington, D.C./MS Harrison

9 November 1957 Acqui, Italy

Dear Nancy—

I came here to take the cure—recommended by Anita Loos! The baths have been beneficial—walking without a cane. The mud baths are much less appalling than they sounded—powdered volcanic earth they look.

I am mailing from Milan a blanket for little Joel—the dignified and thoughtful—bless him. Is his appetite undiminished.

If I am not mistaken the woman in *Parade's End* was Violet Hunt. Ford Madox Ford loathed her. She frankly told me her story at a London party—Gertrude—after my retelling it to her—scolded me for telling her. No she wasnt Lady Brett in *The Sun Also Rises*—very different indeed. Violet Hunt was ever so good looking and very distinguished. Lady Brett was Lady Dove something and was common to the quarter until they went to Spain and you know what she was there. The Canadian girl was Stella Ford—without benefit of the law or clergy.

Yes *A Legacy* is a distinguished accomplishment and so is Sybille Bedford. I met her several times a few years ago. She's German—separated from an English husband and lives in Rome.

Do I sound like a dull unwitty columnist. The dull and unwitty are not so unsympathetic as being a columnist.

Fondest love to you all.

Alice

To John Lucas, Northfield, Minnesota/MS Lucas

16 November 1957 — 5 rue Christine, Paris VI

Dear Mr. Lucas—

The Atelier de Juan Gris—the catalogue of which I wished to send you—Louise Leiris said you have received a copy—is fantastically beautiful— breathlessly interesting—excitingly absorbing. The two—largish for Gris—paintings of women were a great surprise. There is something you must know—Kahnweiler confided to me as he sometimes does—and which he must to you too—that Picasso had acknowledged frankly and fully that he was prepared to accept Gris now—as he had not formerly—as the great painter he knew him to be. Very hush hush. It is a nice secret.

Affectionate greetings to you all.

A.B.T.

Atelier de Juan Gris: An exhibition of paintings (1926/27) by Gris at Galerie Louise Leiris. The paintings of women are *Femme* (1926) and *La Femme au Panier* (1927).

To William Alfred, Cambridge, Massachusetts
MS Harvard

10 December 1957 — 5 rue Christine, Paris VI

Dear William—

You will be happy that your prayers have been answered—that I had the blessing yesterday of confessing and of receiving Holy Communion.

The baptism of my youth counted and through Madame Azam I saw the priest Friday and he arranged for yesterday. After Holy Communion he gave me a missal a rosary and these cards. Now I have everything to learn to live in the peace of our Lord Jesus Christ.

My deep gratitude to you for your prayers that made this blessing possible.

Alice

To Carl and Fania Van Vechten, New York/MS Yale

[26 December 1957]
Christmas Day

5 rue Christine, Paris VI

Dearests—

What there is to tell you on this blessed happy day will perhaps surprise my own Papa Woojums more than it may Fania darling—in any case you will share the deep satisfaction of knowing the happiness that has come to me. On the fête of the Immaculate Conception I was admitted to the Catholic Church—confessed and was given Holy Communion. It was not far from accomplished for some time but the end came suddenly quickly because I had been baptised as a child. One day about a month ago I spoke to Madame Azam and she gave me the name of an English priest with whom I had a long conversation and he made the rest possible. There is everything to learn but with a catechism and a missal I shall make up for lost time. Then last week Bernard turned up and we had a long conversation about what had happened to me and Baby. They had had much discussion about the church and Baby's Judaism—which was a kind of ethical conception—a modern version of the Mosaic law which of course included no future life and that is what is such a comfort to me now—the peopled heaven—not only God and Jesus but the angels and saints. Dearests I hope you are pleased in my new happiness. For the present I am not telling any one but I shall write to Donald [Gallup] in a day or so.

I love you with all my heart.

Always your loving devoted grateful

M.W.

1958

To Virginia Knapik, Paris/MS Knapik

9 January 1958 — 5 rue Christine, Paris VI

Dearest Virginia—

The simple way you accepted my new life gave me the deepest contentment—the greatest pleasure. It is wonderful to be part of the great Catholic Church—where I should have been long ago.

God bless you for all you have done for me.

Alice

To Virginia Knapik, Paris/MS Knapik

7 April 1958 — 5 rue Christine, Paris VI

Dearest Virginia—

This is not alone to thank you for the delicious lunch but to tell you both that Harold's music impressed me deeply. It is of a splendor that we dont know today. It is entirely original both in its composition and its rhythm. It is entirely revolutionary—like nothing or nobody else's—as Gertrude's writing and Picasso's painting of nearly fifty years ago. And music is the quickest of the arts because some of it is *heard and understood* at once. So all happiness for the music and you two.

Alice

To Edward Weeks, Editor, The Atlantic Monthly, Boston
MS The Atlantic Monthly

29 April 1958 5 rue Christine, Paris VI

Dear Mr Weeks—

Thank you very much for your too kind words. It is a great pleasure and honor for anything of mine to appear in *The Atlantic Monthly*—which published Henry James and Gertrude Stein. Who am I who should find myself—however distantly—in such overwhelming company.

Cordially and appreciatively
Alice Toklas

The Atlantic Monthly: Toklas' article "Fifty Years of French Fashion" was published in the June 1958 issue.

To Carl Van Vechten, New York/MS Yale

21 May 1958 5 rue Christine, Paris VI

Dearest Papa Woojums—

Days—ages have passed without a minute free. Max [White] has been coming six times a week for four or five hours to work on the book. It is going swimmingly and wont take as long as he originally thought it would. And we are agreed that the reminiscences should be centered on Baby and her work. That mine be discarded—possibly to throw light on her method. You agree —dont you? I am nothing but the memory of her.

Then I had to make an inventory of the pictures—their sizes—dates when painted and their present value for Edgar Allan Poe for his reassurance. He will be breathless with surprise when he sees the value Georges Maratier put upon them—which he kindly did—saving the fee of an expert—which he is. I sent it to the lawyer to send to E.A.P. (I do not communicate with the grumpy grandpapa.) He said over the phone—This is a blow he wont recover from!

In the meantime everyone has come to Paris and here—some amusing—others less so. The nicest by far Anita Loos who has been here doing over a Colette play she translated into a French film—surrounded by C.'s widower—agents—lawyers—and notary public. She telephoned me the day before she left and she and the *N. York Herald* dramatic critic lunched with me at a very good small restaurant way back of Montmartre that Edward [Waterman] had recommended to me. There is a young chef who owns it and he cooks exceedingly well. James Beard said we should keep our eye on him. Anita is delicious—so good looking—witty—and original. She said she had not seen you in some time but she was going to telephone you as soon as she gets back to N. York. She is working in Italy until the end of this month and then sails from Naples.

Maurice Grosser was here on his way to Portugal (in a wee car) where he is going to paint. He says Paul Bowles is in Portugal and Jane is in N. York having her eyes treated (very serious).

The accounts in the U.S. papers are doubtless very exaggerated about the political situation here. It is confused and discouraging but not alarming. All the many political parties are in disagreement with each other and between each other inside their parties. De Gaulle may come in for a few months—he wont have a majority long. You mustnt worry about me. It is quiet and supplies are plentiful.

Hugs and kisses from

M.W.

work on the book: Toklas was working with Max White on her memoirs for Holt. There had been some question of her obligation to Harper and to relieve herself of it she unwillingly supplied recipes for a book that was published as *Aromas and Flavors of Past and Present* (1958). In conversations about this book Toklas disassociated herself from the introduction and comments of Poppy Cannon.

To W. G. Rogers, New York/MS Rogers

26 May 1958 5 rue Christine, Paris VI

Dearest Kiddie—

Your A.P. sent someone from their Paris office to interview me. He shouldnt have been allowed in if he hadnt come from a friend's friend. Far fetched? He was—I have been told lately—a typical American journalist—not my idea of one. He asked me what the Paris Museum of Modern Art thought of the pictures—when I saw Picasso last? What I thought of François Sagan's last book. What I thought of her and Menotti's ballet. I spare you my answers. If I gave him a glass of cognac—not Russian—it was because I wanted to get rid of him quickly. Before he left he said in the ten years he had lived in Paris he was sorry never to have run up the stairs and come in to see me. What he has done to my answer to that I dont venture to surmise.

5 rue Christine was sold to a company who has sold the flats. The tenants all bought their flats except me. The French law protects aged ladies so I can stay on for the rest of my days. The hallways

and stairs have been repainted dark green and pale buff—quite handsome.

I am going next week for two days to Switzerland if planes are flying. And later to Acqui to take the cure again—arthritis is bad again—too cold and damp and too much heavy work in the household. Madeleine is a.w.o.l. had to be dismissed—substitute doesnt hear—see or understand. Do you know Anita Loos? Enchanting. Virgil is due for the summer. Knoedler has opened their Paris gallery with a Soirée de Paris show—have you seen their catalogue? Excellent. Why doesnt Mildred send a verse to *The N. Yorker.* Tell her *de ma part* they need her.

Love to you both from

Alice

To John Schaffner, New York/MS Columbia

29 May 1958 5 rue Christine, Paris VI

Dear Mr. Schaffner—

The work with Max White is advancing rapidly though he doesnt like to hear me say so. He is working without me—having a fair amount of notes I supplied in the course of his questionings and my conversations with him.

With affectionate greetings
Alice Toklas

To John Schaffner, New York/MS Columbia

17 June 1958 5 rue Christine, Paris VI

Dear Mr. Schaffner—

It is indeed very strange news that I have to tell you. Three days ago I had a letter from Max White announcing quite inexplicably that he was giving up the collaboration—destroying the notes he had taken—the work on them he had done (he had shown me three excellent typewritten pages) returning to Holt at once one half the advance royalties (the rest later)—and was leaving Paris in a few days. He is no longer at his hotel—his present address is unknown.

All this has left me stunned. The time—about four hours a day six days a week—and the effort have been wasted. I have no idea what prompted him to take this decision. Since it was I who suggested his collaboration I feel guilty—to you and to Holt who have been so kind and patient—re Harper as well as Max White. Have you anything to suggest.

Please have a solution to the present difficulty.

With warmest greetings.

Ever cordially
Alice Toklas

To John Schaffner, New York/MS Columbia

20 July 1958 — 5 rue Christine, Paris VI

Dear Mr. Schaffner—

The revelation of Max White's financial situation leaves me aghast. I am sorrier than I can say that you and Holt were put —through my mistake of having chosen Max White as a collaborator—in such a humiliating situation—and a time consuming one. It was the worst possible judgement that lead me to it.

About Mrs. Barry—once more I shall be making difficulties for you. My objection to her as a choice is that both her experience and reputation are of a kind of feminine journalism that are not to my taste. For example her opinions concerning paintings—books—people shocks me. How could we work together? It is indeed shameful that this is my third refusal with nothing but Max White as a choice. What can I say—what can I do but throw myself upon you again.

No I am not discouraged with the new contretemps—but the weather and the arthritis do—I am trying to get to the baths at Acqui and some sunshine there.

Cordially
Alice Toklas

To Charles Norman, New York/MS Virginia

25 July 1958 — 5 rue Christine, Paris VI

Dear Mr. Norman—

Certainly you may use the quotation from Gertrude Stein for the British edition of your book. She was an enthusiastic admirer of

The Enormous Room and recommended it to the young writers.

It is a great pleasure for me to see the recognition E. E. Cummings has achieved as the chief American poet.

Cordially
Alice Toklas

Norman: An editor and writer, Norman wrote *The Magic Maker: E. E. Cummings* (1958).

To John Schaffner, New York/MS Columbia

28 July 1958 5 rue Christine, Paris VI

Dear Mr. Schaffner—

Thanks a lot for your prompt answer and your understanding of my reason for objecting to Mrs. Barry.

Donald Sutherland—whom I have known intimately for many years and for whom I have the greatest admiration—is too perfect a choice. I should not presume to suggest him. He is a Greek scholar—has written on aesthetics—poetry—and is published in the more important university and literary reviews. As for Mr. Robert Wernick I don't know of him. As a magazine writer I wouldn't be attracted to him.

Alas that Sutherland's name should have been mentioned—so very much beyond my need.

Always cordially and appreciatively.

Alice Toklas

To Samuel Steward, Chicago/MS Bancroft

7 August 1958 5 rue Christine, Paris VI

Sam dear—

Yes Max was a surprise—he just disappeared into thin air. Harold came down at once after having first gone to Max's hotel. They only knew he had left. He had dined at the Knapiks—stayed on until midnight and not mentioned his imminent departure. Harold and I went over the situation pretty thoroughly and concluded that I was well out of a mess. By the time we came to this there was nothing but relief. The publishers were pleased —they had found him difficult and are now hunting for a successor. I tell you all this because it is a very real Max story.

No Sam dear—the past is not gone—nor is Gertrude (life everlasting—Father Taylor—my confessor—has made that clear). It left me in a dither when suddenly it came to me—where was Gertrude. She is there waiting for us.

I pray for you—my dear.

You know Gertrude told Hemingway—in the early days—he couldnt earn his living doing newspaper work and write—he should like Sherwood [Anderson] earn his living running a laundry. Keep tattoo and writing apart.

Love from your devoted
Alice

ALICE B. TOKLAS AND GERTRUDE STEIN, VENICE, 1908

. . . the past is not gone—nor is Gertrude.

To John Schaffner, New York/MS Columbia

17 August 1958 5 rue Christine, Paris VI

Dear Mr. Schaffner—

It is—don't you think—a happy coincidence that your letter came while I was telephoning to Jo Barry to make an appointment with him to come to see me on Tuesday evening the nineteenth. He would be very pleasant to work with—though he has no such familiarity with the work of Gertrude Stein as Max White had—but it will be my task to make it known to him. The only question is will he (J.B.) have time to do any other work than his reporting to the *N. York Post* (poetical—literary—artistic happenings in Paris and France). I shall let you know the result Wednesday morning of our conversation. He will want to collaborate—but will he be able to manage it.

Alas no he wasn't—he has just received a wire for more work from his N. York office—and he has a contract for two books to be finished this autumn—we talked it over until midnight. He has persuaded me to start at once to do the book alone. The memories do not frighten me—the relation to G.S.'s work will not be such easy sailing—but that is not what interests Holt—that is my affair—that is where I shall miss Max White. J. Barry will look over and discuss with me say five thousand words.

Appreciatively and cordially yours

Alice Toklas

To William Alfred, Cambridge, Massachusetts
MS Harvard

26 August 1958 — 5 rue Christine, Paris VI

Dear William—

The first steps in the Franciscan mysticism are showing me the long happy way ahead. Every evening it is read and reread. You and Bernard Faÿ are my godfathers for the life of the spirit.

About Gertrude's place. In the beginning there was the undeniable knowledge that she had no conviction of a future life. The good Father Taylor—who heard my first communion [*sic*]—and Bernard both told me that she was in Heaven and that I should pray to her there. Of course this is a great comfort. Bernard says he has known this a long time and was waiting always for me to come back to Holy Church.

Thank you for quoting Saint Teresa—she had Alphonsus of Madrid did she not as her spiritual guide. The last time I was in Madrid—five or six years ago—I went to mass at her church and it was her fête day—was that not beautiful.

Many tender thoughts from

Alice

To Harold and Virginia Knapik, Paris/MS Knapik

Saturday Evening [October 1958] — Acqui, Italy

My dearest dears—

When you disappeared at the station I felt like Blackie deserted and devoted. Then there was nothing to do but look out of the window at the Mediterranean. The only other person in the compartment was a nice man—he looked like an engineer—returning to his parents' home in Milan. He supplied me with matches—which we had forgotten but refused a Pall Mall because they werent strong enough. The train stopped endlessly. It took an hour before we left Nice. Finally at Ventimiglia they examined passports—luggage (not mine!) and changed money. I went into the dining car and sat down at an empty seat next to the door where they served me a copious but execrable lunch. When I returned a couple had gotten on at San Remo—she smelled of garlic—hair and——but they were kindly and helped get a porter at Savonna when we got there late. We turned our backs and said goodbye to the Mediterranean. Great wild mountains—widening out into deep wild valleys—occasionally fortified—a castle on top of one—endless tunnels—a wee bit of cultivation as we neared Acqui—a young Jesuit seminarian got me and my bags off—and even found a taxi. The station no distance from the hotel. The town considerably larger than Grasse—richer and poorer—a nice room—a splendid bath—the water from springs piping hot with a force of a fire hose. Unpacked a bit—dozed and 7:30 went down to dinner. A minestrone (refused)—a pâté (refused)—a trout like our good California flounders—fresh and juicy—lemons—a tomato salad—4 cloves garlic—a lemon pie—good pâte—all well cooked—little salt and no pepper—but both on the table—the dining room full—forty or fifty. Now to bed! Ever lovingly and gratefully—A.

Sunday morning

Have seen the doctor—nice man—prescribes 10 baths in 3 groups—1 day between 3 baths. Says ankles and legs are phlebitic. And now after the bath commenced (not mud more like powdered soapy—volcanic earth—put on in great slabs—wrapped up in sheets of rubber plastic very hot and soothing—then bathed to remove the application and 20 minutes in my bed)—dressed and had lunch—ham—butter—exquisite—green *cannellone*—roast chicken—*beignets aubergines*—excellent excellent apple.

Last evening glorious red sky—this morning covered—it is trying to rain now. They merely say it is autumn. Today is the fête of the raisin (*vendange*) and the gaily uniformed bands are marching up the street under my window—cymbals drums fifes—odd toyish instruments—drum majors—and each has a half dozen brass. The music is quite simpleminded. Fortunately I dont have to go out to enjoy it.

You were both angels to me. Please believe that I am *always* gratefully devotedly lovingly

Alice

Blackie: A cat that had lived at the house in Magagnosc where Toklas and the Knapiks vacationed in 1957.

To William Alfred, Cambridge, Massachusetts
MS Harvard

[9 October 1958] Acqui, Italy
The fête of Saint Francis of Assisi

Dear William—

The special prayers for you through Saint Raphael the Archangel I have said every day. It would be very comforting if they were answered and the lonesomeness from which you suffer should be relieved by the answer of the young girl in Rome. Maybe she is answering you satisfactorily now.

Unfortunately Father Taylor has been away from his church. Not being able to walk I could not go to Communion but the baths here have helped the walking so tomorrow I shall go to church and feel purged. Acqui is a quiet town in Lombardy—all the smallest villages have churches. It is a plain countryside without any of the beauty of Umbria and Tuscany. The sky is blue—the clouds are heavy. It is not cold yet. Before returning to Paris in about two weeks I may spend a day or two in Milan.

In Paris before leaving I saw Mercedes de Acosta—who is very good to me. She belongs to several churches which is confusing but she prays in all of them which is worse still. She has written her memoirs which are to be published soon. Have I written you that Max White suddenly gave up working on the memoirs with me and tore up the notes I had given him—so there was nothing for me to do but to commence over. It is slow work—the plan was to use Gertrude's work to describe her. A copy of *The Making of Americans* which has kept me company these many years will be the point of departure. The agent and the publishers have been patient and kind—Carl Van Vechten and Donald Gallup of Yale University too.

Dear William I send you many loving thoughts and prayers.

Alice

To Gilbert Seldes, New York/MS Marion Seldes

24 November 1958 5 rue Christine, Paris VI

Dear Mr Seldes—

Mildred [i.e. Muriel] Draper's beauty fascinated me before she spoke. It was at Doneys (?) the confectioner in Florence in 1910 (?). She had a drooping eyelid which seemed romantic to me. A few days later we met her at Mabel Dodge's at Arcetri and then for the rest of that summer and the next at the Drapers' home in Arcetri. Muriel was astonishingly direct outspoken and American —though she used Italian exclamations. The baby held in her arms was saintlike. Then they moved to London where Paul [Draper] was to study voice culture.

In the early summer of 1914 Gertrude Stein and I went to London and at Covent Garden we saw in a box in one of the upper tiers a fabulous woman—more beautiful and more sensational than any of the English women of those days. She had ashen colored hair—brushed from her forehead—from her head rose an exaggeratedly tall and large *turquoise bleu aigrette*—the color of her very low cut dress. A large opal flamed from the base of the *aigrette.* During an intermission I walked across the opera house under her box. It was Muriel. My memory is that Paul came down joining G.S. and me asking us to dine with them one evening within the week. G.S. and I were staying at the time with the [Alfred] North Whiteheads and when we said we were to dine with friends living in Edith Grove Mrs. Whitehead said—"how amusing—that is where seamstresses live." And Miss Emily Dawson—a cousin of Logan Pearsall Smith—the first Mrs. Bertrand Russell—and Mrs. Bernard Berenson said "you will meet everyone at her house—all the duchesses and everyone else." The house at Edith Grove had been two houses connected cleverly to make one. The music room was very large—a Coromandel screen was its chief ornament. Dinner was served at once in a smallish room dimly lighted with candles—a gold framed mirror with gold sconces. Poorly lighted though it was the furniture appeared to be copies. We were six at table—a Scotch or Yorkshire novelist and a cabinet minister. Conversation was dull and heavy. Muriel was wearing sapphire blue and sparkling with many opals. Soup—deep tomato colored—was served in white Wedgwood—the food was good and served quickly. Muriel led us into the big room—where people were gathering. There was Robert de la Condamine—May Sinclair—the Baroness von Huten—an American novelist married to a German. A great many people sat on large cushions on the floor—later in the evening Arthur Rubinstein came and played. Someone remarked if Muriel was not like a Titian to which the Baroness von Huten remarked: "I protest I protest!"

In 1934 we were in the U. States where G.S. was lecturing at colleges and a wire came to her from Muriel from Moscow welcoming G.S. back to the U.S. (It is now in the G.S. collection at Yale University Library.) That was the last time we heard from Muriel. She is a vivid happy memory today of transcendent beauty courage and independence unique in my over eighty years experience.

Cordially
Alice Toklas

To Ned Rorem, New York/MS Rorem

27 November 1958 5 rue Christine, Paris VI

Dear Mr. Rorem—

Excellent news of the N. York Philharmonic doing your symphony. Leonard Bernstein was brought to see me lately. What an utterly charming creature he is. He spoke to me of Paul and Jane [Bowles]—Jane's health is a great sadness to me—she is very attaching—her inability to work steadily made me impatient with her—but now I am ashamed and wish I hadnt been. You ask after Brion Gysin—he is here and painting beautifully—working hard. Do you know everyone works in Paris—except the workingmen. If you dont want to work go to Italy. Though I should be pleased to see you again.

Let me know how your symphony is received.

Warm greetings to you—dear Mr. Rorem.

Alice Toklas

Ned Rorem: Rorem had lived in France and Morocco from 1949 to 1958. He composed an opera based on Stein's play *Three Sisters Who Are Not Sisters.*

1959

To Princess Dilkusha de Rohan, London/MS Texas

29 January 1959 5 rue Christine, Paris VI

Dilkusha dearest—

Bless your courage and levelheadedness. Praying for you did help me bear all you were going through. It wasnt possible to pray for specific things. If God would watch over you He would know and He did and does. And it gives me a feeling of being close to Him. And to you whose prayers from long ago brought me back to Holy Church. You are a wonderful group—you and Denise Azam and Bernard and naughty sweet Edward Waterman. You know Frederica Rose said to me when I told her it would make too many complications if I told [Francis]—"No dont tell Francis—he would come right over to see you and bring a Cardinal for lunch!"

Lady Duff Cooper came to see Gertrude several times—she was lovely then but at Pierre Balmain's collection two years ago I thought age had coarsened her and her face had lost its flower-likeness—but she has beautiful manners—almost royal.

I had to go to Pierre's collection because I was being paid to do a 4 minute B.B.C. broadcast—through Janet Flanner it was arranged.

Could anything be more ridiculous at my age and situation. It will pay for a pair of winter sandals.

Dearest Dilkusha get well—keep well and God will give you peace.

Love to you always
Alice

To L. Arnold Weissberger, New York/MS Weissberger

7 March 1959 — 5 rue Christine, Paris VI

Dearest Arnold—

Delighted to hear from you and to know that you all are coming over and that I shall be in Paris in June when you expect to be here. You will have a good lunch at my restaurant as my guests. I haven't cooked for over two years now. I am a tired old woman—no denying it. I hobble about.

You are a real Romeike press clipping bureau. (Is it still in existence.) I used to read its advertisement with ravishment when I was young in San Francisco in the *Argonaut*. And then I came over here and Gertrude's *Three Lives* were published and we subscribed to Romeike's. It was breathlessly exciting. And thanks for the clipping. Give my love to the adorable Anita Loos.

And much love to you all and *à bientôt*.

Alice

To L. Arnold Weissberger, New York/MS Weissberger

16 April 1959 5 rue Christine, Paris VI

Dear Arnold—

The two cheques for ten and twenty dollars *(Brewsie and Willie)* came this morning just as I was going off to my milliners where I had ordered a new hat. "Put on plenty of feathers"—I had told her. And she had! It is a wow. Wait until you see it. Not satisfied with that extravagance I went across the Place Vendôme and bought a bottle of Jicki at Guerlain and a pretty kerchief next door.

I shall be delighted to meet Olivia de Havilland (such a romantic name) and you will lunch with me.

Love to you all.

Devotedly
Alice

To Anne Low-Beer, San Francisco/MS Low-Beer

20 April 1959 5 rue Christine, Paris VI

Dearest Anne—

It is just these last few days that I am feeling more cheerful now that my ticket is bought and the valises are getting ready for the day after tomorrow departure for Acqui—forgive this dull preamble and the reference to lava baths!

In hunting for some papers I found the most adorable photograph of your blessed mother. Naturally I supposed it had gone to Yale years ago—fortunately it is here for you. It was taken either shortly before you were born or shortly afterwards. It is too lovely. Georges Maratier when he saw it years ago exclaimed at her being so very French. She has been constantly in my thoughts these last days. I have been doing my memoirs—(the advance from a kind editor pays for my trip). She made my childhood and youth joyous—my girlhood happy—in spite of her own tragedies. Life without her was dull—the radiance she diffused was missing—I fear to go on without her in the picture.

My days are filled with routine comings and goings—a few friends —many duties. The household is fatiguing but must be accomplished—the modern conveniences of nearly thirty years ago have become hopelessly outmoded.

A very nice gifted milliner remembers a little toque she made that dear Bela took back to you and wants to make another. Do you happen to know someone who is returning? If not I shall have to find someone—otherwise there is the everlasting duty to consider.

All my thanks to you—Anne dear—and my devoted love.

Alice

Bela: Dr. Bela Low-Beer, Anne's husband.

To Louise Taylor, England/MS Taylor

28 June 1959 Piscop, Seine et Oise

Dearest Louise—

I was terribly ill for three weeks—and have just gotten here to rest and pick up which I am doing. It is a charming place in a big park—a natural lake under my window with a white horse and a white cow wandering under the fine trees. On Monday I get to work on the memoirs. The white ducks are bathing in the lake. The white cow and horse are being brought in and the mallard ducks are fighting. Heaps of love to you both from

Alice

To Parker Tyler, New York/MS Texas

4 September 1959 5 rue Christine, Paris VI

Dear Mr. Tyler—

Gertrude Stein became acquainted with the work of Pavlik through Jane Heap. Six young painters were showing their pictures in the early twenties at a gallery in the rue Royale. She commenced with Pavlik and bought quite a few of them. Later she bought pictures of Kristians Tonny—Genia Berman and Christian Bérard—of the same neo-romantic group. None of them were satisfying. Eventually she took them down from the walls—still later she exchanged them for other pictures. There was no break between them—Pavlik found other patrons. Neither she nor I ever heard that he had a change of heart—neither from him nor from anyone else.

Cordially
Alice Toklas

Parker Tyler: Tyler was doing research for *The Divine Comedy of Pavel Tchelitchew, A Biography* (1967).

ALICE B. TOKLAS, PAVEL TCHELITCHEW, AND GERTRUDE STEIN, NEAR BELLEY, 1927

To Princess Dilkusha de Rohan, London/MS Texas

18 October 1959 5 rue Christine, Paris VI

Dilkusha dearest–

Have you seen Sylvia Beach's book? *Shakespeare and Company.* I have just been paid thirty-five dollars by *The New Republic* for a review of it–that will mend the springs and recover the arm-chair–the horsehair has worn out. The first idea was to buy a new chair but the price for a plain one was staggering. Virgil Thomson has just done over his flat–it has all the American conveniences–it is astonishing how appliances diminish work and take no room at all. To think this was a modern installation twenty years ago!

The people who bought the flat above me seem to be pleasant. He is an architect–and she is a very good looking intelligent woman–but the mess they have made here–their workmen hammer and pound–the plaster comes down and I get nervous about the pictures–it would be ruinous to pastels but what is it doing to gouaches–it frightens me.

My love–my prayers–my thoughts are always with you–dearest Dilkusha.

Alice

1960

To Mercedes de Acosta/MS Rosenbach

[17 April 1960] Easter Morning 5 rue Christine, Paris VI

Mercedes—dearest most wonderful—surprising and adorable of women—

Your book has left me breathless—excited and very happy. No matter how much I expected you have exceeded that by atomic distance. From the beginning its appearance was a delight—its title was a delight (and the reason of it too)—the photographs were most suitably informal and attractive. When I got to reading it I was ravished. You are astoundingly wise—generous and universal—not only in relation to the great figures but to the little people. I curtsy before you for your tremendous accomplishment. It is your heart that keeps you so modest. Pardon all my surprise. For example your story of Garbo is a classic—at the end you have made her one of the great heroines of all time—just as you have left Marlene Dietrich a warm but ordinary woman.

All my loving thoughts and blessings—dearest—darling Mercedes.

Alice

book: Mercedes de Acosta's memoir *Here Lies the Heart* (1960).

To Noël Murphy, Orgeval, France
MS Library of Congress

20 April 1960 5 rue Christine, Paris VI

Noël dearest—

What a lovely day you gave me. Such evidence I have of it now. The lillies of the valley are delicately sturdily fragrant—I love them and you. My heartfelt thanks. And the lunch—the *ratatouille* only as French Italians can make it. The Mediterranean all the way to Grasse has been influenced by Nizza. When I came to France fifty-three years ago I had no idea that such was the case. San Francisco was more Alsatian French. We came to the right country—didn't we. Did you know that Mrs. Mackay wanted to buy the Arc de Triomphe to pay the 1870 war debt. Nice California emotion.

Much love and many thanks from

Alice

To Virginia Knapik, Chicago/MS Knapik

23 April 1960 5 rue Christine, Paris VI

Virginia dearest—

Life is hectic—real and earnest—at least every other day! I had lunch at another restaurant—exhausting—fatiguing and unhealthy. I burn holes in everything. When I have settled in my convent in Rome—peace and quiet having descended upon me I shall be O.K. again. Mercedes [de Acosta] threatens a visitation there and Naomi [Barry] too. It is possible. It is close and doesnt rain. The man who edited the Sherwood Anderson letters was to come to see me about Gertrude and him. He probably couldnt find the bell and I sat up until 11 o'clock and then found a note from him in the door with no address!

They were wonderful at the Embassy about the passport. I had forgotten my old passport—so I had to go over again with it—and they said to bring photographs. Then they gave me a fistful of papers to fill out—which took all my spare time for three days (where are your divorced husbands and wives and their children by previous marriages). Then I got there with the papers filled and the photos and the old passport and I fell asleep on a chair and a nice young woman led me to her desk and in a very little while a man came and asked me to swear allegiance and fidelity (which I havent had to do since 1914) and I thanked him and said I was going to go to Italy in a month—what would I do. Oh—he said—you can come for the new one the day after tomorrow (which was today). Oh—I said—can I send a responsible person for it. Yes—was the answer—if she has a word from you. And so Madeleine brought it to me this morning.

Dearest get rested—blessings to you and to Harold.

Love from
Alice

To Anita Loos, New York/MS Loos

Sainte-Jeanne d'Arc
8 May 1960

5 rue Christine, Paris VI

Dearest Anita—

My friends see you—why cant I? From Acqui I am going down to Rome to stay with friends for about a week—then back here until about the 15th of July.

Janet [Flanner] is in fine form. You will have seen that her old enthusiasm for the General has cooled but she has taken on very warmly Monsieur K. Carl Van V. is nearly as old as I am but not nearly as tired so he can go about and enjoy himself.

Have you read Mercedes de Acosta's book—*Here Lies the Heart.* There is a classic description of Greta Garbo. A friend said to me one day—You cant dispose of Mercedes lightly—she has had the two most important women in U.S.—Greta Garbo and Marlene Dietrich.

Someone sent me an uninteresting—illustrated book called *The Jazz Age.* On looking through the illustrations I found to my horror one of Gertrude *en face* one of Ezra Pound—a few pages further one of you!

Dearest Anita—much love to you—many tender thoughts from your devoted

Alice

To Bernard Faÿ, Fribourg, Switzerland/MS Faÿ

[June 1960?] Acqui, Italy

Dear Bernard—

Your letter—as one from you always does—gave me the deepest pleasure but the last one brought me that encouragement so much needed just then. Everything you said about Gertrude was a joy to me. My prayers are for her as you said that they should be—that all was well with her—and that has been my comfort. You were her dearest friend during her life and now you have given her that eternal life.

At once let me apologise for illegibility—writing is done by feeling not by sight. It was necessary to have a secretary to whom to dictate but she was a great nuisance and it was a relief to be rid of her—which leaves a lot of work to be done after returning to Paris. The Edgar Allan Poes—first senior aged ninety—then son—who came over in February to see me have resigned and Mrs. Allan Stein is threatening to appoint a legal guardian for the pictures and to avoid insurance to lend them to a museum until I die. It is a nuisance but my nice lawyer—Russell Porter—will do what he can.

In Rome amongst the few people I met the one or rather the ones to whom I became attached were the Gervasis. Frank Gervasi came up to Culoz the day it was liberated to see Gertrude and shortly afterward he was flown back to U.S. He took Gertrude's manuscript *Wars I Have Seen* to Random House. He then disappeared. It was only in Rome the other day that he reappeared. It was a pleasure to see him again. He had a letter—some rhymes and a poem from Gertrude and a sweet warm memory of her.

Eyes are tired. I shall write again from here where I stay for about two weeks.

All my heartfelt thanks for everything.

Devotedly
Alice

insurance: Toklas carried an insurance policy on the paintings. At the time of Gertrude Stein's death a French expert had valued thirty-nine paintings and two folios of drawings at $28,475. (The highest valuation on any of the pictures was $2,500.) It was on this valuation that the insurance policy was drawn. In 1958, a Fine Arts Policy was instituted to provide additional coverage for the pictures, though at nowhere near their market value, which would have been prohibitive for Toklas.

To Virginia Knapik, Chicago/MS Knapik

[9 August 1960] Monastère du Précieux-Sang, Rome

Dearest Virginia—

Here I am with the good sisters—comfortable and very happy—my little room (very convent) is hot but will be appreciated next month—the nights are cold—the air blows in from the sea fifteen miles away. Dawn comes slowly but dusk is rapid—so I have time to dress for mass in the chapel at six-thirty—then coffee at seven-forty—bath when the water is hot later. John Brown and Simone come to see me—took me for a drive Sunday. The avenue under the window is above Trastevere but I havent seen the church yet—and the whole quarter has been cleaned up and built up astonishingly since when we knew it. I am in a parlous state from the amount of undercooked pâté I ate at the Browns. I have taken enough laxative to kill a dog. Here the food is simple and nourishing and there are vegetables. There is a wonderful soup—but I am waiting for winter for that. If winter isnt going to be perfect what is? The arthritis is better. I walk down one flight and a half to chapel and back to my room and down two flights and back for lunch without a stick and there is an elevator so dont send me stockings and no shirtwaists. Madeleine has washed the one you brought me from U.S. and it is as good as new. Here the wash is as good as Mad's. I think the nuns do it. Can that be? I brought a quantity of blouses.

The trip down was wonderful—jet in one hour and forty minutes—second class—$50 the round trip. John Brown had an embassy auto drive us to the Paris airport and a friend of his called for us and drove us along the Appian Way!

Alice

To John Schaffner, New York/MS Columbia

21 August 1960 Monastère du Précieux-Sang, Rome

Dear John—

Thank you a lot for your letter which moved me. Your and Robert Lescher's generosity shames me—undeserved as it is. The heat has dried out a great deal of the winter's moisture and would be entirely encouraging if it didn't prevent working but by the end of the month the equinox will bring refreshment and I shall become a steady regular uninterrupted worker.

So very gratefully but definitely I am thanking and refusing your and Robert Lescher's offer of a secretary and a further advance from Holt. Neither of them would be a help—on the contrary they would be an embarrassment—you understand this—don't you? A month hence I shall have something to send you. John Brown—my good friend—cultural attaché at our embassy here—will find someone to type it. So there we are. You should have had this information long ago. Try to forgive me—please.

I am quite comfortable and very happy here—the nuns are a cloistered order but there are three who go out into the city.

Life is extremely simple but it suits me.

Let me know please that you are satisfied.

To you all my fondest good wishes always—

Alice

Robert Lescher: Then an editor at Holt, Rinehart and Winston. It was Lescher who had first suggested the possibility of a memoir to Schaffner.

To Carl and Fania Van Vechten, New York/MS Yale

21 October 1960 Monastère du Précieux-Sang, Rome

Dearests—

Happy Wedding Anniversary to you sweet darlings—forty-six years married today. I pray God that He is leaving darling Fania's eyes in peace—that she is not in pain. As you see I am helping my tired old eyes by writing large.

I have just returned from a lunch party in my honor at the William Peppers'—they seem not to be any relation to your Peppers. It was Arnold Weissberger who sent them the letter of introduction. She has written four cook books—is considerable of a cook—paints and wears considerably too much thin gold jewelry. I liked him a lot—he is the manager of *Newsweek* for the Mediterranean coast. They have a great house in a garden way out in the suburbs. I was called for by some people I knew some years ago in Paris—delightful Southerners—John and Virginia Becker. They called for me in the Princess Caetani's car! There were four other people at table whose names I did not catch—conversation lively. I shall be seeing them—the Peppers—again. When Arnold wrote to introduce the Peppers he ended with: Eugène Berman is living in Rome now. I think I should tell him you are there now. And I answered: Please dont.

In twenty-nine Baby saw at a show of young painters Genia's pictures and bought two—classical landscapes—Roman architecture. He brought them to the rue de Fleurus. We were leaving in a day or two for Bilignin. Genia said he would like to paint it. Baby asked him to come down there which he did shortly after we got there.

Our Paris servant did not want to go to the country but I had a very pretty intelligent young girl who had worked one year at the hotel in Belley before we found Bilignin. She was very pretty—her coloring was ravishing. One evening Baby wanted Thérèse to

ALICE B. TOKLAS, BILIGNIN, 1934

Photograph by Carl Van Vechten

"PORTRAIT OF ALICE B. TOKLAS," BY EUGÈNE BERMAN
INK, 1929

Department of Special Collections, Research Library, University of California, Los Angeles

bring her something and rang for her but she didnt answer. Baby rang several times but there was no answer. Baby went down the hall and knocked on Thérèse's door—no answer. Baby opened the door. No Thérèse—the bed had not been slept in. Baby heard voices beyond from the room Genia occupied. There was no clue—neither Baby nor I believed Thérèse was in bed with Genia—definitely not. She came from a family of honest women.

Thérèse said after he left—*"Le jeune peintre est très Russe."*

Gratefully—devotedly—
M.W.

Princess Caetani: Marguerite (Chapin), Princess of Bassiano, published the reviews *Commerce* (Paris, 1924–32) and *Botteghe Oscure* (Rome, 1948–60).

Genia: The artist Eugène Berman.

To Jane Eakin, Paris/MS Eakin

27 October 1960 Monastère du Précieux-Sang, Rome

Dearest Jane—

Have you ever used a Schaeffer cartridge pen? If not do not. They are easy to refill but difficult not to empty on your hand or the paper.

I was so glad to get your letter—paprika to excess in U.S.? Unknown here but pepper is more than pepper—sweet and gently spiced. The Italian cooking is daily more delicious—if macaroni is cut out—their vegetables are cooked like the Chinese and there are baby green peas now that it has grown cold—do come down and taste raw pin mushroom salad and raw white truffles and spring turkey—no more food until you both come down.

I had to give up the Durrell novels—my eyes gave out. The days are so short—dark at five o'clock and sunrise beautiful beyond words at seven. And two more winter months to go to the shortest day and then two before they are as long as today. Ghastly—except that there [are] wild flowers in January—like California—and one eats out of doors. Rome is not southern enough—I am bored with winter. But the color here is indescribably beautiful—even when it is grey or black.

Tender thoughts—much love.

Devotedly
Alice

Jane Eakin: An American painter who was then living in Paris.

To Princess Dilkusha de Rohan, London/MS Texas

21 November 1960 Monastère du Précieux-Sang, Rome

Dearest Dilkusha—

For days I've been trying to tell you what has been happening to me—the more that happens the less time there is in which to tell it.

Xavier [Fourcade] took me last Saturday to a Papal audience at the Vatican. It was momentous and moving. There were two rows of seats around the walls of a large room—we were in the first—near where the Pope entered. The five steps to the throne were covered in brilliant red carpet, His Holiness is small. His gestures precise—descriptive. His voice showed the peasant origin. He spoke in Italian—the blessing naturally in Latin. There were four *messeigneurs* in their scarlet capes who answered in English—French—German and Spanish. When it was over I was weak.

Waugh's son is like his father—I dislike them heartily.

Thanks a lot for letting me read Louise's letter and the good news that she returns from her trips looking and feeling so well. It is sad that she must part with the Chelsea flat. If I had had the inclination and the money to have kept Bilignin and the rue Christine the French law would not have permitted me to do so—only one home. Picasso was required to give up the flat in the rue de La Boëtie and he had plenty of political influence.

About my writing being more legible—that comes from the pains I take to make it so. It takes me three quarters of an hour to write one of these pages held under a strong lamp and more than a foot from my eyes and there is little print that I can read.

Tender thoughts—dearest Dilkusha—blessings and love from

Alice

1961

To Pierre Balmain, Paris/MS Balmain

4 January 1961 Monastère du Précieux-Sang, Rome

Pierre dear—

You cant half fancy the pleasure seeing you gave me—it was a revival of those happy days that are only memories now. As for all your gifts my very modern Santa Claus!! when they were all opened and put away I was quite overwhelmed. You are much too good to me. You must have devastated Doneys. The convent dessert is a baked apple—Canadian of course—excellent but monotonous. Now there is a luscious *marron glacé!* Thanks and thanks again.

Next time you go through Rome take time to lunch with me—no not at the convent! There is an old restaurant—new to me—where one eats rather well.

A thousand good wishes for the success of the new collection. I am sorry to have to wait for my return to see it.

You are in my thoughts often—and in my prayers. May the Lord bless and protect you.

Devotedly
Alice

Vent Vert is more flowerlike than ever.

ALICE B. TOKLAS AND GERTRUDE STEIN, 1928

. . . those happy days
that are only memories now.

To Virginia Knapik, Toronto/MS Knapik

12 January 1961 Monastère du Précieux-Sang, Rome

Virginia dearest—

It was lovely to get your letter—but on account of my eyesight I must ask you for the future to right *dark* on a white paper—otherwise it is too great a strain—such is old age.

Yesterday Dame Judith Anderson and her niece spent the day with me on her way to Monaco where they are the guests of the Prince and his American princess. Judith brought me a bag of passion fruit she picked two days before in her garden. They brought me to the convent gate in a taxi and very emotionally kissed me good bye seven times and naturally forgot to give me the bag. Off to Monaco she has given the bag to her hotel to deliver to me—but will they. If you dont know this fruit you must —Hediard before the last war had passion fruit syrup which made *the* most delicious ice cream. What are the Hawaiian nuts *The N. Yorker* advertises.

While we are on eating they are translating into Italian the cook book with an advance of two hundred dollars—which comes handily to make up the deficit of too many guests for lunch at restaurants. Did you know one called Alfredo a la Scofa with a gold fork and spoon Mary Pickford gave them a generation ago. I have been given them twice—*trop d'honneur*—but the thickest chicken breasts cooked with a cream sauce is *non pareil.*

You told me not to smoke the butts so I don't.

It is warmer but it pours a deluge and is dark. The convent was so well heated I opened a window and in popped Sister Saint Paul. She was horrified.

Je t'embrasse my *chère.*

Devotedly
Alice

To Russell Porter, Paris/MS Porter

20 January 1961 Monastère du Précieux-Sang, Rome

Dear Mr. Porter—

Thank you for your letter and for having wired to Mr. Poe.

It is unfortunate for me that he should have left so long a time to lapse before acting upon the will of Gertrude Stein. In it is stated that for my maintenance pictures should be sold. Mr. Poe now requires the consent of Allan Stein's three children. Mr. Poe does not propose coming to Paris until February.

There are two things to be noticed. Mr. Poe Senior appointed an expert to place a value upon the pictures for their insurance. He was unfamiliar with any of the pictures and asked me to name the painters to him and the value of each picture.

In the meantime it is I who am paying the rent of the flat—the next term is due on the 15th of this month—its upkeep—the char.

As for paying doctor's bills for me—the baths at Acqui are all I envisage.

Thank you again.

Cordially
Alice Toklas

will of Gertrude Stein: Toklas had been drawing a monthly allowance of $400 from the Stein estate. From this money she paid all household and personal expenses. As records and her correspondence show, this allowance was often late in coming.

To Russell Porter, Paris/MS Porter

5 February 1961 Monastère du Précieux-Sang, Rome

Dear Mr. Porter—

After having received the copy of Mr. Poe Junior's letter that you forwarded to me a much more conciliatory one came in which he advised me to sell at once a picture to Monsieur Kahnweiler —Picasso's dealer. Did you receive a copy of this letter? Because if not I shall send the original to you.

I wrote to M. Kahnweiler at once offering him either of the two green Picasso pictures in the salon at 5 rue Christine in Paris.

Then yesterday came a letter entirely reversing this. You must have received a copy of this letter. In it Mr. Poe writes that he wishes to consult with Monsieur Dupré and the Stein children before any picture or pictures are sold and the minimum price decided upon. Mr. Poe quotes the price at auction in New York of four impressionist pictures and adds that the price of the Picasso picture has reached its highest point. I answered this at once. You will understand the tone of my letter. If you have not received a copy of this last letter of Mr. Poe I shall send it to you.

Yours cordially
Alice Toklas

Monsieur Dupré: Bernard Dupré, a French lawyer who represented Roubina Stein and was the guardian for her children, Michael and Gabrielle, until they came of age.

To Russell Porter, Paris/MS Porter

6 February 1961 Monastère du Précieux-Sang, Rome

Dear Mr. Porter—

A letter from Mr. Kahnweiler has just come. He will pay sixty thousand dollars for the Picasso *Green Still Life* in the salon at 5 Christine.

I have warned Mr. Poe that I should deduct the remittances of the three months he withheld without warning. Should I not deduct $1200. Please let me know.

How mistaken Mr. Poe was. Can we prevent him from taking any pictures from the flat.

Ever cordially
Alice Toklas

Green Still Life: A 1909 picture now in the collection of Mr. and Mrs. John Hay Whitney.

To Russell Porter, Paris/MS Porter

11 February 1961 Monastère du Précieux-Sang, Rome

Dear Mr. Porter—

E. A. Poe Junior wrote me to sell a Picasso picture to M. Kahnweiler—which I did for sixty thousand dollars. A few days later he wrote me that he [Poe] was going to consult M. Dupré and the Stein children concerning the sale of a picture. I have answered him that I could not go back on my word to M. Kahnweiler as [Poe] had his to me.

Mr. Poe says he will arrive here by plane at 11:10 on February 25th and that I should meet him at twelve o'clock at his hotel. It will take him more than two and a half hours to get to his hotel. I have asked him to come to the convent which will be quieter than his hotel. Please try to persuade Mr. Poe of this. And that I insist upon being paid from the sale of the picture the remittance for the three months withheld without warning.

Always cordially
Alice Toklas

To Sandy Campbell, Rome/MS Campbell

16 February 1961 Monastère du Précieux-Sang, Rome

Dear Sandy–

Let us not postpone lunching further than Tuesday. It is understood that you are my guests for the warm garlic artichokes and whatever delectable *plats* may follow.

On Tuesday then at half after twelve.

Warm greetings to you all.

Alice Toklas

LUNCH AT THE TRE SCALINI, ROME, 1961
ALICE B. TOKLAS, JOSÉ QUINTERO, ISABEL WILDER,
DONALD WINDHAM, AND LYNDALL BIRCH

Photograph by Sandy Campbell

To Virginia Knapik, New York/MS Knapik

10 March 1961 Monastère du Précieux-Sang, Rome

Virginia dearest–

No reading or writing any more. A secretary with the largest fattest pink legs comes to take dictation every afternoon and improves my English! I am fed up with Rome–Roman ruins and Renaissance palazzos but not with the food–*marvellous.* I have learned how they cook the artichokes but they must be cut fresh from the garden. I have become intimate with a man who has written a great cook book and cooked an ineffable lunch. Harold here would do the same. The market in Paris is not comparable –but I dont want to live in Rome–Les Quatres Chemins? So much love to you and Harold. Blessings.

Alice

Les Quatres Chemins: One of the vacation houses Toklas had rented with the Knapiks.

To Sandy Campbell, Rome/MS Campbell

16 March 1961 Monastère du Précieux-Sang, Rome

Dear Sandy–

Waiting for the water to be piping hot I missed seeing you. The freesias are a joy–their perfume–color and form are exquisite. Thank you. On Saturday you and Donald and James "illegible" must lunch with me at Fontanella–where they have white truffles and where the artichokes are fair—will you call for me around half after twelve? At one o'clock I am ravenous.

Devotedly
Alice

Sandy Campbell: Campbell, an actor, was in Rome with his friends Donald Windham, the novelist, and William (not James) LeMassena.

To Russell Porter, Paris/MS Porter

2 May 1961 Monastère du Précieux-Sang, Rome

Dear Mr. Porter—

Your letter which I have just received has surprised me greatly. You will remember that I wrote you that before Mr. Edgar Allan Poe Junior came over he wrote me to sell a picture to cover the insurance of the pictures—my monthly allowances—and possible hospital expenses. When he came here to Rome we had an amiable and long conversation. He asked me to write to you the gist of it and said he would telephone you between his air flight—Rome—Paris—U.S.A.

About my sale of the drawings—there was nothing clandestine about it. I made no secret of it. I asked Picasso's consent. He came to the flat and telephoned to Kahnweiler. They looked at the drawings and agreed upon the dealer who should show and sell them. For the show Kahnweiler wrote an appreciative and touching introduction about Picasso and Gertrude Stein.

I would remind you that Mrs. Allan Stein came to me three or four years ago to ask me to sell a picture for her as she was in debt. I refused saying I lived frugally so as not to have to do so myself—that she need not keep a car.

They [the drawings] are not missing—they were sold which I have the right to do according to Gertrude Stein's will.

These are the facts.

Always cordially
Alice Toklas

sale of drawings: In aid of seeing through to publication all of Stein's heretofore unpublished works, Toklas had in 1954 quietly and at far less than their market price sold a group of about forty Picasso drawings (1903–7) from the exhibition, *Picasso: Dessins, 1903–1907,* which was mounted by Galerie Berggruen et Cie with the cooperation of Galerie Louise Leiris. The catalogue had a preface, "A la mémorie de Gertrude Stein," by Daniel-Henry Kahnweiler. Included in the sale was at least one drawing, *Deux Femmes Debout* (1906), that belonged to Toklas.

To Fernanda Pivano, Milan/ MS Pivano

9 June 1961 — 5 rue Christine, Paris VI

Nanda dearest—

This letter was awaiting me on my return from Acqui but other surprises—unpleasant—were here.

Now you must know the shocking news that greeted my entrance to the flat. The walls were bare—not one Picasso left—the children of Allan Stein want them loaned to a museum where they would be adequately insured which of course I could not do. Two good lawyers are defending the case. Isnt it a bore?

The weather is abominable. It is dark—like a partial eclipse of the sun and it rains heavily for several hours every day.

Paris has been wonderfully decorated for the visit of the Kennedys

—huge flags on very tall white flagpoles. I got a glimpse from a taxi of the Place de la Concorde and the Champs Elysées.

Dearest—I send you both warmest—most devoted love.

Alice

This letter: The Italian publisher Rizzoli had written to Toklas inquiring about Italian translation rights to one of Stein's books.

The walls were bare: There had been in France in the previous three months two spectacular robberies of paintings. Roubina Stein, fearing that the collection at the rue Christine might be endangered, secured entry into the apartment. Using the inventory list prepared at the time of Stein's death she found that certain pictures were missing and that a portfolio of Picasso drawings could not be found. Without any attempt to get in touch with Toklas, she went to the courts and had the pictures declared "endangered" by Toklas' absence from the apartment. (It should be understood that Toklas always took great care to insure that either Madeleine or the concierge should visit the apartment several times a week. The concierge had strict instructions never to reveal that Toklas was out of Paris no matter who inquired.) By court order, the day before Alice returned from Rome, the paintings (including those that belonged to Toklas and were not part of the Stein estate) were removed from the apartment and cached in the vault of the Chase Manhattan Bank in Paris.

To Princess Dilkusha de Rohan, London/MS Texas

23 August 1961 — 5 rue Christine, Paris VI
Sunday

Dilkusha dearest—

The pictures are gone permanently. My dim sight could not see them now. Happily a vivid memory does.

Through a friend I have a Spanish maid *(soubrette)* aged 34—dressed at the Prisunic—who has two afternoons a week free and

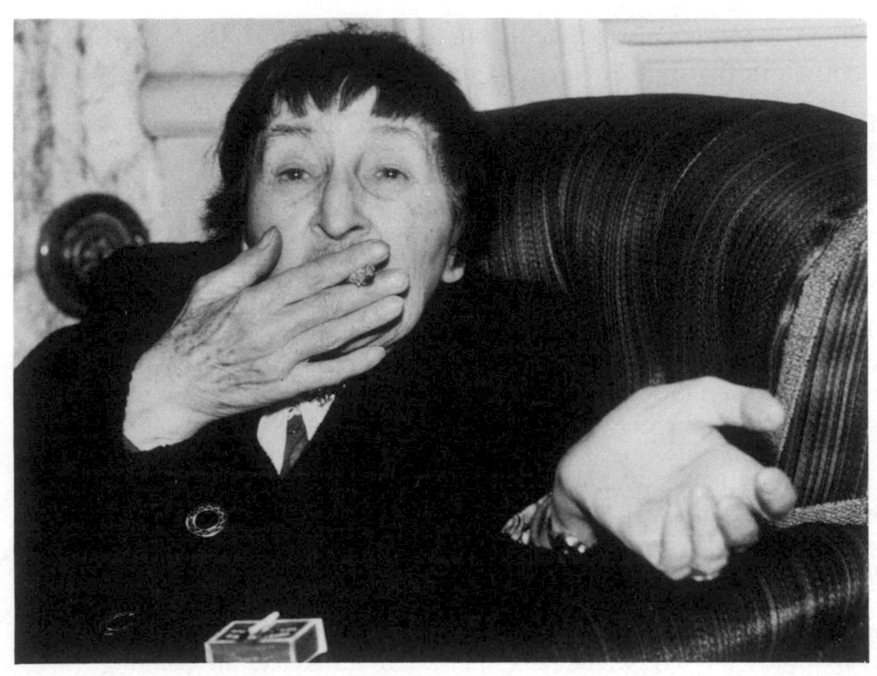

ALICE B. TOKLAS, 5 RUE CHRISTINE, 1961

The pictures are gone permanently.
My dim sight could not see them now. Happily
a vivid memory does.

every evening from eight o'clock to midnight—large wages and social insurance. She lives for her class in luxury. She is a good marketer—a fair cook and doesnt want to learn.

This is my depressing news.

Except—my editor—who is a darling—he and his handsome young wife have come to Paris to talk over the manuscript with me as far as I have gotten—215 pages—he is going to find a secretary for the rest to be paid for from advanced royalties.

My eyes are still dimmer—that is why I dont write to you oftener. I may cease—don't worry—it's not a surprise to me. I cant have much news. The telephone rings—the *soubrette* jabbers and brings an incredible message to me. [Robert] Lescher (editor) thinks she is useless but amusing.

The painters and writers cook book for which I was asked to do a foreword is out any day now.

Now I must put order in my little corner for my doctor is coming —the knee much better—arthritis much worse—fatigue enormous.

Dont worry about me—I am 84 years old. All old people fall—an aunt skating on the ice—a granduncle jumping off a street car.

So very much love. You are always in my thoughts and prayers.

Alice

To Sandy Campbell, Rome/MS Campbell

26 August 1961 Ville d'Avray, Seine et Oise

Dear Sandy—

It was very cheering to get your letter forwarded from Paris to this nursing home where I am being treated by massage and exercise so I can walk again. The leg doesn't hurt so much anymore and they think I will be cured in less than a month. It is very dismal here. Though the sun shines today, most days are dark, and the hospital bed gets littered with my few possessions. This nursing home is a fit subject for a novelette. There are ten people on the staff and they all hate each other. In any case they never agree, and they come bouncing into my room as if it were a way station and say: "Is she here?" and they take messages for the telephone which never get delivered. The maid is a very young Italian girl from near Venice, not the seaside, and she planks things down on my chest and leaves me to *me débrouiller* myself. I ring for her to take away the tray and she leaves the door wide open, during which time other people come to visit or to look on.

Love and devotion
Alice

I can walk again: Toklas had tripped, and in an attempt to avoid hitting her head had broken her kneecap. During this illness, and later, in the last few years of her life, Toklas sometimes dictated letters. These usually have more conventional punctuation.

To John Schaffner, New York/MS Columbia

11 November 1961 — 5 rue Christine, Paris VI

Dear John—

At a lecture by John Brown to which I had hobbled I had a moment's conversation with Sylvia Beach and when I asked for news of Bryher and H.D. she gave me the very sad news of the death of H.D. a month ago. I wrote to Bryher this morning to Burier la Tour—asking for the letter to be forwarded in case of her absence. It is impossible to believe in Bryher without H.D. They came together to the rue de Fleurus years ago and then Bryher asked us to lunch at Burier la Tour bringing Thornton

Wilder with us. He [Wilder] was a great admirer of H.D.'s poetry and had been one of her father's at Yale. He told me he thought Bryher Napoleonic in many ways.

Thank you both for the generous check of six hundred and three and 35/100 dollars. It's most unfortunate that so much time has been lost—though I still hope to get the book finished not too long after the new year.

Alice

To Princess Dilkusha de Rohan, London/MS Texas

26 November 1961 5 rue Christine, Paris VI

Dearest Dilkusha—

Pierre Balmain came to see me the other evening accompanied by an utterly charming young Chinaman whom he met in Peking. Pierre wanted to see Francis' [Rose] book. The woman who read aloud to me bored me and frequently I "absented" myself to avoid hearing her unpleasant voice. So that all unconscious of what Francis had written about Pierre and Pierre's mother I gave him the book. Pierre's mother was the widow of a doctor—opened a luxury shop of infinite taste—sold her pearls to pay his [Balmain's] first term at the rue François Premier. Well when Pierre read Francis' description of his mother as a "greengrocer" imagine his horror. His first thought was to challenge the statement but he quickly realised that it was only one of Francis' endless lies. His [Rose's] American edition will be in endless hot water. At the time he was staying with us with Cecil at Bilignin he writes of seeing Göring—Hitler—and Mussolini daily in Berlin. So I beg of you not to correct the book for America. Your name must not get mixed up with his!

Just as I was about to write to you about Janet [Flanner] she telephoned—she is coming tomorrow morning to read me the five pages she has written about the pictures. Pray God she has not been indiscreet. She is wonderfully thin and fidgety—she has had a complicated arthritis and has aged. She is seventy years old.

I am three quarters Pole. The Knapiks who are pure [Polish] hate no one. I dont think I hate anyone now. My father confessor returned to England and a wonderful successor is an old old friend of Bernard. He helps me.

God's blessings—love.

Devotedly
Alice

Francis' book: Saying Life: The Memoirs of Sir Francis Rose (1961).

To Russell Porter, Paris/MS Porter

28 December 1961 Monastère du Précieux-Sang, Rome

Dear Mr. Porter—

I am shocked and surprised at not having received a remittance for so long a time. What has happened to Mr. Poe or his son? I have been living on the advance royalty of my editor at Holt for a book he commissioned. This money I was keeping to pay my expenses for the cure at Acqui—which I sadly need for the arthritis has become painfully acute. My expenses at the convent where I am living as a paying guest are as low as a plain convent. I am well heated—the food is very coarse—but is adequate. My personal expenses are even less than in Paris—except postage which is an important item—manuscripts and books are unasked for but must be returned. In the meantime my eyes are a great trouble. I can write only by holding the paper within about ten inches of my eyes under a strong light.

What can you do to make Mr. Poe activate—wire him. You will remember the difficulty you once had to get an answer from him. It is urgent that he sends me the money by wire at once—for I am down to bedrock.

It has not been easy for me to write these things to you. Gertrude Stein—in her generosity to me—did not foresee that such an occasion could arise.

Will you please let me know at once what you have done to relieve the situation.

Cordially
Alice Toklas

1962-1966

To L. Arnold Weissberger, New York/MS Weissberger

23 January 1962 5 rue Christine, Paris VI

Dear Arnold—

I'm getting well—none too quickly—but still not too bad. I went to Pierre Balmain's opening yesterday & sat on a little chair between the Princess Isabelle of France & our ambassador, Gen. Gavin, and his goodlooking wife. The show was astonishingly beautiful. And I was there in all the glory that Pierre had provided, but came back stiff and tired.

I walk to the sitting room alone without the nurse.

Devotedly
Alice

To Louise and Redvers Taylor, England/MS Taylor

3 August 1962 5 rue Christine, Paris VI

My dears—

Got back from Acqui Sunday evening walking without a cane. The baths did a lot of good but the house doctor stuffed me with the most frightful medicines from which I am now recovering.

Going over closets—armoires—for putting in order my possessions before they fall into the hands of the Armenian widow of Allan Stein—I came upon a blank book—cover missing—written in the large "English" handwritings *à la mode* of my youth—so that I can read it now. Here are two recipes you'll find easy to make and tasty.

Home Made French Mustard

3 teaspoons dry (English) mustard. 1 teaspoon flour. Add enough water to make a paste. Let these come to a boil. When cold add pinch salt—pinch sugar and 1 teaspoon oil.

Doody's Ice Cream

1 cup heavy cream beaten until stiff. 1 glass Raspberry jelly—whites of 5 eggs beaten stiff. Mix gently—freeze.

Mocha Torte

Spread the following on 3 layers sponge cake: Add the yolks of 4 eggs to 1 cup strong cold coffee. ½ cup sugar. Bring to boil in double boiler. Remove from fire. When cold add drop by drop to 1 cup butter.

Mrs. Moore's Creamed Crab

1 pint rich cream
1 picked crab
½ glass sherry—pinch pepper & salt
Yolks 4 eggs—stir well in double boiler.
Do not boil—serve hot.

This is all for today—my eyes have given out. Much much love.

Devotedly
Alice

To Pierre Balmain, Paris/MS Balmain

17 January 1963 — 5 rue Christine, Paris VI

Dearest Pierre—

Your postal from So. Africa with the small wild lions came weeks ago. Everyone enjoyed it and finally a few days ago I gave it to Jo Barry to give to his young son. The postal from Palermo didnt arrive—there were post office strikes here and in Italy.

Then on Thursday your marvellously beautiful shawl came. It is ravishingly beautiful. I sat down to write to tell you what pleasure it was giving me when a huge basket came from Hediard's—such delicacies I dont remember having seen gathered together before. I put the avocados in the refrigerator but ate half of one the day before yesterday and the other half today.

Even with the magnifying glass I cant see what I have written—forgive me. Now it is orange marmalade and jelly which will help to swallow sleeping pills.

May our Lord bless and protect you.

Yours devotedly
Alice

To Princess Dilkusha de Rohan, London/MS Texas

20 March 1963 — 5 rue Christine, Paris VI

Dilkusha dear—

Madeleine is coming tomorrow morning at the crack of dawn so that there will still be hot water for a bath. It's a fearful bore. The little Spanish maid has caught cold. Her room is better heated than mine! A nice young Englishman comes to read aloud to me. He's just finished Synge's *Playboy of the Western World*—tremendous! I haven't read it for nearly fifty years! What a genius he was.

The little Picasso chairs have gone beyond the reach of the Armenian's grasp. I shall miss them.

Alice

Picasso chairs: Two small eighteenth-century chairs with needlepoint seats and backs, executed by Toklas in the late 1920's, after designs by Picasso. The chairs were given to YCAL.

To Donald Sutherland, Boulder, Colorado
MS Sutherland

16 May 1963 5 rue Christine, Paris VI

Dear Donald—

I don't know the date—Jacintha has taken the paper away and the calendar doesn't help me. I am in a devil of a mess but everyone is helping to get me out of it. The woman who bought the flat when the house [was sold] several years ago sent a *huissier* yesterday morning at seven thirty who said the police would come with an expulsion order. Jo Barry and Doda Conrad are at work. Doda is getting Malraux to work. It appears he's all powerful! Madeleine thinks that if General de Gaulle is not going to save me I had better go to a hotel at once.

If there is no other news it is because no one comes except to help. But there will probably be good news soon. Neither you nor Gilberte must take on the police eviction!!

Much love to you both.

Devotedly
Alice

Jacintha: Jacintha Abas, Toklas' *femme de ménage.*

expulsion order: When 5 rue Christine was sold, each tenant had been given the opportunity to buy his apartment. Believing that because of her advanced age she would not be evicted, Toklas refused. French law did, however, provide that an apartment could not be vacant more than four months in a year without a legitimate reason, and while Toklas was in Rome (1960/61) the owner sued for possession. Through the intervention of friends the matter was delayed. When it came to be decided, it was suggested by the authorities that she move permanently to the south for her health. When the bailiff presented Toklas with her final expulsion order she was in bed with a broken hip. Very politely they read her the notice and then noted her reply: "I was born in 1877. If I leave this apartment it will be to go to Père Lachaise." Although friends again intervened, a year later Toklas was evicted from the apartment she had for so many years shared with Stein.

To Louise and Redvers Taylor, England/MS Taylor

25 May 1963 — 5 rue Christine, Paris VI

My dears—

Dont be worried—the news is not so bad as it sounds. The French law has changed from giving me the flat because of my age to giving it to the owner after my seventieth year. But influential people are at work—a cabinet minister—a cultural officer—Virgil Thomson. Malraux has telephoned my French lawyer to say he is in communication with the prefecture. None of these are discouraged in the least so you are not to be.

I am not going to use your adorable lovely little handkerchief for tears—oh no oh no—but with a new dress!

Dont worry—everything is going better than any one hoped.

My heartfelt thanks and love.

Your devoted
Alice

To Louise and Redvers Taylor, England/MS Taylor

[4 November 1964] [16 rue de la Convention, Paris XV]

Dearest Red and Louise—

You can't imagine how glad I'm going to be to see you here in Paris on December 11th. Having lost a lawsuit I was evicted from the rue Christine. After more than 3 months at the American Hospital and over two weeks at the convalescent home where I was well treated by a blind masseur, Madeleine moved my furniture and objects here. Well, here I am at my age in a new home, very modern—but with no right to drive nails in the walls—in a country of painting! You will see it on the 13th, when I hope to be well enough to walk about again. I think of you always and pray for you.

Devotedly
Alice

new home: With the help of Janet Flanner and Doda Conrad, Toklas had been moved to an apartment on the left bank, several miles from the rue Christine.

To Harold and Virginia Knapik, New York/MS Knapik

9 January 1965 16 rue de la Convention, Paris XV

Dearest Harold and Virginia—

I'm still in bed in the flat, waiting for something to turn up. The flat holds nearly all of Gertrude's furniture. But there is a carpenter in the building next to it who makes most dreadful noises. When he gets too noisy I scream *'taisez-vous!* & sometimes it's effective, but not always. The walls are so thin one hears everything. A neighbor sneezed the other day and I heard it distinctly. That is why you can't drive nails in the wall. An earthquake would bring us all into the court five flights below and I don't promise to survive. I wish to goodness you were here. I think I've said it already, but I say it again.

Don't send me any more coffee, my dear. I have my old coffee I used to have at rue Christine, quite conveniently. And if not, my dreadful Spaniard can go to Fauchon.

It's been dark and cold, but now darker than cold. I don't remember anything like it, in spite of which come back. I'll try to find someone who will take the miniature furniture to you.

Endless and always dearest love to you both.

Alice

To Wendell Wilcox, Chapel Hill, North Carolina
MS Wilcox

15 January 1965 — 16 rue de la Convention, Paris XV

Dear Wendell—

I was delighted to hear from you. Sam may well have brought good news, better than the real news, for I've been in bed for a year now. The new apartment is quite alright and I'm growing accustomed to it. The rue Christine was a fond memory of Gertrude, and I was forcibly ejected by the owner who has done it over to suit herself. When she came to look at it years ago, she said: You have a great many pictures, and I said, "They dont go with the apartment." She didnt know one picture from another then and now she is an expert.

This flat is very modern—with underground heat. When it falls down, it will be an awful crash. Five stories to go. I dont think I'm ever going to become attached to it.

Fond love to you both, and best wishes for the New Year.

Alice

To Benjamin G. Benno, New York/MS Benno

[22 March 1965] 16 rue de la Convention, Paris XV

Dear Benno—

One of my most vivid and happiest memories was the visit of Gertrude Stein and me to your flat, very high up at the top of a great number of stairs. Gertrude Stein said to me afterwards—"His pictures are so much under the influence of—or rather he understands Picasso so well, that they will be sold a hundred years hence, not as false Picassos, but as real Picassos." I wonder if you ever came to see her in Paris and saw her Picassos.

After this war, when we got back to Paris, she bought a Dora Maar which is the only picture I have here. I miss the old flat that was filled with memories of Gertrude Stein. If you ever come to Paris I should like to see you again. I have a cataract which is to be removed shortly and then I shall be able to see the documents you sent me—for which I thank you.

Always cordially
Alice Toklas

Benno: A painter whom Stein and Toklas had met in Paris in the 1930's.

To Robert A. Wilson, Copenhagen/MS Wilson

30 April 1965 16 rue de la Convention, Paris XV

Dear Mr. Wilson—

I shall try to get the packages done as you directed. But we are not certain what the difference between twine and string may be. Jacintha will be in a state of despair if I can get her to do them, because she doesn't like doing things except as they are done in Spain.

Don't bother to come down here specially.

I've taken to filter-tipped cigarettes as a step to not smoking, I think.

Your gifts are a great delight to me. The Japanese matches are wonderful.

Gratefully and cordially
Alice Toklas

Wilson: Robert Wilson, owner of the Phoenix Book Shop in New York, had gone to see Toklas. He arranged to buy from her some copies of the Plain Edition that she still had.

To John and Patricia Lucas, Rome/MS Lucas

24 July [1965] 16 rue de la Convention, Paris XV

To all of you, dearest Lucases—

It was so nice to hear from you going to all those lovely places, though I know Pamplona very little, having had a prejudice on account of Hemingway. It's not very likely I shall see Spain again, so I can dream about Gibraltar and the street that leads down from it, and I envy you all your Spanish experiences.

Devotedly
Alice

To Wendell and Esther Wilcox,
Chapel Hill, North Carolina/MS Wilcox

2 August [1965] 16 rue de la Convention, Paris XV

Dear Wendell and Essie—

It certainly is strange that you have never been to New York till now. New York needs you more than you need it. However have you gotten on all these years without landing there? I suppose that Chicago filled all your plans, but here we are now with New York claiming you.

I send you both my dearest love and will write to you again as soon as my eye is completely cured. The doctors are all away on a vacation. Last time he came he said, "Look at me now. Can you see me." To which I replied, "Yes, for first time." Which he didn't think was funny, but I did.

Alice

To Harold and Virginia Knapik, New York/MS Knapik

9 January 1966 16 rue de la Convention, Paris XV

Dearest Virginia and Harold–

I'm so glad to hear from you, but I am sick of waiting for you to come back to Paris. I'm going to have the masseur who should have been coming months ago. I was waiting to have enough money to pay him as a matter of fact. I don't know what is to become of me. For the present moment I'm living on the proceeds of the bank. The Armenian's lawyer is trying to make some sort of settlement without selling any of the pictures. But how he's going to manage it I'm sure I don't know.

Do come back soon. I shan't last forever.

A bientôt
Alice

Index

Index

Index

Index

Index

Index